Acts

The People's Bible

ROLAND CAP EHLKE
General Editor

ARMIN J. PANNING
New Testament Editor

G. JEROME ALBRECHT
Manuscript Editor

Acts

RICHARD D. BALGE

NORTHWESTERN PUBLISHING HOUSE
Milwaukee, Wisconsin

Second printing 1993

The cover and interior illustrations were originally executed by
James Tissot (1836-1902).

Library of Congress Card 87-63118
Northwestern Publishing House
1250 N. 113th St., Milwaukee, Wl 53226-3284
© 1988 by Northwestern Publishing House.
Published 1988
Printed in the United States of America
ISBN 0-8100-0286-8

CONTENTS

ILLUSTRATIONS

CONTENTS

EDITOR'S PREFACE

The People's Bible is just what the name implies — a Bible for the people. It includes the complete text of the Holy Scriptures in the popular New International Version. The commentary following the Scripture sections contains personal applications as well as historical background and explanations of the text.

The authors of *The People's Bible* are men of scholarship and practical insight, gained from years of experience in the teaching and preaching ministries. They have tried to avoid the technical jargon which limits so many commentary series to professional Bible scholars.

The most important feature of these books is that they are Christ-centered. Speaking of the Old Testament Scriptures, Jesus himself declared, "These are the Scriptures that testify about me" (John 5:39). Each volume of *The People's Bible* directs our attention to Jesus Christ. He is the center of the entire Bible. He is our only Savior.

The commentaries also have maps, illustrations and archaeological information when appropriate. All the books include running heads to direct the reader to the passage he is looking for.

This commentary series was initiated by the Commission on Christian Literature of the Wisconsin Evangelical Lutheran Synod.

It is our prayer that this endeavor may continue as it began. We dedicate these volumes to the glory of God and to the good of his people.

Roland Cap Ehlke

ACTS
INTRODUCTION

The Book of Acts is a continuation of the Gospel of Luke. It is Volume II of the account which the author prepared for "most excellent Theophilus" (Luke 1:3). Its narrative begins where the Gospel of Luke ends, with the appearances of the risen Christ and his ascension. (Compare Luke 24:36-51 with Acts 1:1-11.) Since the author does not address Theophilus with the formal title "most excellent" in Acts as he did in the Gospel, some scholars suppose that Theophilus had become a believer in the time between the two writings.

The author described his method of gathering information and setting it down at the beginning of his first writing (Luke 1:3). He "carefully investigated everything" and he set about "to write an orderly account." He gathered information from eyewitnesses and, especially in his reports of official proceedings, he probably used written accounts and records. There are four sections in *Acts* (16:10-17; 20:5-15; 21:1-18 and 27:1-28:16) where the writer uses the personal pronoun "we," and that suggests that he was with Paul personally during these events.

Author

Luke's authorship of the third Gospel and of this writing was not questioned until modern times. The second-century teachers of the church assumed that both volumes were written by the man to whom Paul refers as "our dear friend Luke, the doctor" in Colossians 4:14, who sends greetings in

Philemon 24, and who was with Paul when the latter wrote his last epistle (2 Timothy 4:11).

Luke's authorship was challenged by certain German scholars in the nineteenth century. However, from about 1900 until now, even those who are inclined to question everything about the Bible do not generally question that Luke wrote this book. There is nothing in the book or in history that compels us to doubt that Luke wrote both volumes of this history for Theophilus although he does not mention himself by name in either Acts or the Gospel.

Title

Luke did not provide a title for either of his accounts. One of the ancient manuscripts of the New Testament gives Volume II the heading "Acts." Another calls it "Acts of the Apostles." The second title, especially, could be misleading, since the book does not report all of the acts of all of the apostles. Only once are all of the Eleven mentioned (1:13) and the election of Matthias to replace Judas is reported in 1:26. Thereafter, only Peter, James and John are mentioned. There is no reason at all to assume that the other nine apostles failed to carry out the Lord's great commission, but Acts does not report their activities.

In chapter 9, Luke reports the conversion of Saul of Tarsus, who became the Apostle Paul. Luke reports the work of Peter and Paul in considerable detail but has little to say about the other apostles. He also recounts the work of men like Stephen and Philip, as well as Paul's mission companions, especially Barnabas. The book is really an account of "some acts of some apostles."

Some have suggested that this book could be titled "the continuing Acts of Jesus," for throughout the book we have the record of how Jesus was present with his grace and power to spread abroad the salvation which he had won. Others have proposed that it be called "The Acts of the Holy Spirit," for the writing is also the story of how the promised Spirit empowered the followers of Jesus to witness to their Savior. Someone has pointed out that just as in the Creed the Second Article moves on to the Third Article, so the story of Jesus' work in the Gospel of Luke moves on to the story of the Holy Spirit's work in the Book of Acts.

Content and Purpose

Luke's history in Acts shows how the promise and instruction of Jesus, recorded in 1:8, was carried out. Our Savior said, "You will receive power when the Holy Spirit comes on you; and you will be my witnesses in Jerusalem, and in all Judea and Samaria, and to the ends of the earth." The book reports the events of Pentecost and then traces the ever-widening course of the gospel.

The story begins in Jerusalem, reports the work in the Holy Land, follows Paul to Asia Minor and the European continent and finally ends with Paul continuing his work as a prisoner in Rome. The time span of all this is from A.D. 30 to about 62. That is, it covers the time from Pentecost to the time of Paul's two years of house arrest in Rome. Thus, we could say it covers the first generation of the New Testament church's history.

Among the important points which Luke makes for Theophilus which the Holy Spirit inspired him to write for our sakes, too, are these:

1) He reports Jesus' continuing activity in the interest of his church and for the salvation of sinners, as well as the coming of the Holy Spirit and the power he gave to believers to witness.

2) He records what the message of the church was from the very beginning. We learn that it focused on the

crucified and risen Savior, that it was a message of repentance and the forgiveness of sins, that the apostles regularly based their message on Old Testament Scripture and the facts of salvation history. Acts is full of examples of their preaching and teaching.

3) He shows how the break between Christianity and Judaism came about, also describing relations between Jewish and Gentile Christians.

4) He provides information on what the attitude of the Roman authorities was before A.D. 64, when the first government persecution against Christians broke out in Rome.

Without this book we would have only a scanty record of the apostles' activity and the gospel's spread. We would have little knowledge of church life in the first generation of the church. We would have only hints from the epistles as to the matters which are reported in vivid detail in Acts. We also have a clearer understanding of the epistles because of the historical information which Acts provides.

Time and Place of Writing

It is clear from the last verse of Acts that Luke wrote after Paul had been under house arrest at Rome for two years. Since the author was not reluctant to report the deaths of other Christians in his writings, there is no reason to think that Paul was dead at the time Acts was written. Nor does Luke say anything about the outcome of Paul's trial before Caesar. He is silent about the burning of Rome in A.D. 64 and about the cruel persecution under Nero which followed. These events would all have had a bearing on the story of Paul and would have been a concern to a man like Theophilus.

Tradition says that Paul was released after his trial and that he made a mission tour to Spain in keeping with the plans he outlined in Romans 15:28. We know from 2 Timothy that he was arrested and imprisoned a second time. Tradition says that he was condemned and beheaded, sometime between A.D. 64 and 66 (although some historians reckon that he was executed as late as A.D. 69).

Since none of these events were reported in Acts, although all of them would have been of interest to Theophilus, we conclude that Luke wrote Acts before Paul's death. We conjecture that he wrote even before the burning of Rome in A.D. 64. Let us say he wrote between A.D. 62 and 64, probably from Rome.

Theme and Outline

"YOU WILL BE MY WITNESSES"
I. Peter and His Co-workers Witness in Jerusalem and its Environs (1-12)
   A. "You Will Be My Witnesses" (1:1-11)
   B. Preparation and Equipping (1:12-2:4)
   C. "God-fearing Jews from Every Nation" (2:5-41)
   D. The Word of God Spreads in Jerusalem (2:42-6:7)
   E. Stephen's Witness Sealed in Blood (6:8-8:1)
   F. Philip's Work in Samaria and Judea (8:1-40)
   G. The Conversion of Saul (9:1-31)
   H. Salvation for the Gentiles (9:32-11:26)
   I. The Jerusalem Church Preserved in Famine and Persecution (11:27-12:25)
II. Paul and His Companions Witness in Asia Minor and Europe (13:1-21:16)
   A. Paul's First Mission Tour: Asia Minor (13:1-14:28)

Luke

PART I
PETER AND HIS CO-WORKERS WITNESS IN JERUSALEM AND ITS ENVIRONS

ACTS 1 — 12

"You Will Be My Witnesses."

1 **In my former book, Theophilus, I wrote about all that Jesus began to do and to teach ²until the day he was taken up to heaven, after giving instructions through the Holy Spirit to the apostles he had chosen.**

The "former book" to which Luke refers is his Gospel. We would call "the former book" Volume I and the Book of Acts Volume II.

Theophilus means "one who loves God." It was a very common Greek name, and by itself it does not prove that the man was a Christian. It was often used by Jews living outside Palestine, and Theophilus may have been a Jew living in the Hellenistic world of the Roman Empire. In Luke 1:3 the author used the title "most excellent" Theophilus in addressing his first reader. That may mean that he was an aristocrat or an official. Luke does not use the title here. Since Christians did not address one another with formal titles, this may mean that Theophilus became a Christian after reading Luke's Gospel, that "Volume I" was God's instrument to convert him.

Luke's Gospel ended with a summary of the risen Lord's instruction to his disciples, his promise of the Holy Spirit, and his ascension. This account begins with a similar summary and sets the stage for the events to be recorded in Acts. The expression "Jesus began to do and teach" simply means that Jesus did it. We could add, "He finished what he began."

The apostles he had chosen were the Eleven as listed in verse 13. Judas Iscariot was dead. The word "apostles" means that they were sent out by him to deliver his message. John 20:22,23 sheds further light on the instruction they received through the Holy Spirit: "(Jesus) breathed on them and said, 'Receive the Holy Spirit. If you forgive anyone his sins, they are forgiven; if you do not forgive them, they are not forgiven.' " The Spirit of God was present and active in the lives of these men even before Pentecost. They were instructed to preach God's gospel and God's law.

³After his suffering, he showed himself to these men and gave many convincing proofs that he was alive. He appeared to them over a period of forty days and spoke about the kingdom of God. ⁴On one occasion, while he was eating with them, he gave them this command: "Do not leave Jerusalem, but wait for the gift my Father promised, which you have heard me speak about. ⁵For John baptized with water, but in a few days you will be baptized with the Holy Spirit."

At various times during those forty days Jesus stood among these men, spoke with them, showed them his hands and feet, invited them to touch him and ate a piece of broiled fish in their presence (Luke 24:36-42). Paul tells us in 1 Corinthians 15:6 that on one occasion more than 500 believers saw him alive. He appeared again and again, so that there would be no doubt that he had risen and was alive.

"He spoke about the kingdom of God," which is not a place but an activity, not God's realm but his reign. God rules in people's lives by the preaching of repentance and the forgiveness of sins (Luke 24:47).

Verse 4 reviews and restates what was written in Luke 24:49. The gift which Jesus' Father promised is the Holy Spirit. The words "promise" and "gift" remind us that the Holy Spirit does not come by our activity or effort but from God. Even the apostles could only "wait for" him, trusting God's promise.

"For" at the beginning of verse 5 is used in the sense of "seeing that." The promise of the Spirit, of baptism with the Holy Spirit, had been preached by John as he announced the coming of Christ. He said, "I baptize you with water. But one more powerful than I will come, the thongs of whose sandals I am not worthy to untie. He will baptize you with the Holy Spirit and with fire" (Luke 3:16). John preached "a baptism of repentance for the forgiveness of sins" (Luke 3:3), and the apostles had received the forgiveness of sins in that baptism. What they were to receive in the future was the baptism with the Holy Spirit which would give them the power to do their apostolic work (Acts 1:8). The story of Pentecost in chapter 2 describes how this promised gift, this baptism with the Holy Spirit, was given.

A footnote in the NIV informs us that the Greek expression may be understood as "in" water rather than "with" water. "With" seems to suit the sense better, since it provides a contrast: "with water . . . with the Holy Spirit." "In" would simply remind us that John did his baptizing at the Jordan River. It would not be teaching that baptism must be by immersion.

⁶So when they met together, they asked him, "Lord, are you at this time going to restore the kingdom to Israel?"

Jesus' resurrection had demonstrated beyond a doubt that he is the Lord's Anointed. Would he now do what many hoped the Lord's Anointed would do? A popular hope among the Jewish people was that the Messiah would bring back the days of David and Solomon, when the kingdom of Israel was at its greatest. They hoped that Israel would not only be free from Roman domination but would also be a world power. Even the select group of the apostles still needed instruction about Messiah's purpose and the nature of God's kingdom.

7He said to them: "It is not for you to know the times or dates the Father has set by his own authority. 8But you will receive power when the Holy Spirit comes on you; and you will be my witnesses in Jerusalem, and in all Judea and Samaria, and to the ends of the earth."

It was not for them (or us) to know when God will bring his great plan to completion. It is enough to know that he has a plan for his kingdom and that his will is gracious and good. He has his calendar, and he has marked the day and made a note of the hour. We are not to calculate the time of our Lord's second coming, the date of judgment day.

Before his resurrection, when he was in his state of humiliation and not exercising his divine knowledge to the full, Jesus had said he did not know the day of God's judgment: "No one knows about that day or hour, not even the angels in heaven, nor the Son, but only the Father" (Mark 13:32). Here he does not say, "I do not know," but, "It is not for you to know."

From his word we know that his kingdom is not political but spiritual. We know that it is not limited to the Jewish people but includes all believers, the spiritual Israel. We know that our Lord will come again with glory, to judge both the living and the dead.

11

The apostles were not to busy their minds with what they could not know. Rather, they were to be occupied with the great mission assignment that Jesus was giving them. Beginning at Jerusalem, they would go out as his witnesses in ever-widening circles. Judea is the area in which Jerusalem is located, the southern part of Palestine. Samaria is the area to the north, between Judea and Galilee.

Witnesses are people who tell what they have seen and heard. The apostles had seen his deeds and heard his words. They had witnessed his obedient life and death, they had seen him alive from the dead. It would be their mission to tell this to the farthest parts of the earth. The Book of Acts describes in part how they carried out that assignment. Through the writings of the New Testament they continue to witness to this day.

What they had seen and heard qualified them to be witnesses. Power from the Holy Spirit would equip them for this work. Here Jesus himself tells what the baptism with the Spirit will be. It will be an enabling and equipping power. For example, on Pentecost (2:32), at Solomon's Colonnade (3:15), and before the Sanhedrin (5:30-32) Peter would be able to testify clearly and fearlessly that God raised the crucified Jesus to life. "We are witnesses," he could say.

"You will be my witnesses" is a promise. We, of course, are not witnesses in the same sense that the apostles were. But we have received the Holy Spirit who enables us to trust Christ, to know what he has done for us and for all people. This gives us the ability and the responsibility to speak of him and his salvation, beginning at home and continuing in ever-wider circles.

9 After he said this, he was taken up before their very eyes, and a cloud hid him from their sight.

He Appeared to the Eleven as they Sat at Meat

13

10They were looking intently up into the sky as he was going, when suddenly two men dressed in white stood beside them. 11"Men of Galilee," they said, "why do you stand here looking into the sky? This same Jesus, who has been taken from you into heaven, will come back in the same way you have seen him go into heaven."

It was in the vicinity of Bethany (Luke 24:50), on the Mount of Olives (Acts 1:12), a short distance east of Jerusalem. This is the only account in the New Testament of what they actually saw when Jesus ascended.

This being taken up and hidden from their sight made it clear that they must not expect him to establish a political kingdom with visible glory. It brought home to them that they must wait for the promised Spirit to empower them for their mission task. It signaled that he would no longer appear and disappear as he had been doing during the forty days since his resurrection.

They did not see the resurrection, but they saw him alive afterward. They did see the ascension, but from now on he would be hidden from their sight.

The sudden appearance of the "two men," the description of their clothing, and the fact that they had a message from God make clear that they were angels. The description is similar to that in Luke 24:4, where the angels appear to Peter and John at Jesus' empty tomb. Angels are spirits, but at times they assumed human form to communicate with men.

The apostles kept straining to see Jesus after the cloud hid him from their sight. The angels' question reminded them that they had a mission to carry out and that they must not spend their lives gazing at the sky. Jesus will be returning, and there is work to do before that.

The angels' words are also an answer to the disciples' question about the kingdom (v. 6). The disciples would be workers in his kingdom of grace, bringing God's gracious rule into people's lives. The perfect fulfillment of that kingdom will occur when Jesus returns visibly.

The heaven to which Jesus ascended is not the realm of astronomers, the sky with its stars and planets. It is not a place where he is confined or to which he has retired. It is the state of glory in which he who shares our humanity enjoys all the power and glory which he had with the Father from eternity. God "raised him from the dead and seated him at his right hand in the heavenly realms, far above all rule and authority, power and dominion, and every title that can be given, not only in the present age but also in the one to come. And God placed all things under his feet and appointed him to be head over everything for the church, which is his body, the fullness of him who fills everything in every way" (Ephesians 1:20-23). He fills the whole universe (Ephesians 4:10).

Our Savior did not retire when he ascended to heaven. He has not deserted us. He is involved and he is in charge. The apostles' acts and the church's work in every generation are his doing. This work is not only done for him; it is done by him.

He will return from heaven, visibly, say the angels.

> "Look, he is coming with the clouds,
>   and every eye will see him,
> even those who pierced him;
>   and all the peoples of the earth will mourn
>   because of him.
>
>   So shall it be! Amen"
>   (Revelation 1:7).

A Replacement for Judas

¹²Then they returned to Jerusalem from the hill called the Mount of Olives, a Sabbath day's walk from the city. ¹³When they arrived, they went upstairs to the room where they were staying.

Those present were Peter, John, James and Andrew; Philip and Thomas, Bartholomew and Matthew; James son of Alphaeus and Simon the Zealot, and Judas son of James. [14]They all joined together constantly in prayer, along with the women and Mary the mother of Jesus, and with his brothers.

The hill was called the Mount of Olives because many olive groves were (and are) situated on it. People can still walk on the Roman road which went from Jerusalem up and over the hill.

The Sabbath day's walk was set at 2,000 paces, from one-half to three-quarters of a mile. The expression was thought to go back to the time when Israel was wandering through the desert. The distance was supposed to be reckoned from the farthest tent on the fringe of the camp to the place of worship at the center. At the time of Jesus' ministry the expression and the distance were used to determine how far one could walk without violating the Sabbath prohibition against work. The expression was often used simply to estimate distances, as it is here. It was an expression like our "about a stone's throw."

The base of the Mount of Olives is 2,000 paces from the city. The distance to the vicinity of Bethany is 2,000 paces in the other direction. There is no question of Sabbath violation here, since the ascension took place on a Thursday, forty days after Easter.

The room where they gathered may simply have been an upper-story room. It may have been a kind of penthouse, a room built on the flat roof of the house. Such rooms are still to be seen in Israel and the Middle East.

The eleven men mentioned in verse 13 are listed in the Gospels at Matthew 10:2-4; Mark 3:16-19; and Luke 6:14-16. Matthew and Mark call Judas son of James "Thaddaeus." It was not unusual for a man to be known by more than one name. Thomas is also called Didymus, and Peter is known by his original name, Simon, as well as the Aramaic form, Cephas. Bartholomew, "Son of Tolmai," gives us the family name of the man known in John's Gospel as Nathanael (John 1:46; 21:2). To call Simon "the Zealot" is to say that he belonged to a sort of "freedom party" of political activists, people who were not only zealous in the Jewish religion but who also sought freedom from Roman rule.

It was a mixed group of ordinary men with ordinary names. The Lord would accomplish extraordinary things through them.

The Eleven and those with them prayed because they were believers. They prayed together because they were united in what they believed. They devoted themselves to prayer. We are not told what they prayed for, but the petitions of the Lord's Prayer would probably provide a good summary of their prayer concerns. Their prayer was in response to the words and the works of Jesus. "Constantly" suggests that they prayed faithfully and frequently, not that they did nothing but pray.

This verse contains the only reference to Jesus' mother outside the Gospels. The Greek word for "his brothers" could include "sisters." When we think about who Jesus' brothers might have been, we are reminded that Jesus, speaking from the cross, committed Mary to the care of the Apostle John. We also recall that the brothers mentioned in John 7:2-5 did not believe in him. Were they brought to faith after the resurrection? Were they Mary's stepsons, children of Joseph by an earlier marriage? Were they children born to Mary and Joseph after the birth of Jesus? Were they cousins, since the Greek word for "brothers" was sometimes used for other relatives? The Bible does not give us sure answers to these questions, and so we cannot answer them in a definite way. Neither the questions nor the answers have a bearing on the facts of our salvation.

The "brothers" *may* even be among the "believers" who are mentioned in verse 15. See the footnote in NIV: "brothers."

15In those days Peter stood up among the believers (a group numbering about a hundred and twenty) 16and said, "Brothers, the Scripture had to be fulfilled which the Holy Spirit spoke long ago through the mouth of David concerning Judas, who served as guide for those who arrested Jesus — 17he was one of our number and shared in this ministry."

Peter was a leader in the sense that he took the initiative in doing something necessary and constructive. Since Jesus had chosen twelve men to judge the twelve tribes of Israel, Peter and the others felt that a replacement for Judas should be selected. The Eleven did not lord it over the other believers and make a selection without consulting them. "A group numbering about a hundred and twenty" were present.

The particular Scripture to which Peter seems to be referring is verse 9 of Psalm 41:

> "Even my close friend, whom I trusted,
>   he who shared my bread,
>   has lifted up his heel against me."

We read in John 13:18 that Jesus himself quoted this verse with reference to Judas who betrayed him.

This Scripture verse and those quoted in verse 20 have their fullest meaning in the story of Judas's betrayal and his fate. They "had to be fulfilled," according to what God foreknew and what his Spirit foretold.

It is evident that Peter believed that the words of men in the Scripture are the word of God. He does not say that David spoke but that the Holy Spirit spoke through David's mouth. David was the instrument or channel, but God was the author and source. Scripture comes from God, and Scripture must be fulfilled. That was the conviction of the apostles, as it is ours.

"This ministry" is the work of preaching the gospel which the Lord graciously assigned to his disciples. Peter's choice of words emphasizes apostolic service more than apostolic status. Judas had had a share in that service, but he had forfeited it by his treason.

18(With the reward he got for his wickedness, Judas bought a field; there he fell headlong, his body burst open and all his intestines spilled out. 19Everyone in Jerusalem heard about this, so they called that field in their language Akeldama, that is, Field of Blood.)

The NIV treats these verses as an explanation on Luke's part by placing them outside the quotation marks and inside parentheses. It is also possible to read verse 18 as part of Peter's speech and take only verse 19 as Luke's explanatory note. In either case Luke is informing Theophilus of what happened to Judas, information he had not included in his Gospel.

We are told in Matthew 27:5-8 that "Judas threw the money into the temple and left. Then he went away and hanged himself. The chief priests picked up the coins and said, 'It is against the law to put this into the treasury, since it is blood money.' So they decided to use the money to buy the potter's field as a burial place for foreigners. That is why it has been called the Field of Blood to this day."

There is some irony in Luke's words. Judas did not intend that the thirty pieces of silver be used to buy a field. He was not planning to do charity work when he struck the bargain to betray Jesus. He did not give the money for that purpose or make the purchase himself. But in a sad sense he bought it, because that was how "the reward of his wickedness" was used.

Luke here adds a detail concerning Judas's death that is not found in Matthew's Gospel. When the traitor hanged himself, he fell such a distance that his abdomen ruptured, with the result that "all his intestines spilled out."

Tradition located the potter's field south of the Valley of Hinnom, well removed from the southern wall of the city. Its name signified that it was bought with blood money. The phrase "in their language" reminds us that this is not part of Peter's speech but part of Luke's explanation. Peter continued with two quotations.

20"For," said Peter, "it is written in the book of Psalms,

> **" 'May his place be deserted;**
> **let there be no one to dwell in it,'**

and,

> **" 'May another take his place of leadership.'**

21Therefore it is necessary to choose one of the men who have been with us the whole time the Lord Jesus went in and out among us, 22beginning from John's baptism to the time when Jesus was taken up from us. For one of these must become a witness with us of his resurrection."

Psalm 69:25 speaks of those who are enemies of the Lord and of his anointed king, David. It speaks of them in the plural, "May *their* place be deserted; let there be no one to dwell in *their* tents." Peter applies the passage to the one who betrayed the Lord's Anointed, Jesus, and uses the singular, "*his* place."

Psalm 109:8 speaks in a similar tone of the same or similar enemies, and Peter again applies it to Judas, whose place of leadership is empty. He concludes that someone must be chosen to take Judas's place, someone who has the same qualifications that the other apostles have. That is, he must have been with Jesus from the beginning of the Savior's ministry ("John's baptism") to the day of his ascension. Like the others, he must be one who had seen and heard and touched and eaten with, who had also been instructed by, the risen Christ.

Peter was describing what an apostle in the strictest sense was and what an apostle did. An apostle was a man with whom Jesus associated ("went in and out"). He was a man who saw Jesus after the Lord rose from the dead and who then testified to this in the world.

²³So they proposed two men: Joseph called Barsabbas (also known as Justus) and Matthias. ²⁴Then they prayed, "Lord, you know everyone's heart. Show us which of these two you have chosen ²⁵to take over this apostolic ministry, which Judas left to go where he belongs." ²⁶Then they cast lots, and the lot fell to Matthias; so he was added to the eleven apostles.

The group of believers who were present nominated two men who met the qualifications which had been outlined by Peter. With the word "Lord" the assembly was addressing Jesus, who had chosen the original Twelve. Thus, in praying to him, they were addressing him as God. They were confident that he had made his choice and that he would indicate who that choice was. He would name the new apostle through them.

We are not absolutely sure how this drawing of lots was carried out. One method which the Jews used at the time was to write names on pebbles or pieces of broken pottery, then place them into a container and shake them vigorously. The name which flew out first was the choice. The expression "the lot fell" would seem to suggest this method. However, the Greek word which NIV translates as "he was added" can mean "he was chosen by a vote."

21

Whatever the method was, the assembly's confidence that the Lord would make his will known in this way was in accord with Proverbs 16:33: "The lot is cast into the lap, but its every decision is from the Lord."

Matthias was chosen, and we may assume that he faithfully carried out his assignment. Neither he nor Joseph Barsabbas is mentioned again in the New Testament, but that does not mean they played no role in the church's mission. Remember, we have *some* acts of *some* apostles in this writing.

Sometimes it still happens that two men are equally qualified for a position of leadership in the church. When an election results in a tie it is proper to draw lots in some way to determine the Lord's choice. In general, however, such choices should be made on the basis of knowledge, using sanctified common sense.

The Coming of the Holy Spirit

2 When the day of Pentecost came, they were all together in one place. ²Suddenly a sound like the blowing of a violent wind came from heaven and filled the whole house where they were sitting. ³They saw what seemed to be tongues of fire that separated and came to rest on each of them. ⁴All of them were filled with the Holy Spirit and began to speak in other tongues as the Spirit enabled them.

Pentecost is the Greek name for the important Jewish observance of the Feast of Harvest (Exodus 23:16) or, as it was also called, the Feast of Weeks (Exodus 34:22). Pentecost means "fiftieth;" the feast took place fifty days after the Passover Sabbath (Leviticus 23:11,15,16). Every pious Jew tried to be in Jerusalem for this Feast. Those who could not come to Jerusalem observed it in the synagogues throughout the Roman empire and beyond. Freewill offerings were brought (Deuteronomy 16:9-11).

That Sunday came as it came every year, but God had special events in mind for this Pentecost in A.D. 30. What Jesus had promised concerning the Holy Spirit would now take place.

The "all" who were "together" most likely included the entire group mentioned in 1:13-15. They may have been in the house where the upper room was located, or in one of the meeting rooms of the temple area, or in another place. They were gathered for worship and prayer, no doubt. Since they were sitting, they were most likely listening to one of the apostles speak.

The sound which filled the whole room did not merely come from the sky. It came from the dwelling place of the Most High. It came from God.

Just as Luke speaks of a sound "*like* the blowing of a violent wind," so he speaks of "what *seemed to be* tongues of fire." He makes clear that the sound and the tongues were not natural phenomena but signs from God.

Here was the fulfillment of John the Baptist's prediction: "He will baptize you with the Holy Spirit and with fire" (Luke 3:16), and Jesus' promise, "In a few days you will be baptized with the Holy Spirit" (Acts 1:5). The baptism with the Holy Spirit and with fire was occurring there in that room on that day.

The tongues of fire came to rest on each person present. All received the baptism of the Spirit, for each would have work to do in carrying out the great commission.

Loudly and clearly all of them spoke in languages other than the language they normally spoke. They did not all speak at once, but each spoke as the ability was given. This was not babbling or incoherent speech; it was perfectly understandable to those who knew the languages.

The believers were now equipped and prepared to begin carrying out the assignment which the Lord had given to his church. The dramatic signs — the sound, the fire, the ability to speak in other tongues — were signs of that. Such signs did not always accompany the preaching of the apostles or the testimony of other believers. However, the Spirit sent by Jesus is always present and active when the gospel is spoken. He gives the word its power, and he gives believers the power to speak the word.

"God-fearing Jews from Every Nation"

5Now there were staying in Jerusalem God-fearing Jews from every nation under heaven.

Some of them had come for the Feast. Some of them had come to live out their days in the homeland. All of them were "God-fearing," that is, they tried to live in faithfulness to the God of Israel and in compliance with the law of Moses.

"Every nation under heaven" is explained in verses 9 to 11, although it need not be limited to the nations mentioned there. Because of wars and persecutions, also because of their business activities, Jews had been scattered throughout the Roman Empire and beyond it. They were known as Jews of the Diaspora, the "dispersion."

6When they heard this sound, a crowd came together in bewilderment, because each one heard them speaking in his own language. 7Utterly amazed, they asked: "Are not all these men who are speaking Galileans? 8Then how is it that each of us hears them in his own native language?"

Each person in the crowd heard and understood someone of the apostles speaking the language of his homeland. It was not the Aramaic of Judea, which most of them understood, or the Greek of the Roman Empire, which virtually all of them would have understood. Nor did they hear the dialect of Galilee, which they might have expected the apostles to speak. How could the natives of a small and rustic region speak in the languages of many nations? What the people heard threw them off balance.

Some people say that the miracle of Pentecost was not in the apostles' speech but in the people's hearing. But verse 4 says that the apostles spoke "in other tongues." The speaking was the miracle, not the hearing. The apostles' speech was not babbling which the hearers then interpreted. It was coherent and intelligible speaking of foreign languages.

[9]"Parthians, Medes and Elamites; residents of Mesopotamia, Judea and Cappadocia, Pontus and Asia, [10]Phrygia and Pamphylia, Egypt and the parts of Libya near Cyrene; visitors from Rome [11](both Jews and converts to Judaism); Cretans and Arabs — we hear them declaring the wonders of God in our own tongues!"

For the homelands of these people, see the map on page 294. There were representatives from three continents included in this listing: Asia, Africa and Europe. The apostles were to go into all the world, but on this day people from all the world were gathering around them in Jerusalem.

The Holy Spirit had equipped the apostles to proclaim God's great saving work in many languages. The confusion of tongues which resulted at Babel when men tried to glorify themselves by building a great tower (Genesis 11:1-9) was reversed on Pentecost. Then the Spirit moved men to glorify God in languages that were understood by all who heard. This "reversal of Babel" still occurs when missionaries learn new languages in order to declare the wonders of God to people in world mission fields.

[12]Amazed and perplexed, they asked one another, "What does this mean?"

[13]Some, however, made fun of them and said, "They have had too much wine."

It was natural for everyone who heard to inquire about the significance of such an event. But some of them refused to believe either the message or the miracle. They preferred to discredit both by an "explanation" that slandered the Lord's spokesmen. They accused them of drunkenness.

¹⁴Then Peter stood up with the Eleven, raised his voice and addressed the crowd: "Fellow Jews and all of you who live in Jerusalem, let me explain this to you; listen carefully to what I say. ¹⁵These men are not drunk, as you suppose. It's only nine in the morning!"

Peter addressed the crowd in a manner and with a message that showed the charge of drunkenness to be false. The Eleven stood with him in support of what he had to say. What he said was the testimony of all the apostles.

Nine in the morning was the hour of morning prayer, and the Jews did not eat until after that hour. Wine was drunk only with meals, and since it was too early for breakfast, it was also too early to have had too much wine. Peter did not need to defend himself, because his speech made it obvious that he was not drunk. He defended "these men," the Eleven who were standing silent while he spoke. Peter continued:

¹⁶"No, this is what was spoken by the prophet Joel:
¹⁷" 'In the last days, God says,
I will pour out my Spirit on all people.
Your sons and daughters will prophesy,
your young men will see visions,
your old men will dream dreams.
¹⁸Even on my servants, both men and women,
I will pour out my Spirit in those days,
and they will prophesy.
¹⁹I will show wonders in the heaven above
and signs on the earth below,
blood and fire and billows of smoke.

²⁰**The sun will be turned to darkness**
   and the moon to blood
   before the coming of the great and
   glorious day of the Lord.
²¹**And everyone who calls on the name of the**
   Lord will be saved.'"

Peter's real answer to the charge of drunkenness lay in his explanation of what was happening and why it was happening. The speaking in other languages was the sign that the Holy Spirit was being poured out, as God had promised through the Prophet Joel (Joel 2:28-32). The prophet uttered these words about 870 B.C.

The presence of the Holy Spirit was especially evident in the miracle of languages. Not everything else which Joel prophesied was going to happen in detail that day, but the gift of speaking in other tongues was a sign that the entire prophecy would be fulfilled in God's good time and in his way.

The phrase "in the last days" is Peter's interpretation of Joel's expression "afterward." The "last days" refers to the time after God sent his Son and his Son completed his redeeming work. The sending of the Spirit was the evidence that the work of redemption is complete, that when Christ comes again it will be as judge of all. We live in "the last days."

God promised through Joel that all people, male and female, old and young would receive the Spirit. All would proclaim God's message to others after receiving his revelation. "All people" includes Jews and Gentiles, "all whom the Lord our God will call" (v. 39), those who repent and are baptized for the forgiveness of sins (v. 38). This outpouring, which began on Pentecost, continues today wherever the gospel is preached.

27

The references to wonders in heaven and signs on earth are reminders of the time when God delivered Israel from Egypt. Joel's reference to them and Peter's quotation of them are an announcement of God's great deliverance of all people through Christ's saving work.

At the same time Joel's prophecy speaks of Christ's second coming, his coming in judgment. Jesus spoke of it in similar language: "When you hear of wars and revolutions, do not be frightened. These things must happen first, but the end will not come right away. . . . There will be . . . fearful events and great signs from heaven. . . . There will be signs in the sun, moon and stars. . . . The heavenly bodies will be shaken" (Luke 21:9,11,25,26). Every war and revolution, every eclipse, every storm, every earthquake and every erupting volcano remind us that we live in the last days and that we may expect our Lord's return at any time.

Joel calls it the great and *dreadful* day of the Lord (Joel 2:31). Peter interprets that by calling it the *glorious* day of the Lord. It will be a dreadful day for those who have rejected the grace of God, but a glorious day for those who wait in hope. Everyone who calls on the Lord who has revealed himself in Jesus Christ will be saved in the day when Christ returns.

22"Men of Israel, listen to this: Jesus of Nazareth was a man accredited by God to you by miracles, wonders and signs, which God did among you through him, as you yourselves know."

Peter was reminding his fellow Jews of something they knew: God had acted through Jesus. As God-fearing Israelites they would want to know the significance of those miracles, wonders and signs. Those works, said Peter, were God's certification that Jesus came from God and did God's work. Those works bore witness that Jesus' message was

God's message. They attested to the fact that he was the promised Messiah, Israel's hope.

23"This man was handed over to you by God's set purpose and foreknowledge; and you, with the help of wicked men, put him to death by nailing him to the cross."

Who had put Jesus to death? Was it the "some" of verse 13, who were now trying to discredit the Twelve? Was it all who were within earshot of Peter's sermon? Peter was addressing the "men of Israel" (v. 22). Those who had plotted Jesus' death and accused him before Pilate were representing all of Israel. They acted for the nation. Not every Israelite had rejected or would reject the Messiah, but as a nation the Jews had done so.

The Romans had the authority and the skill to nail Jesus to the cross, but those wicked men did what they did to help the Jews put him to death.

Yet none of this could have happened if it had not been in accord with "God's set purpose and foreknowledge." The men who crucified Jesus were responsible for what they did. They were not helpless, mindless robots. But their actions served God's purpose, which was to offer his Son for the sins of the world. God willed the cross because it was an essential part of his plan of salvation.

24"But God raised him from the dead, freeing him from the agony of death, because it was impossible for death to keep its hold on him."

Peter's words are a hard saying. God's people had rejected and killed God's Anointed One. God had acknowledged him as his Anointed One by raising him from the dead. Obviously they were on the wrong side of God, not God's people but God's enemies! Peter was preaching the law to convict them of their sin. That he succeeded in doing this becomes clear in their reaction at the end of his sermon (v. 37).

"The agony of death" does not mean that Jesus continued to suffer during the time he lay in the tomb. The word translated "agony" here is literally "birth-pains." Death was "in labor" while Jesus lay in the grave. It could not hold the Lord of life indefinitely and had to give him up. This, of course, is picture language. Death did not give life to Jesus as a mother gives life to her newborn. Rather, God raised him from the dead, and thus death could not hold him.

²⁵**"David said about him:**

> **" 'I saw the Lord always before me.**
> **Because he is at my right hand,**
> **I will not be shaken.**
> ²⁶**Therefore my heart is glad and my tongue rejoices;**
> **my body also will live in hope,**
> ²⁷**because you will not abandon me to the grave,**
> **nor will you let your Holy One see decay.**
> ²⁸**You have made known to me the paths of life;**
> **you will fill me with joy in your presence.' "**

Now Peter quoted Psalm 16:8-11 in order to show his hearers that what happened to Jesus was in accord with their own Scriptures. It was King David who sang these words and, as Peter would show (vv. 29-32), David was really speaking of the resurrection of Christ.

The psalmist says that he keeps his eyes on the God of free and faithful grace. The Lord will help him and keep him steadfast. This fills David with joy and hope, and he is confident that God will not simply leave his body to decay in the grave. David is one of God's "holy ones," one of his saints, and God had showed him that he would enjoy eternal life with him.

²⁹"Brothers, I can tell you confidently that the patriarch David died and was buried, and his tomb is here to this day. ³⁰But he was a prophet and knew that God had promised him on oath that he would place one of his descendants on his throne."

The prophecy in Psalm 16 could not have had its final and perfect fulfillment in David. "David rested with his fathers and was buried in the City of David" (1 Kings 2:10). If his tomb had been opened, they would have discovered that his body had decayed.

Then what did David's words mean and how were they fulfilled? God had promised him: "When your days are over and you rest with your fathers, I will raise up your offspring to succeed you, who will come from your own body, and I will establish his kingdom. He is the one who will build a house for my Name, and I will establish the throne of his kingdom forever" (2 Samuel 7:12,13).

> "The Lord swore an oath to David,
>   a sure oath that he will not revoke:
> 'One of your own descendants
>   I will place on your throne'" (Psalm 132:11).

Every Jew knew that that "descendant" was the promised Messiah, and Peter was inviting them to conclude that the "Holy One" whose body would not see decay was the Messiah. To make sure they did not miss the point, Peter went on:

³¹"Seeing what was ahead, he spoke of the resurrection of Christ, that he was not abandoned to the grave, nor did his body see decay. ³²God has raised this Jesus to life, and we are all witnesses of the fact."

David had prophetic knowledge that his holy descendant would rise from death. Peter and his fellow apostles had firsthand knowledge, historical knowledge. They had seen the risen Christ, spoken with him, eaten with him. More than 500 persons had seen him at one time (1 Corinthians 15:6). "God has raised this Jesus to life." Jesus of Nazareth is the fulfillment of Israel's Scriptures, the whole meaning of Israel's religion and the heart of Israel's faith.

"God has raised this Jesus to life" was the heart of the message which the apostles preached in all the world and which they recorded in the pages of the New Testament. It is the foundation of our faith. His death was the sacrifice for our sins and God raised him to life to declare that the sacrifice was accepted. His death was for our forgiveness and God raised him to life to declare that we are forgiven. He died to destroy the devil and God raised him up to declare that hell has been defeated.

[33]"Exalted to the right hand of God, he has received from the Father the promised Holy Spirit and has poured out what you now see and hear."

They put him to death, but God exalted him to his right hand. That is, Christ exercises the power of God and enjoys the honor of God. What he had from eternity according to his divine nature he now has and uses according to his human nature as well.

He has the authority to send the Spirit whom he promised to send, and he sent him. Jesus sent the Spirit of truth to testify about him and to equip his apostles to testify about him (John 15:26,27), to guide them into all truth (John 16:13).

"What you now see and hear" refers to the miracles of Pentecost, the signs of the Spirit's presence and activity. The signs say that Jesus has poured out his Spirit on all people, as Joel prophesied (vv. 17-21).

Notice that all three persons of the Trinity are mentioned here, separately and distinctly.

³⁴"For David did not ascend to heaven, and yet he said,
" 'The Lord said to my Lord:
"Sit at my right hand
³⁵until I make your enemies
a footstool for your feet." ' "

Again Peter quoted David, this time from Psalm 110:1. David did not ascend to heaven, and so his words must have their ultimate fulfillment in him who did ascend. Just as Psalm 16:8-11 was a prophecy of Jesus' resurrection, so this verse is a prophecy of his exaltation.

Jesus quoted these words of Psalm 110 (cf. Matthew 22:44; Mark 12:36; Luke 20:42,43) to demonstrate that David's Son is also David's Lord. In the psalm the Lord Jehovah speaks to David's Son and calls him David's "Lord." He promises to give him victory over his enemies. That is the meaning of the picture of the footstool, for it was the custom of victorious kings to place their feet on the necks of those whom they conquered.

God has given Jesus power and authority to subdue sin and death and Satan. The Son of God hid his power when he came as a servant to redeem us. Now the work of redemption is completed and God has exalted him: "Sit at my right hand." The sending of the Spirit on Pentecost is a sign that this is so. The final manifestation of this victory will occur on the day of judgment. This is what David said about Jesus and what God did for him.

³⁶"Therefore, let all Israel be assured of this: God has made this Jesus, whom you crucified, both Lord and Christ."

His glory had been hidden during his earthly service. Now God made it public and open by exalting him.

Peter said, "You crucified" this Lord and Christ. Their representatives had done it by their insistence: "Crucify him!

33

We have no king but Caesar." As a nation they were of the same spirit. What a terrible thing they had done, crucifying the one of whom David prophesied, the one who is the Lord himself and their promised Messiah!

See what God did! See what you did? They asked: "What shall we do?"

37 When the people heard this, they were cut to the heart and said to Peter and the other apostles, "Brothers, what shall we do?"

The Holy Spirit did his work through Peter's sermon. He brought them to realize that they had earned God's judgment. They did not say, "*We* didn't crucify him." They did not say, "He is *not* the Christ." They did not say, "You have had too much wine." They were cut to the heart, and their question showed that God had prepared them to hear the gospel.

38 Peter replied, "Repent and be baptized, every one of you, in the name of Jesus Christ for the forgiveness of your sins. And you will receive the gift of the Holy Spirit. 39 The promise is for you and your children and for all who are far off — for all whom the Lord our God will call."

"Repent" means more than "regret." They already regretted their past rejection of Christ and their part in his crucifixion. "Repent" means "turn from your sinful unbelief to faith in Jesus, from your self-righteousness to trust in his redeeming work." The word of God which Peter had preached and the promise of forgiveness in baptism had the power to work such repentance.

From Peter's words we see that baptism is a means by which God gives us his saving grace: it is "for the forgiveness of your sins." That forgiveness, merited by Christ's perfect life and death, is mediated to sinners in baptism. Baptism in the name of Jesus Christ is baptism on the basis of who he is and what he has done. On that basis God sends our sins away, which is what "forgives" really means. What God sends away is gone!

Notice that "the gift of the Holy Spirit" is imparted with baptism. It is not something that comes separately or later. This may not be clear in the NIV, but it is clear in the original language.

The promise of the Spirit, who works repentance and is active in baptism and gives forgiveness, is for all who hear Peter's words. It is also for their children. It is also for those who were not there that day, including you and me. It is for Jews scattered throughout the world as well as for Gentiles, for all whom God has called or ever will call by the message which Peter proclaimed that day.

" 'Peace, peace, to those far and near,'
     says the Lord. 'And I will heal them' " (Isaiah 57:19).

Notice that children are included in the promise. They also need the forgiveness of sins and the gift of the Holy Spirit. They also, therefore, are to be baptized. God's Old Covenant with Israel included them, and it is unthinkable that the New Covenant would exclude them.

Peter's sermon did not really end in verse 39. He continued, and the rest of what he said is summarized for us in the next verse:

40 With many other words he warned them; and he pleaded with them, "Save yourselves from this corrupt generation."

"Be saved" would be a more literal translation than "save yourselves," and it would help us remember that salvation is entirely God's gift. It is not something we accomplish or contribute to. How could they be saved? Peter had already told them (v. 38).

"Corrupt generation" does not refer simply to the people of that time. Nor is it limited to the Jewish people. It refers to all unbelieving people in every age. They are headed for damnation, and Peter's words show the way of salvation, of rescue from eternal punishment.

41 Those who accepted his message were baptized, and about three thousand were added to their number that day.

Peter's message was God's effective word. Peter planted the seed and God made it grow. The exalted Christ added three thousand believers to his church that day.

The Lord did that by means of the gospel in word and sacrament: "Those who accepted his message were baptized . . . and . . . were added." The gospel persuades and changes people. Sometimes great numbers, sometimes seemingly insignificant numbers, but God's way of doing it is by the gospel.

The Word of God Spreads in Jerusalem
The Fellowship of Believers

42 They devoted themselves to the apostles' teaching and to the fellowship, to the breaking of bread and to prayer.

The apostles taught all the things which Jesus had commanded them to teach (Matthew 28:20). Their teaching is preserved for our instruction and inspiration on the pages of the New Testament. The believers were devoted to living it as well as learning it.

"Fellowship" is sharing. They shared a common faith, a devotion to the apostles' teaching, the blessings of word and sacrament. And so they were a fellowship, a group that shared in worship and in the Lord's work. They shared their joys and woes, their needs and opportunities.

"The breaking of bread" probably includes more than just eating together. It most likely refers to the *Agape*, or love feast, which often preceded the celebration of Holy Communion. Whether receiving the Lord's Supper or simply eating together, this breaking of bread was an expression of their unity in Christ and their joy in his salvation.

Prayer was an important activity in the life of the Jerusalem church. It is still an important sign of vitality in a modern congregation. Like the other activities of the early church, praying together was an expression of their unity and their devotion to the apostles' teaching.

[43]Everyone was filled with awe, and many wonders and miraculous signs were done by the apostles.

The wonders and miraculous signs were really done by God and were performed *through* the apostles. *Through* would be a better translation than *by* here. It was not their power but his which filled everyone with awe. These works were signs that the apostles' teaching was from God. "Everyone," including those who were not yet believers, could see that God was at work through these men.

[44]All the believers were together and had everything in common. [45]Selling their possessions and goods, they gave to anyone as he had need.

Our expression "all for one and one for all" catches the meaning of the statement that "all the believers were together." They had come from many lands and many cultures, but they were united by faith in the Savior.

Verse 45 explains what it meant that "they had everything in common." We will find a more detailed description of this sharing in chapter 4:32-35.

What prompted them to do this? We are not told that the apostles commanded them to do so or that they were trying to put some economic theory into practice. We can only conclude that they did it out of love for the Lord and for their brothers and sisters in Christ. They were devoted to the fellowship.

[46]Every day they continued to meet together in the temple courts. They broke bread in their homes and ate together with glad and sincere hearts, [47]praising God and enjoying the favor of all the people. And the Lord added to their number daily those who were being saved.

They met at the temple because it was the house of the Lord and they were the Lord's people. It was the Father's house and they were his children. They gathered there daily, perhaps at the hours of prayer.

They gathered in one another's homes to share the common meal. They rejoiced that the Lord had come to save them, that he was present in their lives and that he would come again to take his church to heaven with him.

Even those who were not in the fellowship of believers had to like and respect those Jerusalem Christians. In our day, too, it ought to be possible for unbelievers to say of us, "Those Christians are helpful neighbors and good citizens." Our lives cannot make believers of them, but the way we live might at least remove some hindrances to their faith. Our words and actions might convince some that they ought to give the gospel a hearing.

The Lord continued to bless the apostles' work by adding daily to the group of believers. The expression "those who were being saved" could just as well read "the saved." It refers to those who were called to faith by the gospel. It reminds us that the church is not an organization that simply seeks members regardless of what they believe. It is the community of the saved, of believers in Jesus as Lord and Christ.

Healing and Preaching at the Temple

3 **One day Peter and John were going up to the temple at the time of prayer — at three in the afternoon. ²Now a man crippled from birth was being carried to the temple gate called Beautiful, where he was put every day to beg from those going into the temple courts. ³When he saw Peter and John about to enter, he asked them for money. ⁴Peter looked straight at him, as did John. Then Peter said, "Look at us!" ⁵So the man gave them his attention, expecting to get something from them.**

The word translated "temple" in verse 1 is the same word that is translated "temple courts" in verse 2. The term refers to the whole temple area as distinguished from the sanctuary. The temple belonged to the people of God, and so it belonged to those who trusted and served the Lord's Anointed, Jesus. That is why his followers could properly continue to meet and pray there.

Peter and John are often mentioned together in Acts, working as partners. These two men, along with John's brother James, had been part of the inner circle of Jesus' disciples.

Three in the afternoon — the ninth hour as the Jews reckoned it — was one of three hours of prayer. The others were 9:00 a.m. and sunset. There was a daily sacrifice at 3:00 p.m. called "the evening sacrifice." It was an hour of "peak activity" at the temple.

The temple gate called "Beautiful" was probably on the east side of the temple, leading from the court of the Gentiles to the court of women. That is how the first-century Jewish historian Josephus described it. It must have been a busy place if it was a good place for a beggar to sit.

Peter looked straight at the man and commanded the man to look straight at him. Usually people do not really look at beggars, and beggars do not usually look directly at those from whom they beg. Peter's demand signaled that something more than the ordinary giving of alms was going to take place. At this point the beggar did not realize what was going to happen and certainly did not "have faith to be healed." Since he had been lame from birth, there was no reason to hope that he would ever be cured.

⁶Then Peter said, "Silver and gold I do not have, but what I have I give you. In the name of Jesus Christ of Nazareth, walk." ⁷Taking him by the right hand, he helped him up, and instantly the man's feet and ankles became strong. ⁸He jumped to his feet and began to walk. Then he went with them into the temple courts, walking and jumping, and praising God.

Here is one example of the "many wonders and miraculous signs . . . done by the apostles" (2:43).

"In the name of" means "by the power and authority of." Peter and John were not miracle workers. Rather, the Lord worked through them. They were only instruments of his power and authority.

The man would not receive what he had asked for, money. He would receive much more, a gift that would make it unnecessary for him ever to beg again.

The healing was instantaneous, not gradual. There was no healing process, no period of rehabilitation. He walked and he jumped, things he had never done before. This was not the result of his faith or of a decision on his part. It was the power and grace of Jesus Christ that gave him strength and ability to do what he had no hope of doing.

He knew where this healing had come from and he praised God. The name of Jesus reminded the crippled man of all he had heard about the man from Nazareth. As a person who had spent every day in the temple area, he had certainly heard a great deal, probably most of the things we know from the four Gospels. Now he had been healed in the name of that man.

⁹When all the people saw him walking and praising God, ¹⁰they recognized him as the same man who used to sit begging at the temple gate called Beautiful, and they were filled with wonder and amazement at what had happened to him. ¹¹While the beggar held on to Peter and John, all the people were astonished and came running to them in the place called Solomon's Colonnade.

Since it was the hour of prayer and evening sacrifice, a great many people saw the man. They knew what his condition had been, and they were awestruck and dumbfounded at the sight.

Solomon's Colonnade was a roofed porch which ran along the eastern side (perhaps around all four sides) of the temple wall. It enclosed the outer court of the temple. People assumed it was part of the original temple of Solomon. It may have been built over the rubble of that first temple.

The beggar would not leave the side of his benefactors. After the time of prayer, perhaps cutting short their own devotions, the people gathered around the three men.

¹²When Peter saw this, he said to them: "Men of Israel, why does this surprise you? Why do you stare at us as if by our own power or godliness we had made this man walk?"

As he had done on Pentecost, Peter addressed his hearers as "Men of Israel." This was to remind them of their responsibility as people who had been especially blessed in receiving God's written word and God's revealed religion. It was to challenge them to react responsibly to the miracle they had witnessed and the message he would preach.

The healing had not taken place through the power and godliness of Peter and John. They did not want their countrymen to admire them. They wanted Israel to acknowledge its Savior. The address in verses 13 to 26 proclaims Jesus as Lord and Christ in much the same way and for the same purpose as Peter's sermon on Pentecost.

[13]"The God of Abraham, Isaac and Jacob, the God of our fathers, has glorified his servant Jesus. You handed him over to be killed, and you disowned him before Pilate, though he had decided to let him go. [14]You disowned the Holy and Righteous One and asked that a murderer be released to you. [15]You killed the author of life, but God raised him from the dead. We are witnesses of this."

With "the God of our fathers" Peter was identifying with his hearers and insisting that he and John were true Israelites. He would not wash his hands of his people but would try to win them to faith in Christ.

The God of their ancestors had glorified Jesus as Isaiah foretold:

"See, my servant will act wisely;
    he will be raised and lifted up and highly exalted. . . .
By his knowledge my righteous servant will justify many,
    and he will bear their iniquities.
Therefore I will give him a portion among the great,
    and he will divide the spoils with the strong"
(Isaiah 52:13; 53:11,12).

Surely the descendants of Abraham, Isaac and Jacob could not disown the one whom God had glorified. But they had! Through their representatives they had. "Pilate tried to set Jesus free, but the Jews kept shouting, 'If you let this man go, you are no friend of Caesar' " (John 19:12). See Luke 23:13-23 also.

Would they continue to disown him?

Israel's Messiah was holy, dedicated to do the will of his Father and blameless in carrying it out. He was righteous, conforming perfectly to the standard of God's law. "But the chief priests and the elders persuaded the crowd to ask for Barabbas and to have Jesus executed. 'Which of the two do you want me to release to you?' asked the governor. 'Barabbas,' they answered" (Matthew 27:20,21).

Again, it was not only the Pharisees or the chief priests or the Sanhedrin who did this. Peter charged his hearers with complicity and responsibility in the crime: "You killed the author of life." What a devastating preachment of the law!

"You killed the author of life." Here is a great paradox and mystery. The divine originator and guardian of life was put to death. Peter was saying, "That man is God and God died as that man." What man was required to do and could not do — keep God's law — God came and did for us. He came as a man to do it. The work of salvation is divine work, and he who lived and died for our salvation is divine. The God-man's work was successful and accepted by God, for "God raised him from the dead."

Peter and John were witnesses that God had done this, and the healing of the crippled man was further testimony. It was a further attestation of the fact that Christ is alive and that he acts in grace and power.

16"By faith in the name of Jesus this man whom you see and know was made strong. It is Jesus' name and the faith that comes through him that has given this complete healing to him, as you can all see."

The name of Jesus is the revelation of his grace and power. That name, or revelation, created faith in the crippled man. It created the faith which enabled the man to receive the complete healing which had filled the crowd with wonder and amazement. Jesus' grace and power to make him strong were there before the man believed. The man's faith laid hold of them. Twice Peter mentioned "name" and "faith" to emphasize that no power in him and John or in the crippled man had been responsible for this miracle of healing.

[17]"Now, brothers I know that you acted in ignorance, as did your leaders. [18]But this is how God fulfilled what he had foretold through all the prophets, saying that his Christ would suffer."

Peter did not mean to say that ignorance is innocence. They could not be excused for disowning God's servant and killing the author of life. But Peter was leading into the thought that God in his grace had used their evil act for his good purpose and that the gracious Lord was ready to forgive their sins. His words were in the spirit of Jesus, who prayed from the cross, "Father, forgive them, for they do not know what they are doing" (Luke 23:34).

God did not order them to act as they did or will that they do it. He did not cause their ignorance. But through their ignorant actions he accomplished what had to occur because his word had prophesied it.

Popular Jewish belief did not think of Messiah as suffering. It still does not. I once heard a hero of the modern state of Israel say, "A Messiah who suffers and dies cannot be Israel's Messiah." But God foretold it and God fulfilled it and his Christ *did* suffer.

His suffering was not an accident or tragic mistake. It was God's way of delivering all sinners from eternal suffering.

[19]"Repent, then, and turn to God, so that your sins may be wiped out, [20]that times of refreshing may come from the Lord, and that he may send the Christ, who has been appointed for you — even Jesus."

Repent of your past sins and turn to God by confessing that he whom you killed is in fact God's Anointed and your Savior. In that way the wiping out of sins which he accomplished for all will be yours. "Times of refreshing" are times when sins are wiped out and there is peace with God. God sends the Christ when the gospel is preached and when people believe in him. The times of refreshing and the sending of Christ do not refer to a thousand-year reign of the Messiah, as some people believe. Rather, the times of refreshing are simply the day of salvation, the day when a sinner is brought to faith in the Savior.

Verse 21 makes clear that Peter did have the ultimate time of refreshing and the second sending of Christ in mind, too:

[21]"He must remain in heaven until the time comes for God to restore everything, as he promised long ago through his holy prophets."

The Christ who came as a baby, who comes to the hearts of sinners and makes them saints, will come again on that day which God has set as the time to restore everything. As heaven received him visibly, so will he return visibly (Acts 1:11).

The results of the fall will be reversed, and then "the creation itself will be liberated from its bondage to decay and brought into the glorious freedom of the children of God" (Romans 8:21). Years after he spoke these words recorded in Acts 3:21, Peter wrote: "In keeping with his promise we are looking forward to a new heaven and a new earth, the home of righteousness" (2 Peter 3:13).

John, who was there with Peter when the crippled man was healed, received this revelation from the Lord: "I saw a new heaven and a new earth, for the first heaven and the first earth had passed away" (Revelation 21:1). The healing of the cripple was an example and a foretaste of what God will do when his appointed time comes. All that the prophets preached and foretold spoke of Christ and his coming to restore everything.

The original language does not say, "He must remain in heaven." That could suggest that Jesus is confined to a particular place. The Greek says, "Heaven must receive him." In God's plan heaven must accept him as its Lord, for he is the maker of heaven and earth.

As we saw in the discussion of the ascension (Acts 1:9-11) and in Peter's sermon on Pentecost (2:33), Jesus' ascension means that he now uses his eternal divine power in the interest of his church, although he is no longer visible.

[22]"For Moses said, 'The Lord your God will raise up for you a prophet like me from among your own people; you must listen to everything he tells you. [23]Anyone who does not listen to him will be completely cut off from among his people.' "

Peter quotes an example of Old Testament prophecy concerning Christ, Deuteronomy 18:15,16. Jesus is that prophet to whom Israel was to listen and whom they were to obey. Like Moses, he came from Israel. Like Moses, he is a mediator between God and man. Like Moses, he is the deliverer from slavery.

The consequence of failing to listen to and obey this promised prophet is set down in verse 23, which combines the warnings of Deuteronomy 18:19 and Leviticus 23:29. To reject him in unbelief is eternally fatal.

[24]"Indeed, all the prophets from Samuel on, as many as have spoken, have foretold these days. [25]And you are heirs of the prophets and of the covenant God made with your fathers. He said to Abraham, 'Through your offspring all peoples on earth will be blessed.' [26]When God raised up his servant, he sent him

first to you to bless you by turning each of you from your wicked ways."

As with "all the prophets" in verse 18, so in verse 24 Peter was not speaking so much of specific passages as of the whole message and ministry of those men. They all proclaimed the Christ who was to come, and the entire Old Testament focuses on him.

The offspring promised to Abraham (Genesis 22:18; 26:4) through whom all peoples on earth will be blessed, is Christ. Paul wrote in Galatians 3:16, "The Scripture does not say 'and to seeds,' meaning many people, but 'and to your seed,' meaning one person, who is Christ."

The people of Israel were heirs of, they shared in, what the prophets foretold and what God promised to Abraham, Isaac and Jacob. How tragic if these favored people should continue to deny their inheritance and refuse their birthright! Christ came to be a blessing to all people. How can his own people refuse that blessing?

"Raised up" in verse 26 is not a reference to the resurrection but to the entire earthly ministry of Jesus.

The gospel of salvation was offered first to the Jews. That had been the case in Jesus' own ministry, and it was happening there in Jerusalem as Peter preached.

Notice that just as creation and redemption are God's work, so is conversion. God sent his servant to bless Israel by turning (converting) them. Notice, too, that individuals rather than nations are converted: "each of you."

Peter's sermon was interrupted at this point, and he and John were hustled off to jail. But what a powerful law and gospel sermon it was. The sermon would bear fruit (4:4).

Peter and John Witness to the Sanhedrin

4 **The priests and the captain of the temple guard and the Sadducees came up to Peter and John while they were**

speaking to the people. ²They were greatly disturbed because the apostles were teaching the people and proclaiming in Jesus the resurrection of the dead. ³They seized Peter and John, and because it was evening, they put them in jail until the next day.

There was negative reaction to Peter's preaching, and he was interrupted. The priests were those responsible that week for various temple duties. The captain of the temple guard was responsible for order in the temple courts and was second only to the high priest in rank. The Sadducees were one of several schools of religious thought among the Jews. They came from various priestly families and effectively controlled what happened in the temple. The high priest was chosen from their circles, and he presided over Israel's high court, the Sanhedrin.

The apostle's preaching greatly disturbed them. For one thing, "they were teaching the people" without authorization from the Sanhedrin. More important, Peter was proclaiming Jesus as the Messiah. The Sadducees did not believe in a personal Messiah. Most significantly, Peter was preaching that Jesus rose from the dead. The Sadducees did not believe in resurrection. Now, if Jesus really rose, they could not deny that there is such a thing as resurrection.

Although they were like "freethinkers" in religion, the Sadducees were very conservative in political matters. They were satisfied with things as they were under Roman rule, and they did not want any preaching that might in any way disturb the status quo. That was why they had conspired against Jesus.

It was too late in the day for a hearing, and so they kept Peter and John in custody overnight.

⁴But many who heard the message believed, and the number of men grew to about five thousand.

The aristocracy and power structure were determined to stop the preaching of the apostles. But the message was already doing its work. "Men" here does not mean "people." It means "males." With women and children, therefore, the number of Christians must have exceeded 10,000. These statistics are not given by Luke to bolster the reputation of the apostles. Rather, they are a testimony to the power of the gospel.

5The next day the rulers, elders and teachers of the law met in Jerusalem. 6Annas the high priest was there, and so were Caiaphas, John, Alexander and the other men of the high priest's family.

The Sanhedrin was made up of seventy (or seventy-two) rulers, elders, and teachers of the law. The rulers were those who supervised the temple with its priests and administered the temple treasury. The high priest and his highest assistants, including the captain of the guard, would make up this group.

The elders were laymen of mature age, respected for their piety and wisdom. In the gospels they are usually mentioned last and may have been the least influential. Many of these were Pharisees.

The teachers of the law were professional interpreters of the Scriptures. Many of these, also, were Pharisees.

Verse 6 mentions the chief Sadducees. The Jews still recognized Annas as high priest, although the Romans had deposed him 15 or 16 years before. Annas's son-in-law Caiaphas was the officially recognized high priest from A.D. 18 to 36. As such he presided over the Sanhedrin at the trial of Jesus and now at this judicial hearing for Peter and John. John and Alexander cannot be definitely identified.

7They had Peter and John brought before them and began to question them: "By what power or what name did you do this?"

49

The body which had tried Jesus of Nazareth and condemned him to die now sat in its customary semicircle and
questioned two of Jesus' followers. Verses 9 and 14 suggest
that the healed man stood with them, or that he was at least
present.

Their opening statement was very similar to a demand
they had once made of Jesus when he taught in the temple
courts: "Tell us by what authority you are doing these
things" (Luke 20:2). On neither occasion was the question
friendly or sincere.

They did not ask how the crippled man had been healed.
They simply referred to "this," refusing to acknowledge the
miracle and suggesting that it was unauthorized and therefore wrong. "Where do people like *you* get the authority to
do such things?"

**8Then Peter, filled with the Holy Spirit, said to them: "Rulers
and elders of the people! 9If we are being called to account today
for an act of kindness shown to a cripple and are asked how he
was healed, 10then know this, you and everyone else in Israel: It is
by the name of Jesus Christ of Nazareth, whom you crucified but
whom God raised from the dead, that this man stands before you
completely healed. 11He is**

> **'the stone you builders rejected,
> which has become the capstone.' "**

In this time of crisis Peter was filled with a special measure
of the Spirit. The Holy Spirit had been present and active in
his life before this. Now the Spirit equipped him in a special
way with the courage and ability to witness to the power and
name of Christ. Jesus had promised this: "When you are
brought before synagogues, rulers and authorities, do not
worry about how you will defend yourselves or what you
will say, for the Holy Spirit will teach you at that time what

you should say" (Luke 12:11,12). That same Spirit enables us to answer concerning our faith and hope in Christ.

In a way, Peter put his questioners on trial. What kind of people find fault with "an act of kindness shown to a cripple"? And what will they do now with Jesus Christ of Nazareth whom they once crucified but whom God raised from the dead? It was by his name that the miracle had been done. Not witchcraft, not idolatry, but his power and grace accounted for the complete healing. Who or what else could have done such a thing?

The "capstone" in a building may be the keystone at the top of an arch, without which the arch and the building would collapse. It may also be the cornerstone, which in ancient architecture determined the lines for the whole building. Without a cornerstone or with a badly laid cornerstone there could be no sound construction. In either case, the capstone was *the* important stone which the building absolutely needed.

To call Jesus the capstone here was to say that without him Israel's faith could not stand. Rejecting him was rejecting the fulfillment of all God's promises. Jesus quoted the same Psalm (118:22) against the members of the Sanhedrin (Luke 20:17). Jesus had told them this prophecy would be fulfilled. Peter was telling them that it had been.

What the builders of Israel's religion rejected, God chose as the key component of their faith. Obviously they could not be good builders. Obviously they were at odds with God.

[12]**"Salvation is found in no one else; for there is no other name under heaven given to men by which we must be saved."**

Physical healing for the crippled man and eternal salvation for all who believe — both come from Jesus Christ of Nazareth. God has given this name to men as the revelation of his saving grace. The name "Jesus" means "Savior." What he is called he is. What his name means is what he does.

Salvation is surely found in him. It is found in him alone. Without this conviction there can be no evangelism, no home missions, no world missions. Without this certainty the church would lose its reason for being.

The words "we must be saved" remind us that the living God is committed to this salvation in Jesus Christ of Nazareth. The "we" also says that even those who condemned Jesus and asked Peter and John the hostile question of verse eight can be saved by him.

¹³When they saw the courage of Peter and John and realized that they were unschooled, ordinary men, they were astonished and they took note that these men had been with Jesus. ¹⁴But since they could see the man who had been healed standing there with them, there was nothing they could say. ¹⁵So they ordered them to withdraw from the Sanhedrin and then conferred together. ¹⁶"What are we going to do with these men?" they asked. "Everybody living in Jerusalem knows they have done an outstanding miracle, and we cannot deny it. ¹⁷But to stop this thing from spreading any further among the people, we must warn these men to speak no longer to anyone in this name."

¹⁸Then they called them in again and commanded them not to speak or teach at all in the name of Jesus.

How could such laymen, untrained in the religious schools, speak with such courage? The answer really was that they had been with Jesus.

The Sanhedrin could not deny the miracle, but they would not draw the obvious conclusion that Jesus had risen from the dead and was empowering these men to do such a miracle. The healing was undeniable, but still they denied the name in which it had been done. They could not disprove the resurrection or deny the healing, but they tried to use their authority and power to squelch the apostles' preaching.

[19]But Peter and John replied, "Judge for yourselves whether it is right in God's sight to obey you rather than God. [20]For we cannot help speaking about what we have seen and heard."

[21]After further threats they let them go. They could not decide how to punish them, because all the people were praising God for what had happened. [22]For the man who was miraculously healed was over forty years old.

The men of the Sanhedrin believed that they spoke for God. But in the face of the miracle which they could not deny and Peter's witness to the risen Christ, did they really believe that their injunction to silence could be obeyed? Peter and John would obey the God who raised Jesus from the dead and not the unbelievers who denied it.

The apostles had seen the deeds and heard the words of the Messiah. They had seen him alive from the dead. How could they be silent when their Lord had called and equipped them to be his witnesses? How can we? Silence when we ought to speak amounts to denial.

The Sanhedrin did not release them because it was the right thing to do; they let them go because it was the expedient thing to do. The man had been known for a long time. His condition had existed since birth, more than forty years. The people who praised God for the miracle would not tolerate any punishment of the men through whom God worked that healing.

[23]On their release, Peter and John went back to their own people and reported all that the chief priests and elders had said to them. [24]When they heard this, they raised their voices together in prayer to God. "Sovereign Lord," they said, "You made the heaven and the earth and the sea, and everything in them. [25]You

spoke by the Holy Spirit through the mouth of your servant, our father David:

> " 'Why do the nations rage,
>   and the peoples plot in vain?
> [26] The kings of the earth take their stand,
>   and the rulers gather together
> against the Lord
>   and against his Anointed One.'

[27] Indeed Herod and Pontius Pilate met together with the Gentiles and the people of Israel in this city to conspire against your holy servant Jesus, whom you anointed. [28] They did what your power and will had decided beforehand should happen. [29] Now, Lord, consider their threats and enable your servants to speak your word with great boldness. [30] Stretch out your hand to heal and perform miraculous signs and wonders through the name of your holy servant Jesus."

What the apostles were in the world to do, preach the gospel, was now an illegal activity. The highest authority in Israel had demanded that they stop. What did they do? In perfect unity, not arguing over what they ought to do, they prayed.

The prayer was not a prayer for protection from persecution. It was a prayer of thanksgiving for all that God had done. It was also a petition for courage to continue the work of proclaiming Jesus' name by word and deed. "Lord, don't let your servants be cowed by the threats of your enemies."

They acknowledged him as the almighty creator of the universe. They recounted what the enemies of Jesus had done to him and remembered that his death was in fulfillment of God's prophecy in Psalm 2:1,2. King Herod, Ruler Pilate, the Roman nation and the people of Israel had all conspired against the Lord's Anointed. They did what they wanted to do, and they were responsible for their own actions.

But at the same time, unwillingly and unwittingly, they carried out God's purpose. The prayer does not say it, but implicit in their praise was what they had been preaching: "God raised him from the dead."

Jesus is not dead but alive. His mission is not ended but only beginning. Let the Lord who has the whole world in his hand, who uses even the wickedness of unbelievers for his saving purpose, continue to bless that mission. Let him confirm the apostolic message with more miracles.

[31] After they prayed, the place where they were meeting was shaken. And they were all filled with the Holy Spirit and spoke the word of God boldly.

God gave them a sign that their prayer was answered. They had not asked for a sign or for a special outpouring of the Holy Spirit. They had asked for boldness in speaking the word. The boldness was given with the filling of the Spirit. In the face of threats and opposition they would continue to use the gift they had asked for. The Spirit had prompted them to pray and the Spirit empowered them to preach.

> "The peoples plot in vain. . . .
> The One enthroned in heaven laughs;
> the Lord scoffs at them" (Psalm 2:1,4).

Life in the Jerusalem Church

[32] All the believers were one in heart and mind. No one claimed that any of his possessions was his own, but they shared everything they had. [33] With great power the apostles continued to testify to the resurrection of the Lord Jesus, and much grace was with them all. [34] There were no needy persons among them. For from time to time those who owned lands or houses sold them, brought the money from the sales [35] and put it at the apostles' feet, and it was distributed to anyone as he had need.

We do not read of a generation gap, of class conflict or of social cliques in the Jerusalem church. What we find is people who are "one in heart and mind."

The church's unity expressed itself in a willingness to share. This was not a regulation of the apostles. The right to hold property and have personal possessions had not been abolished. But no one took the attitude "what's mine is mine." Voluntarily, they used what they had to supply the needs of others. That some were in need and some were able to help them indicates that the believers were not all of the same economic and social class. Yet, there was a marvelous unity.

There was certainly a connection between the apostles' continuing testimony and the unity of heart and mind that existed in the Jerusalem church. "With great power" means that their witness was effective. "Much grace was with them all" means that the results of the apostle's work showed in the lives of the believers.

The voluntary sharing was a sign of that. They put their money at the disposal of the apostles, trusting that the Twelve would administer it in an honorable, practical and loving way.

36Joseph, a Levite from Cyprus, whom the apostles called Barnabas (which means, Son of Encouragement), 37sold a field he owned and brought the money and put it at the apostles' feet.

Among the many believers who were providing for needy fellow Christians, Luke mentions one in particular. He is introducing a great mission worker, of whom the Book of Acts will report many more things. This man must have had a gift for encouraging his fellow believers, for the apostles gave him the nickname "Son of Encouragement." We read in Acts 11:23 that he "encouraged them [the Christians at Antioch] all to remain true to the Lord with all their hearts."

As a Levite he would have had occasional duties at the temple. Perhaps that is what brought him to Jerusalem. Cyprus, which had been his home, is the large island in the northeast corner of the Mediterranean. Jews had been settled there as early as the second century B.C. Barnabas would accompany Paul on the first missionary tour, and the first stop would be Cyprus.

5 **Now a man named Ananias, together with his wife Sapphira, also sold a piece of property. ²With his wife's full knowledge he kept back part of the money for himself, but brought the rest and put it at the apostles' feet.**

³Then Peter said, "Ananias, how is it that Satan has so filled your heart that you have lied to the Holy Spirit and have kept for yourself some of the money you received for the land? ⁴Didn't it belong to you before it was sold? And after it was sold, wasn't the money at your disposal? What made you think of doing such a thing? You have not lied to men but to God."

The encouraging generosity of Barnabas had its discouraging counterpart in the deception of Ananias and Sapphira. They were willing to take credit for more charity than they were willing to perform. Peter's evaluation of their action as a lie to the Holy Spirit and as testing the Spirit of the Lord (v. 9) was really God's judgment on the action and the motive. God gave Peter the knowledge of what they had done. God gave him the proper name for their action.

What they did was prompted by Satan, the father of lies. They had not resisted his prompting. It was not only a deceit practiced on the apostles and the believers. It was a lie to the Holy Spirit and therefore a lie to God. Selling one's property and giving away the proceeds was not compulsory. Honesty always is.

⁵When Ananias heard this, he fell down and died. And great fear seized all who heard what had happened. ⁶Then the young men came forward, wrapped up his body, and carried him out and buried him.

⁷About three hours later his wife came in, not knowing what had happened. ⁸Peter asked her, "Tell me, is this the price you and Ananias got for the land?"

"Yes," she said, "that is the price."

⁹Peter said to her, "How could you agree to test the Spirit of the Lord? Look! The feet of the men who buried your husband are at the door, and they will carry you out also."

¹⁰At that moment she fell down at his feet and died. Then the young men came in and, finding her dead, carried her out and buried her beside her husband. ¹¹Great fear seized the whole church and all who heard about these events.

The couple had tested the Spirit of the Lord in the way children test a new teacher, to see what they could get away with, to see how far they could stretch the goodness of God. Tragically, they learned that God will not be deceived and he will not let his grace be abused. Better for us to learn it from this story than by experience.

Verse 11 marks the first time that the word "church" is used by Luke for the community of believers. Pray God that it does not often appear in as somber a context today as it did on that day.

Believers and unbelievers heard about these deaths and of the events which led up to them. The great fear which seized them was the fitting emotion. There was no "natural" cause for the death of the couple. It could only be God's judgment on their hypocrisy.

¹²The apostles performed many miraculous signs and wonders among the people. And all the believers used to meet together in Solomon's Colonnade. ¹³No one else dared join them, even

though they were highly regarded by the people. [14]Nevertheless, more and more men and women believed in the Lord and were added to their number. [15]As a result, people brought the sick into the streets and laid them on beds and mats so that at least Peter's shadow might fall on some of them as he passed by. [16]Crowds gathered also from the towns around Jerusalem, bringing their sick and those tormented by evil spirits, and all of them were healed.

Preaching in Jesus' name had been forbidden by the Sanhedrin. Many people who respected the believers were, therefore, afraid to seek a closer association with them at Solomon's Colonnade where they would be observed by the temple guards and other officials.

Although many people were afraid to meet with the believers at the temple, the gospel which the apostles preached did its work. The Lord kept adding people to his church. Luke has been providing us with numbers of men (3,000 and then 5,000) until now. Here, however, the number of men and women is increasing to the point where Luke no longer has a count to report.

The author does not say that anyone was healed when Peter's shadow fell on him. However, we read in Acts 19:12 "that even handkerchiefs and aprons that had touched [Paul] were taken to the sick, and their illnesses were cured and the evil spirits left them." Also, during Jesus' ministry, "they begged him to let them touch even the edge of his cloak, and all who touched him were healed" (Mark 6:56). The Lord, who healed through the hands of the apostles, may well have accomplished his gracious cures through Peter's shadow, too.

Luke makes a distinction between sick people and "those tormented by evil spirits." He is saying that there were people whose problems were not merely physical. Some had desperate spiritual problems because they were possessed by devils. The living Lord, who dealt with such conditions during his ministry, continued after his ascension to heal all those who were brought to the apostles for help.

¹⁷Then the high priest and all his associates, who were members of the party of the Sadducees, were filled with jealousy. ¹⁸They arrested the apostles and put them in the public jail. ¹⁹But during the night an angel of the Lord opened the doors of the jail and brought them out. ²⁰"Go, stand in the temple courts," he said, "and tell the people the full message of this new life."

²¹At daybreak they entered the temple courts, as they had been told, and began to teach the people.

The Sadducees were not only jealous of the popularity of the apostles; they were also *zealous* for what they considered to be God's honor. They were convinced that the religion of Israel as they understood it was being undermined. The preaching that Jesus is the Messiah and that he has been raised from the dead was a contradiction and confounding of their beliefs. So this time they had all of the apostles arrested, not only Peter and John.

God sent one of his powerful messenger-spirits to free the Twelve. The gospel will have free course in spite of prison doors. God's saving purposes are not frustrated by locks.

The angel of the Lord instructed the apostles to continue preaching the gospel in all its truth and with all it means in the lives of those who believe. They were to do this at the very center of Jewish religion and public life. At daybreak they did just that.

When the high priest and his associates arrived, they called together the Sanhedrin — the full assembly of the elders of Israel — and sent to the jail for the apostles. ²²But on arriving at the jail, the officers did not find them there. So they went back and

reported, 23"We found the jail securely locked, with the guards standing at the doors; but when we opened them, we found no one inside." 24On hearing this report, the captain of the temple guard and the chief priests were puzzled, wondering what would come of this.

25Then someone came and said, "Look! The men you put in jail are standing in the temple courts teaching the people." 26At that, the captain went with his officers and brought the apostles. They did not use force, because they feared that the people would stone them.

The officials did not know what had happened during the night. They were ready to hold another hearing. They were in for a surprise. The angel had freed the prisoners without disturbing the guards. The jail was secure but it was empty!

While the leaders tried to digest this news and weigh its significance, they received a further startling report. The prisoners were in the temple courts, doing what they had been forbidden to do!

Those who rearrested the apostles did so with considerable care and courtesy. The whole population held them in such high regard that the authorities feared mob violence if they were to use force.

27Having brought the apostles, they made them appear before the Sanhedrin to be questioned by the high priest. 28"We gave you strict orders not to teach in this name," he said. "Yet you have filled Jerusalem with your teaching and are determined to make us guilty of this man's blood."

The Sanhedrin had commanded Peter and John "not to speak or teach at all in the name of Jesus" (4:18). What Peter had consistently preached, on Pentecost and since, was that Israel had killed its Messiah and that God had raised him from the dead (2:23,24; 3:13-15; 4:10). That was a call to repentance, but it was also an accusation that those who condemned Jesus to death were guilty of his blood, of opposing God.

As always, the officials feared the people more than they feared God. Perhaps the words they had spoken at Jesus' trial haunted them: "Let his blood be on us and on our children!" (Matthew 27:25). What if the people came to the conclusion that the apostles were right about Jesus? Actually, of course, people who came to that conclusion did not pick up stones to attack the members of the Sanhedrin. They were of a different spirit entirely: they repented and were baptized and were joined to the number of believers.

[29] Peter and the other apostles replied: "We must obey God rather than men!"

The answer of the Twelve established a principle for all Christians for all time. What God's word commands, we must do, even when forbidden to do so by human authorities. What God's word prohibits we must not do, even when commanded to do so by human authorities. It is true that "there is no authority except that which God has established" (Romans 13:1). But when that authority exceeds its bounds by commanding people to break God's law, Christians are bound to obey God rather than the authorities.

These words of Peter are not a general license for civil disobedience or revolution. They apply only when we must choose between doing God's will as it is revealed in his word and obeying the laws of men.

[30] "The God of our fathers raised Jesus from the dead — whom you had killed by hanging him on a tree. [31] God exalted him to his own right hand as Prince and Savior that he might give repentance and forgiveness of sins to Israel. [32] We are witnesses of these things, and so is the Holy Spirit, whom God has given to those who obey him."

³³**When they heard this, they were furious and wanted to put them to death.**

Peter's words in verse 30 allude to Deuteronomy 21:23 to acknowledge that Jesus' death had been a shameful one: "Anyone who is hung on a tree is under God's curse." St. Paul reminds us in Galatians 3:13 that "Christ redeemed us from the curse of the law by becoming a curse for us," and then he quotes that verse from Deuteronomy.

But what did God do with this Redeemer whom Israel had killed? "The God of our fathers raised Jesus from the dead," and "God exalted him to his own right hand as Prince and Savior."

Why has God done this? "That he might give repentance and forgiveness of sins to Israel." Peter was preaching the same message he had preached on Pentecost and since, the message he and the others had been proclaiming in the temple courts a short while before. "You killed him. God raised him from the dead. Repent. Receive God's forgiveness, which is for all, including you."

Every truth must be established in the mouths of two or three witnesses. The apostles were twelve witnesses of how God exalted Christ, "and so is the Holy Spirit." God the Spirit himself bears testimony to the truth of what the apostles taught.

God had given his Spirit to those who obeyed him instead of obeying wicked men. The obedience of the apostles was the obedience of believers who say yes to the word of forgiveness in Christ and then keep on saying yes to all that God has said.

Once again, in the case of the Sanhedrin, the message fell on deaf ears and hard hearts. It made them furious and murderous. They had heard the word of life and wanted to silence the messengers forever.

34But a Pharisee named Gamaliel, a teacher of the law, who was honored by all the people, stood up in the Sanhedrin and ordered that the men be put outside for a little while. 35Then he addressed them: "Men of Israel, consider carefully what you intend to do to these men. 36Some time ago Theudas appeared, claiming to be somebody, and about four hundred men rallied to him. He was killed, all his followers were dispersed, and it all came to nothing. 37After him, Judas the Galilean appeared in the days of the census and led a band of people in revolt. He too was killed, and all his followers were scattered. 38Therefore, in the present case I advise you: Leave these men alone! Let them go! For if their purpose or activity is of human origin, it will fail. 39But if it is from God, you will not be able to stop these men; you will only find yourselves fighting against God."

The Pharisees were the opponents of the Sadducees on various points of doctrine, including the resurrection, which the latter denied. They greatly outnumbered the Sadducees and were more respected by the people. Therefore they were influential in the Sanhedrin, even when it was controlled by the Sadducees.

Gamaliel was regarded as moderate and tolerant in his religious views, and that became evident in the advice which he gave to the Sanhedrin. His most famous pupil was Saul of Tarsus, whom we know as the Apostle Paul. Saul, before his conversion, was *not* moderate or tolerant in his attitude toward Christians.

The fact that Gamaliel recalled the cases of revolutionaries who had failed, Theudas and Judas the Galilean, suggests that what the Sanhedrin feared most was political upheaval. If people believed that Jesus was the Messiah, the King of the Jews, wouldn't that bring on an attempt to throw off Roman domination? The apostles were preaching forgiveness of sins, but the religious leaders weren't listening.

They were assuming that the apostles' Messiah was like the popular Jewish idea of the Messiah as a national liberator. The Sadducees, especially, did not want that, because they were quite comfortable with things as they were.

The first-century Jewish historian Josephus says that Theudas claimed to be Joshua come back from the dead. He promised to part the waters of the Jordan River, march into Judea and take the land away from the Romans. The Roman governor killed him. However, Josephus dates this man about thirteen years after Gamaliel made this address. Either Josephus was wrong about the date, or Gamaliel was referring to an earlier Theudas. It goes without saying that the inspired writer Luke is not in error as he reports Gamaliel's speech.

The same Josephus says that Judas the Galilean led a rebellion at the time of Quirinius's second census for taxing purposes, in A.D. 6 (this was not the census during which Jesus was born, which took place between 8 and 4 B.C.). Judas and his followers took the position that it was not lawful to pay tribute to Caesar. Roman troops under Varus quashed this rebellion.

Gamaliel's suggestion was that time would tell whether the followers of Jesus were from God or not. If they were not, there was no need to kill them now and make martyrs of them. If they were from God, the Sanhedrin would find itself opposing God. The form of verse 39 in Greek suggests that he was willing to grant, for the sake of argument, that the Christian movement really was from God. That does not mean he had become a believer. More likely, he was trying to irritate the Sadducees.

With his counsel of indecision Gamaliel made clear that he had not heeded the call to repentance and faith either. To suspend judgment concerning Jesus of Nazareth is to reject him. "Wait and see" is not good advice when the day of grace has arrived. The gospel will not stay indefinitely while people postpone coming to a conclusion about its claims.

⁴⁰His speech persuaded them. They called the apostles in and had them flogged. Then they ordered them not to speak in the name of Jesus, and let them go.

⁴¹The apostles left the Sanhedrin, rejoicing because they had been counted worthy of suffering disgrace for the Name. ⁴²Day after day, in the temple courts and from house to house, they never stopped teaching and proclaiming the good news that Jesus is the Christ.

Gamaliel's speech persuaded the Sanhedrin not to kill the apostles, but it did not persuade them to treat the apostles fairly.

The apostles suffered. They did not have their wrists slapped. They endured a terrible beating, probably receiving the thirty-nine blows prescribed by Jewish law.

The apostles rejoiced. The Sanhedrin had done its best to disgrace them, but the Twelve considered it an honor to suffer for the sake of Jesus and his truth.

The apostles kept on doing what they had been called to do. They never stopped.

6 **In those days when the number of disciples was increasing, the Grecian Jews among them complained against the Hebraic Jews because their widows were being overlooked in the daily distribution of food.**

For the first time the members of the church are called "disciples." This does not refer to the original disciples of Jesus but to all those who were learning to follow him. A problem of welfare distribution provided all of them with a great learning opportunity.

The Grecian Jews were those who had lived in various parts of the Roman Empire and had come to Jerusalem to live out their lives. Some may have decided on Pentecost to remain and settle where their fellow believers were. Their first language was not the Aramaic of the Palestinian Jews. Their dress and customs and attitudes toward Gentiles differed in some ways from those of the Palestinian Jews.

The Hebraic Jews spoke a language that was common to much of the Middle East. It was related to Hebrew in about the way Dutch or Swedish is related to German. The Grecian Jews spoke Greek, the language which was used all over the Roman Empire. Almost everyone who traveled or had contact with foreigners knew two languages. Yet, there would be some problems of communication within the church at Jerusalem.

The Jews of Jerusalem had developed a system for distributing food money to widows, especially those from other lands. The Christian community set up a similar arrangement, funded by the gifts of people like Barnabas.

There is no reason to think that there was any malice in the neglect of the Grecian widows. Language barriers and differences in social customs would contribute to their being overlooked, as suggested above. A new resident would not have the circle of acquaintances that the natives enjoyed, either.

The complaint, which could have been left to fester until real dissension harmed the church, was immediately dealt with by the Twelve.

[2]So the Twelve gathered all the disciples together and said: "It would not be right for us to neglect the ministry of the word of God in order to wait on tables. [3]Brothers, choose seven men from among you who are known to be full of the Spirit and wisdom. We will turn this responsibility over to them [4]and will give our attention to prayer and the ministry of the word."

The expression "to wait on tables" could as well be rendered "to see to meals." They were not claiming that the work of seeing to meals for widows was beneath them. It would be a mistake to think that the apostles thought that waiting on tables was "unspiritual" work. The ministry of the word of God and waiting on table are both spiritual when they are done by spiritual persons. That is true of every God-pleasing occupation. Service done for Jesus' sake, done as to the Lord, is spiritual service. But the particular service to which the Lord had called the Twelve was to proclaim the word.

The apostles proposed a plan that was both spiritual and practical. It was proposed out of consideration for a minority group in the church.

The seven men for the task were not to be chosen on the basis of availability or popularity or to "get them active in the church." They were to be men recognized as spiritual and practical, men known to have a good supply of sanctified common sense. Why seven were to be chosen is not clear to us today, but it must have been plainly practical for the work that needed to be done.

The apostles were not instituting an office for all time by proposing this plan. But they were giving the church of all time an example of orderly procedure and a practical way of carrying out important Christian service. Pastors should not occupy themselves with congregational business that takes them away from the public and private teaching of God's word, from leading in worship and praying for those entrusted to their care. Congregations should not let their pastors be occupied in that way.

⁵This proposal pleased the whole group. They chose Stephen, a man full of faith and of the Holy Spirit; also Philip, Procorus, Nicanor, Timon, Parmenas, and Nicolas from Antioch, a convert

to Judaism. **⁶They presented these men to the apostles, who prayed and laid their hands on them.**

The seven men all had Greek names, suggesting that they were from among the Grecian Jews or would at least understand them. One man was even a convert from paganism to Judaism. These men would know how to be fair to the foreign-born widows without discriminating against the native-born.

Luke singles out Stephen with a special description, because he will have much more to say about this man later on. We will also hear much more about Philip as the story of Acts unfolds.

The term "deacon" is not used in this narrative. The church has often referred to these seven men as deacons because they were chosen for a particular diaconate. That is, they were servants, chosen for a special service.

The laying on of hands and prayer was to signify that these men had been elected for a specific responsibility and to ask God's blessing on their efforts. It was a Jewish custom and it is a custom which is followed today when church officers are installed. It is a fitting rite but not a divinely instituted ceremony.

⁷So the word of God spread. The number of disciples in Jerusalem increased rapidly, and a large number of priests became obedient to the faith.

"Became obedient to the faith" is another way of saying "believed the gospel" or "trusted in Christ."

We cannot tell how many priests constituted a "large number." It is estimated that there were 8,000 priests in Palestine at the time. The chief priests had hardened their hearts. Many other priests, who had seen and heard the things which had taken place in the temple courts, believed.

"So the word of God spread" is the summary of all that Luke has written thus far about the apostles' work in Jerusalem and the blessing of God on that work. Neither the opposition of the Sanhedrin, the episode of Ananias and Sapphira, nor the problem with the distribution of welfare allotments had prevented the Word of God from spreading.

Stephen's Witness Sealed in Blood

8Now Stephen, a man full of God's grace and power, did great wonders and miraculous signs among the people.

That Stephen was "full of God's grace and power" means that he enjoyed special gifts in addition to the wisdom and faith which were noted at the time of his election as "deacon." He was able to employ those gifts in doing great wonders and miraculous signs.

The signs pointed to God's grace and power, not only present in Stephen but available for all. They were invitations to hear the gospel message.

To this point we have heard of only the apostles doing great wonders and miraculous signs. Now one of the administrators was doing them as well. Later, we shall hear that Philip too performed such works. These men had faithfully used the gifts God gave them and carried out the responsibilities to which the church had elected them. God added more gifts and gave them further responsibilities.

9Opposition arose, however, from members of the Synagogue of the Freedmen (as it was called) — Jews of Cyrene and Alexandria as well as the provinces of Cilicia and Asia. These men began to argue with Stephen, 10but they could not stand up against his wisdom or the Spirit by whom he spoke.

Freedmen were former slaves who had earned or been granted their freedom. Many Jewish freedmen returned to the land of their fathers and would have been included among those people whom Luke calls "Grecian Jews."

Cyrene, the chief city of Libya at that time, had a Jewish community. Recall Simon of Cyrene, who carried Jesus' cross. Alexandria was the capital city of Egypt then, and there were so many Jews there that they enjoyed the privilege of conducting their own civil government, separately from the Gentile population.

Cilicia was the province in the southeastern corner of Asia Minor. Asia was what the Romans called their province in the westernmost part of Asia Minor. Its chief city was Ephesus.

Jews living in such places and others in the diaspora used the Greek translation of the Hebrew Old Testament (the Septuagint), and even in Jerusalem they conducted their services and carried on their discussions of the Scriptures in Greek.

Stephen was probably a member of the larger group of Grecian Jews himself. It is also possible that Saul (who became Paul) was a member of such a synagogue, since his province was Cilicia and he was present at the trial and stoning of Stephen.

The important point that Luke wants to make, however, is that the people who argued with Stephen could not successfully stand up against his wisdom. He spoke by the Spirit, and no one can successfully argue with God.

[11]Then they secretly persuaded some men to say, "We have heard Stephen speak words of blasphemy against Moses and against God."

[12]So they stirred up the people and the elders and the teachers of the law. They seized Stephen and brought him before the Sanhedrin. [13]They produced false witnesses, who testified, "This fellow never stops speaking against the holy place and against the

law. **¹⁴For we have heard him say that this Jesus of Nazareth will destroy this place and change the customs Moses handed down to us."**

Bribery was most likely part of the secret persuasion. Just as in the trial of Jesus, false witnesses were used in the attempt to silence Stephen. To blaspheme Moses was to blaspheme God, for Moses was God's spokesman.

The testimony before the Sanhedrin was not worded in exactly the same way as the charges which had stirred up the people and the elders and the teachers of the law. Then it had been "blasphemy against Moses and against God." The formal charge now was that Stephen constantly spoke "against this holy place and against the law." In that form the charge was similar to the accusation in Jesus' trial, the one on which two witnesses had finally been able to agree: "This fellow said, 'I am able to destroy the temple of God and rebuild it in three days' " (Matthew 26:61).

The form of the charges was an attempt to appeal to the two religious schools which were represented in the Sanhedrin. The Sadducees would regard a threat against the temple as especially repugnant and blasphemous, for their religious concerns focused on the temple and its services. The Pharisees would react most negatively to a change in "the customs of Moses," for their religious concerns focused on the law of Moses and the many traditional regulations which had been added to it.

Since the witnesses were false, we can assume that Stephen had not said these things. What he and the apostles had taught was that salvation is in Jesus Christ, not in the sacrifices or works of the law. Again, they taught that Jesus is the "place" where salvation is found, not the temple. As we read his address before the Sanhedrin, it will be very clear that Stephen did not speak against Moses or God or the law or the temple.

¹⁵**All who were sitting in the Sanhedrin looked intently at Stephen, and they saw that his face was like the face of an angel.**

Stephen was full of the Holy Spirit and so he was God's messenger. Therefore his face was like the face of one of God's messengers. There was a supernatural brightness about him, God's evidence for all to see that this man was his messenger.

7 **Then the high priest asked him, "Are these charges true?"**
²**To this he replied: "Brothers and fathers, listen to me! The God of glory appeared to our father Abraham while he was still in Mesopotamia, before he lived in Haran.** ³**'Leave your country and your people,' God said, 'and go to the land I will show you.' "**

Stephen was not addressing them as brothers and fathers in Christ, fellow believers. Rather, he respectfully addressed them as fellow Israelites and the supreme legal authority in Israel.

"The God of glory" is the glorious God who revealed his glory in his gracious dealings with Abraham and his descendants. The biblical references for Stephen's recounting of God's appearance to Abraham are Genesis 15:7 and Nehemiah 9:7, which specify Ur of the Chaldees as the place in Mesopotamia where God first appeared to Abraham. What God told Abraham at that appearance is recorded in Genesis 12:1, which is quoted in Stephen's speech at verse 3.

Before there was a temple, a Law of Moses, a circumcision covenant or a land of Israel, there was a gracious promise from God; there was a man who believed that promise and was ready to act on it. From the beginning and throughout his address Stephen would reverently recount God's gracious dealings with his people. How could that be blasphemy? Also, at various places in his account, Stephen

73

would speak of how Israel regularly rejected God by rejecting his spokesmen. That was not blasphemy on Stephen's part, either, but a call to repentance.

4"So he left the land of the Chaldeans and settled in Haran. After the death of his father, God sent him to this land where you are now living."

When we compare Stephen's speech with the Genesis story of Abraham, there might seem to be a problem of arithmetic at this point. Genesis 11:26 reads, "after Terah had lived 70 years, he became the father of Abram, Nahor and Haran." Then 11:32 tells us that Terah died at the age of 205. After that death, said Stephen, God sent Abraham to the Promised Land. Genesis 12:4 says, however, that Abraham was 75 years old when he left Haran to go to Canaan. Seventy years plus seventy-five years equals 145, not 205. Did Stephen (and other Jewish interpreters of the Scriptures) have a problem with simple addition? Only if Abraham was Terah's first son. But Genesis 11:26 does not say that he was. It only mentions him first because he was the son whose story the author (Moses) was going to tell.

5"He gave him no inheritance here, not even a foot of ground. But God promised him that he and his descendants after him would possess the land, even though at that time Abraham had no child."

The only land which Abraham ever actually owned in the Promised Land was the Cave of Macpelah, which he purchased as a burial place when his wife Sarah died (Genesis 23:7-17). Otherwise he was a nomad, moving his flocks to wherever grazing was available. The promise was that he and his descendants would possess the land (Genesis 12:6,7), but he was 75 when he left Haran and he had no son (Genesis 15:2). The father of believers simply took God at his word and moved.

[6]"God spoke to him in this way: 'Your descendants will be strangers in a country not their own, and they will be enslaved and mistreated four hundred years. [7]But I will punish the nation they serve as slaves,' God said, 'and afterward they will come out of that country and worship me in this place.' "

Stephen was referring to Genesis 15:13-16, and he used the round number 400 years which is recorded there. Exodus 12:40 gives the exact number of years as 430.

This information from the Lord was a further test of Abraham's faith. That his descendants would be strangers, enslaved and mistreated in a foreign country before inheriting the Promised Land, made the fulfillment of God's promise seem very remote. But Abraham continued to trust God and his promise.

[8]"Then he gave Abraham the covenant of circumcision. And Abraham became the father of Isaac and circumcised him eight days after his birth. Later Isaac became the father of Jacob, and Jacob became the father of the twelve patriarchs."

The twelve patriarchs were the twelve sons of Jacob, the ancestors of the twelve tribes of Israel. Stephen's references are Genesis 17:10-14; 21:4.

As he reverently recounted God's gracious dealing with Abraham, how could anyone accuse Stephen of blaspheming God?

[9]"Because the patriarchs were jealous of Joseph, they sold him as a slave into Egypt. But God was with him [10]and rescued him from all his troubles. He gave Joseph wisdom and enabled him to gain the good will of Pharaoh, king of Egypt; so he made him ruler over Egypt and all his palace.

[11]"Then a famine struck all Egypt and Canaan, bringing great suffering, and our fathers could not find food. [12]When Jacob

heard that there was grain in Egypt, he sent our fathers on their first visit. ¹³On their second visit, Joseph told his brothers who he was, and Pharaoh learned about Joseph's family."

Now began the history of rejection, Israel's repudiation of God's favored representatives. The first example Stephen cited was that of Jacob's eleventh son, Joseph. His brothers, Israel's ancestors, hated him and did their worst to get rid of him. God, however, turned the evil act of the jealous brothers against Joseph to his good and gracious purposes.

Verses 9 to 13 report Stephen's summary of Chapters 37, 39, 41, 42 and 45 of Genesis.

¹⁴"After this, Joseph sent for his father Jacob and his whole family, seventy-five in all."

Here Stephen was quoting the Septuagint, a Greek translation of the Old Testament. Where the Septuagint has "seventy-five," the Hebrew original has "seventy." The Hebrew text combines the sixty-six persons who came from Canaan (Genesis 46:26) with Jacob, Joseph and Joseph's two sons (Genesis 46:27) to total seventy. The Greek translation (Septuagint) counts all nine of Joseph's descendants who were born in Egypt during his lifetime, adds them to the sixty-six people from Genesis 46:26, omits Joseph and Jacob from the count and arrives at the total of seventy-five. The Hebrew text is the inspired text and the translators should not have changed the number to seventy-five. Stephen was not endorsing their error. He was simply quoting a translation which he and other Grecian Jews regularly used.

¹⁵"Then Jacob went down to Egypt, where he and our fathers died. ¹⁶Their bodies were brought back to Shechem and placed in the tomb that Abraham had bought from the sons of Hamor at Shechem for a certain sum of money."

The move to Egypt is reported in Genesis 46:5-7, the death of Jacob in Genesis 49:33 and his burial in Genesis 50:1-13. The Old Testament does not record that the bodies of the other patriarchs were taken back to Canaan, but Stephen's words inform us that this is so.

In verse 16 we see Stephen compressing the Old Testament history in order to say as much as possible in as short a time as possible. Therefore details are blurred in the summary of the burials. Abraham bought the Cave of Macpelah from Ephron the Hittite (Genesis 33:19). It was located at Hebron and *that* is where Jacob was buried (Genesis 50:7-13). *Jacob* had bought a plot of ground to pitch his tent and build an altar at Shechem, from the sons of Hamor (Genesis 33:19). There Joseph's bones were laid to rest (Joshua 24:32).

In none of what Stephen had said thus far was he blaspheming God. The Lord's grace, Abraham's faith, the patriarchs' mistreatment of Joseph and, again, the Lord's grace: these had been the subjects of Stephen's speech. That was not blasphemy, but it was an implicit indictment of the Sanhedrin and their treatment of Jesus. It was also a call to repentance, if they would hear it.

[17]"As time drew near for God to fulfill his promise to Abraham, the number of our people in Egypt greatly increased. [18]Then another king, who knew nothing about Joseph, became ruler of Egypt. [19]He dealt treacherously with our people and oppressed our ancestors by forcing them to throw out their newborn babies so that they would die.

[20]"At that time Moses was born, and he was no ordinary child. For three months he was cared for in his father's house."

These verses are a summary of Exodus 1:6 to 2:4. Whatever information the new king of Egypt might have had, he would not be influenced by what Joseph had done for Egypt at the time of the famine.

"By faith Moses' parents hid him for three months after he was born, because they saw he was no ordinary child, and they were not afraid of the king's edict" (Hebrews 11:23). "We must obey God rather than men!" (Acts 5:29).

21"When he was placed outside, Pharaoh's daughter took him and brought him up as her own son. 22Moses was educated in all the wisdom of the Egyptians and was powerful in speech and action."

For more detail concerning Moses' rescue, read Exodus 2:3-10.

In Exodus 4:10 we read that Moses said, "O LORD, I have never been eloquent. . . . I am slow of speech and tongue." In verse 12 of Exodus 4 God promised: "I will help you speak and will teach you what to say." The content of what Moses said and the way in which he led Israel were from God, and they were, as Stephen said, powerful.

23"When Moses was forty years old, he decided to visit his fellow Israelites. 24He saw one of them being mistreated by an Egyptian, so he went to his defense and avenged him by killing the Egyptian. 25Moses thought that his own people would realize that God was using him to rescue them, but they did not. 26The next day Moses came upon two Israelites who were fighting. He tried to reconcile them by saying, 'Men, you are brothers; why do you want to hurt each other?'

27"But the man who was mistreating the other pushed Moses aside and said, 'Who made you ruler and judge over us? 28Do you want to kill me as you killed the Egyptian yesterday?' 29When Moses heard this, he fled to Midian, where he settled as a foreigner and had two sons."

These verses summarize Exodus 2:11-22. Moses' decision to visit his people was prompted not so much by curiosity as by concern. His concern was commendable but his action in killing the Egyptian was not. God had not yet called him to act on behalf of Israel, and God never called him to take justice into his own hands.

Hebrews 11:24-26 provides an evaluation of why Moses identified himself with his own people: "By faith Moses, when he had grown up, refused to be known as the son of Pharaoh's daughter. He chose to be mistreated along with the people of God rather than to enjoy the pleasures of sin for a short time. He regarded disgrace for the sake of Christ as of greater value than the treasures of Egypt, because he was looking ahead to his reward."

In verses 27 and 28 we have another example of Israel rejecting the man whom God planned to use for their rescue. Midian was east of Egypt, divided into two regions by the Gulf of Aqaba. Moses' two sons, Gershom and Eliezer, are named at Exodus 18:2-4.

30"After forty years had passed, an angel appeared to Moses in the flames of a burning bush in the desert near Mount Sinai. 31When he saw this, he was amazed at the sight. As he went over to look more closely, he heard the Lord's voice: 32"I am the God of your fathers, the God of Abraham, Isaac and Jacob.' Moses trembled with fear and did not dare to look.

33"Then the Lord said to him, 'Take off your sandals; the place where you are standing is holy ground. 34I have indeed seen the oppression of my people in Egypt. I have heard their groaning and have come down to set them free. Now come, I will send you back to Egypt.'

35"This is the same Moses whom they had rejected with the words, 'Who made you ruler and judge?' He was sent to be their ruler and deliverer by God himself, through the angel who appeared to him in the bush."

Sinai (Acts) and Horeb (Exodus) are two names for the same mountain. The call of Moses is recorded in Exodus 3.

When the NIV translates Stephen's words as "*an* angel," it could as well have translated "*the* angel." The Greek would allow either translation. A look at Exodus 3:2, to which Stephen was here referring, makes clear that it should be "*the* angel." It was the Angel of the Lord, the second person of the Trinity before his incarnation, who appeared to Moses at the burning bush.

Israel had rejected Moses as ruler and judge, God sent him to be ruler and deliverer.

³⁶"He led them out of Egypt and did wonders and miraculous signs in Egypt, at the Red Sea and for forty years in the desert."

The story of the deliverance from Egypt is told in Exodus 11 to 14. Stephen's "Red Sea" comes from the Greek translation of the Old Testament. The Hebrew at Exodus 13:18 says "Sea of Reeds," which was a northern extension of the Red Sea.

"By faith he left Egypt, not fearing the king's anger; he persevered because he saw him who is invisible. By faith he kept the Passover and the sprinkling of blood, so that the destroyer of the firstborn would not touch the firstborn of Israel. By faith the people passed through the Red Sea as on dry land; but when the Egyptians tried to do so, they were drowned" (Hebrews 11:27-29).

That had been a special time of grace for Israel. The wonders and miraculous signs of Stephen and the apostles were evidence that a new time of special grace for Israel had dawned. How long would it last? What would Israel do with it?

³⁷"This is that Moses who told the Israelites, 'God will send you a prophet like me from your own people.' "

Peter had also cited this passage in his address to the crowd who gathered when the crippled man was healed (3:22,23). That prophet foretold by Moses (Deuteronomy 18:15) had arrived. He had been put to death, but God had raised him to life. What would Israel do? Throughout the speech, Stephen was not so much defending himself as calling his judges to repentance.

38"He was in the congregation in the desert, with our fathers and with the angel who spoke to him on Mount Sinai; and he received living words to pass on to us."

The assembly in the desert was the congregation of Israel. They were not only a nation; they were also God's "church." Those who trusted the promises of God were a congregation of believers.

"The angel who spoke to [Moses] on Mount Sinai" refers to the Angel of the Lord, who had addressed him at the burning bush. The Angel was God himself, who later gave Moses the living words on the same Mount Sinai.

"Living words" are words which endure and are still valid. Stephen was speaking of "brief sayings," and he meant the Ten Commandments. For the Old Testament account of the giving of the Law see Exodus 19 and 20.

39"But our fathers refused to obey him. Instead, they rejected him and in their hearts turned back to Egypt. 40They told Aaron, 'Make us gods who will go before us. As for this fellow Moses who led us out of Egypt — we don't know what has happened to him!' 41That was the time they made an idol in the form of a calf. They brought sacrifices to it and held a celebration in honor of what their hands had made."

Again, Israel rejected the man whom God had sent to mediate between himself and them. "This fellow Moses" was

81

an expression of their contempt for the God-sent deliverer. They did not really care what happened to him.

They turned to the folly of worshiping the man-made image of a creature. They had not only rejected the man through whom God had led them out of slavery. They also rejected God and returned to their worship of the gods of Egypt. These follies are recorded in Exodus 32.

⁴²"But God turned away and gave them over to the worship of the heavenly bodies. This agrees with what is written in the book of the prophets:

" 'Did you bring me sacrifices and offerings
forty years in the desert, O house of Israel?
⁴³You have lifted up the shrine of Molech
and the star of your god Rephan,
the idols you made to worship.
Therefore I will send you into exile beyond Babylon.' "

The "book of the prophets" here means the Hebrew scroll which contained the prophets from Hosea to Malachi. The particular prophet whom Stephen quoted is Amos (5:25-27). The answer to his questions about sacrifice was "No." They had made sacrifices, but not to God, because their hearts were still set on the gods of Egypt. Therefore he did not accept their sacrifices. When Amos spoke these words, he was also thinking of all the idolatry which followed during Israel's long history, even in his own time.

Around 755 B.C. Amos foretold the Assyrian captivity of the northern kingdom (Israel) "beyond Damascus." The captivity of the southern kingdom (Judah) in Babylon came after that. With the expression "beyond Babylon" Stephen was warning that something even worse would happen to those who rejected Christ.

Once again Stephen was quoting from the Septuagint (Greek) translation of the Old Testament, which did not translate Amos' words literally. The Hebrew says "king" instead of "Molech." It says "pedestal" rather than "Rephan." The point of Stephen's quotation is not lost, however. He simply wanted to remind his hearers of Israel's history of gross idolatry, of which they had been guilty despite God's faithful grace to them.

He did not blaspheme Moses and the law. He regarded them as from God and condemned the way in which Israel's ancestors had consistently rejected both. In acknowledging Moses' greatness and attributing it to God's grace Stephen certainly discredited the false witnesses and the charges they had made.

[44]"Our forefathers had the tabernacle of the Testimony with them in the desert. It had been made as God directed Moses, according to the pattern he had seen. [45]Having received the tabernacle, our fathers under Joshua brought it with them when they took the land from the nations God drove out before them. It remained in the land until the time of David, [46]who enjoyed God's favor and asked that he might provide a dwelling place for the God of Jacob. [47]But it was Solomon who built the house for him."

The false witnesses had accused Stephen of speaking against the temple. Did he?

Stephen did point out that their ancestors had worshiped at the tabernacle for many years before the temple was built. They had been the people of Israel, and God had been their God even then.

The "Testimony" was the law, written on two stone tablets. Those tablets had been kept in the tabernacle, and so one of the terms used for Israel's worship place was "the tabernacle of the Testimony." Some interpreters believe that

83

it had the name because it was a testimony to God's presence. It certainly was that, too.

On the pattern for the tabernacle and its building, see Exodus 25:9,40.

For hundreds of years the tabernacle was the only house of worship Israel had. Even in the glorious reign of the great King David there was no temple, although he expressed a desire to build one. In verses 45 and 46 Stephen was summarizing Joshua 3:14 and 24:18; 2 Samuel 7:2-16 and 1 Kings 8:17-19.

On Solomon's building of the temple, see 1 Kings 6:1,14 and 8:20.

48"However, the Most High does not live in houses made by men. As the prophet says:
49" 'Heaven is my throne,
    and the earth is my footstool.
What kind of house will you build for me?
                            says the Lord.
Or where will my resting place be?
50Has not my hand made all these things?' "

Solomon himself was aware that the Most High "does not live in houses made by men" (1 Kings 8:27). The point of Stephen's quotation from Isaiah 66:1,2 is that the great God has no need for anything man might build. The maker of heaven and earth did not really *need* the temple. What he wants is believing hearts and obedient lives.

The picture of the footstool here is not intended to express the idea of subjecting an enemy (as in 2:35). The image here is that of God's greatness: the whole earth is only like a small piece of furniture for him.

The temple served its purpose as a house of prayer for all nations, a gathering place for God's people, a reassuring sign of God's presence and a place of sacrifice. In that way it served the spiritual needs of Israel. But the need for a temple was never absolute, for God's presence was never limited to that place. And after the great service and sacrifice of Jesus, the temple and its services and sacrifices were not really needed at all. Once the great High Priest, Jesus, had done his saving work, the lessons and reminders of the temple were no longer required.

Stephen's criticism, like Jesus' criticism, was not of the temple as such. That was God's house, serving his people. The problem lay in what the Sadducees and others had made of it: a center of formal worship without heart and spirit. There was too much concern with the externals of the building and of worship, too little concern with the inward condition of the heart.

Stephen was not speaking against the temple but putting it in proper perspective. Stephen was speaking against that lack of perspective which gave the temple too much honor and God too little.

51"You stiff-necked people, with uncircumcised hearts and ears! You are just like your fathers: You always resist the Holy Spirit!"

Here is the theme of Stephen's address: "You are just like your fathers." In what way? "You always resist the Holy Spirit!"

Stiff-necked people are stubborn people, like animals who will not bow to the yoke, who will not yield to reins or leash. Uncircumcised means, in religious terms, pagan or heathen. Their hearts were not with God. Their ears would not listen to him. They were just so many unbelievers.

God called Israel a stiff-necked people after they had worshiped the golden calf (Exodus 32:9). When the nation fell into idolatry at the time of Jeremiah, God's judgment was:

"Their ears are closed (Hebrew *uncircumcised*)
   so they cannot hear.
The word of the LORD is offensive to them;
   they find no pleasure in it" (Jeremiah 6:10)

And: "The whole house of Israel is uncircumcised in heart" (Jeremiah 9:26). Isaiah summarized their history in this way:

"In his love and mercy he redeemed them;
he lifted them up and carried them all the days of old.
Yet they rebelled and grieved his Holy Spirit"
                                  (Isaiah 63:9,10).

[52]"Was there ever a prophet your fathers did not persecute? They even killed those who predicted the coming of the Righteous One. And now you have betrayed and murdered him — [53]you who have received the law that was put into effect through angels but have not obeyed it."

The answer to the questions was "No." There never had been a prophet whom their fathers did not persecute. From Abel to Zechariah (see Matthew 23:29-39), the spiritual ancestors of the Sanhedrin spilled the blood of God's spokesmen.

The Righteous One did what God required of all of you: served God in perfect love and obedience. He did it for all of you. "You betrayed and murdered him."

They had received the law given through angels (the "myriads of holy ones" referred to in Deuteronomy 33:2). Israel boasted in the law. The Sanhedrin accused Stephen of blaspheming the law, but they themselves had not obeyed it.

[54]When they heard this, they were furious and gnashed their teeth at him.

They did not interrupt Stephen just then, but Luke interrupts the address to tell us that the words hit home. They reacted to Stephen's preaching as their ancestors had reacted to that of Moses and the prophets. They ground their teeth in fury.

⁵⁵But Stephen, full of the Holy Spirit, looked up to heaven and saw the glory of God, and Jesus standing at the right hand of God.

Stephen was a man known to be full of the Holy Spirit when he was chosen to help administer the welfare program (6:5). He spoke in the Spirit as he addressed the Sanhedrin. That fullness of the Spirit received special expression now in what he saw and in what he said (v. 56).

In the Old Testament, the visible sign of God's glory was the Shekinah, the pillar of cloud or of fire that went before the Israelites in the wilderness (Exodus 13:21,22). That cloud was an assurance of God's saving presence and his gracious intentions. What Stephen saw gave him the same assurance: Jesus at God's right hand, powerful to sustain Stephen's witness.

In the presence of and with the help of the triune God Stephen completed his testimony:

⁵⁶"Look," he said, "I see heaven open and the Son of Man standing at the right hand of God."

Stephen did not imagine this. He saw it and invited others to see. "The Son of Man" is one of the names of Messiah, used in the prophecy of Daniel 7:13,14. Jesus applied it to himself to affirm that he is the Christ. The Sanhedrin asked him with a direct question whether he was the Christ. He answered, " 'From now on the Son of Man will be seated at the right hand of the mighty God.' They all asked, 'Are you then the Son of God?' He replied, 'You are right in saying I am' " (Luke 22:69,70).

In the minds of the Sanhedrin Jesus' words had been blasphemy and Stephen's were, too. They acted accordingly.

Why was Jesus standing? To welcome his faithful witness? To sustain him in the hour of trial? To judge his adversaries? Probably all of these.

57 At this they covered their ears and, yelling at the top of their voices, they all rushed at him, 58 dragged him out of the city and began to stone him. Meanwhile, the witnesses laid their clothes at the feet of a young man named Saul.

They did not want to hear what they considered to be blasphemy. More, they did not want to hear the condemnation of their actions that lay in Stephen's words.

The trial degenerated into mob action. Without pronouncing sentence they took him out to kill him. It was illegal to carry out the death penalty without permission of the Roman governor, but that did not seem to matter when a mob action resulted in murder.

The young man named Saul approved the action, if he did not participate directly in the actual stoning (8:1). We will meet him again, first as a rabid persecutor of the church, then as the great apostle to the Gentiles. Later, he would confess it to the Lord and acknowledge it before men: "When the blood of your martyr Stephen was shed, I stood there giving my approval and guarding the clothes of those who were killing him" (Acts 22:20).

According to Jewish law, the witnesses had to throw the first stones. They had to take off their outer cloaks to do it. They left them with Saul.

59 While they were stoning him, Stephen prayed, "Lord Jesus receive my spirit." 60 Then he fell on his knees and cried out, "Lord

do not hold this sin against them." When he had said this, he fell asleep.

8 And Saul was there, giving approval to his death.

Stephen's dying prayers were like those of his Lord. He committed his spirit to the Lord, prayed for those who murdered him, and fell asleep. When the expression "fall asleep" is used at the death of a Christian, it expresses the hope of the resurrection to eternal life.

The time of peace and progress for the church would give way to a time of persecution. Stephen was the first martyr, that is, the first to bear witness with his own death to the truth of the gospel. There have been many martyrs since, beginning with the persecution that began that very day.

Philip's Work in Samaria and Judea

On that day a great persecution broke out against the church at Jerusalem, and all except the apostles were scattered throughout Judea and Samaria. ²Godly men buried Stephen and mourned deeply for him. ³But Saul began to destroy the church. Going from house to house, he dragged off men and women and put them in prison.

⁴Those who had been scattered preached the word wherever they went.

Jesus had foretold that the witness to him would be taken throughout Judea and Samaria. Now that began to happen, as an indirect and unintended result of persecution. A general and severe persecution of believers began on the very day of Stephen's martyrdom. Acts 11:19,20 tells us that some of the scattered believers went beyond Judea and Samaria, always witnessing where they were: "Now those who had been scattered by the persecution in connection with Stephen traveled as far as Phoenicia, Cyprus and Antioch, telling the message only to Jews. Some of them, however, men from Cyprus and Cyrene, went to Antioch and began to speak to Greeks also, telling them the good news about the Lord Jesus."

The godly men who buried Stephen included Jews who had been touched by his testimony before the Sanhedrin. They buried and mourned for him because they knew he was not guilty of the charge of blasphemy and that his death had not been based on the verdict of a legal trial.

The apostles stayed in Jerusalem to encourage those believers who remained behind in prison or in hiding. The days of meeting publicly in Solomon's Colonnade were over, but the apostles' work continued.

Saul, meanwhile, was like a raging wild animal in his efforts to destroy the church. He later described his activity during this period: "I persecuted the followers of this Way to their death, arresting both men and women and throwing them into prison" (Acts 22:4). Also: "On the authority of the chief priests I put many of the saints in prison, and when they were put to death, I cast my vote against them. Many a time I went from one synagogue to another to have them punished, and I tried to force them to blaspheme" (Acts 26:10,11). He had approved of Stephen's execution, and he wanted to follow through by destroying the church. The Sanhedrin provided temple guards for the raids which he conducted.

The persecution and scattering did not result in the church's disappearance. On the contrary, it played a role in the planting of new churches. Ordinary Christians shared their faith wherever they went. The enemies of the church did their worst, but God turned their evil intentions to serve his gracious purpose.

⁵Philip went down to a city in Samaria and proclaimed the Christ there.

It was not one of the Twelve but one of the Seven who began the work of preaching to non-Jews. That does not mean that the apostles were disobedient to the great commission or reluctant to begin carrying it out. They did their work where they were until God's providence or special direction placed them elsewhere.

Philip, no longer needed to administer the welfare program for the church in Jerusalem, went north to Samaria. He went "down" because he was leaving Jerusalem, which was always regarded as the highest place, the place where God had his house.

He went to a city in Samaria and proclaimed Christ to people who were the religious opponents and racial enemies of the Jews. The city may well have been Shechem, modern Nablus. It is situated at the foot of the Mt. Gerizim, the center of Samaritan worship. The Samaritans also waited for a Messiah, referring to him as Taheb, meaning "he who restores."

⁶When the crowds heard Philip and saw the miraculous signs he did, they all paid close attention to what he said. ⁷With shrieks, evil spirits came out of many, and many paralytics and cripples were healed. ⁸So there was great joy in that city.

The gospel, accompanied by signs, did its work among the Samaritans as it had among the Jews in Jerusalem.

⁹Now for some time a man named Simon had practiced sorcery in the city and amazed all the people of Samaria. He boasted that he was someone great, ¹⁰and all the people, both high and low, gave him their attention and exclaimed, "This man is the divine power known as the Great Power." ¹¹They followed him because

he had amazed them for a long time with his magic. [12]But when they believed Philip as he preached the good news of the kingdom of God and the name of Jesus Christ, they were baptized, both men and women. [13]Simon himself believed and was baptized. And he followed Philip everywhere, astonished by the great signs and miracles he saw.

The gospel which Philip preached did not only deliver the Samaritans from religious error and ailments of body and spirit. It also delivered them from the longtime evil influence of a practitioner of the occult. This man Simon had people believing that he was a manifestation of God Almighty.

Simon believed and was baptized, but the weakness of his faith becomes evident as the story continues. However, we should not conclude that he was not a believer when he received baptism.

He did seem to be more impressed by the signs and wonders which were a part of Philip's ministry, though, than he was by Philip's teaching. He who had amazed so many by his tricks was astonished by Philip's healing work.

[14]When the apostles in Jerusalem heard that Samaria had accepted the word of God, they sent Peter and John to them. [15]When they arrived, they prayed for them that they might receive the Holy Spirit, [16]because the Holy Spirit had not yet come upon any of them; they had simply been baptized into the name of the Lord Jesus. [17]Then Peter and John placed their hands on them, and they received the Holy Spirit.

We are not told why the apostles sent Peter and John to visit Philip in his mission field. We assume that their purpose was to supervise the work, offering suggestions and help. The Seven had not become the apostles' peers when they were chosen for the work of distributing welfare. They worked under their supervision. Now one of those seven administrators was working as an evangelist. How was he faring? What was he teaching?

On Pentecost and thereafter the Holy Spirit was received in Holy Baptism. In Samaria there was a unique situation in that the Spirit had not been received. We are not told that there was something wrong with the way Philip baptized, or that the Samaritans had failed to meet some standard or fulfill some condition. We are simply told that the Holy Spirit had *not yet* come upon them. The usual and expected thing had not occurred. Their sins were forgiven, but there were no evidences of the Spirit's presence.

Why did God delay the giving of the Spirit? God used this unique situation to demonstrate to the apostles and the Samaritans and to the whole church that the old barriers between Jews and non-Jews had been removed. The church was to be one church, not a Jewish church and a Samaritan church separately. The Lord demonstrated this to the apostles and accomplished this through the apostles as an object lesson on the unity of all believers.

The apostles had not yet begun to make disciples of all nations. Here they were in the position of praying for Samaritans, placing their hands on them. They were present and involved when those former outcasts received the Holy Spirit. It was made clear to them that the gospel, faith and the gift of the Holy Spirit are for all nations and races.

[18]When Simon saw that the Spirit was given at the laying on of the apostles' hands, he offered them money and said, [19]"Give me also this ability so that everyone on whom I lay my hands may receive the Holy Spirit."

The man who had been acclaimed as the Great Power wanted to *buy* the power of God. He had fallen back into his old ways.

We are not told what visible evidence of the Holy Spirit's presence Simon saw. Speaking in tongues would be heard, not seen. There were other special gifts, such as prophecy and healing, but Luke does not mention any of them specifically here.

The buying and selling of church offices and favored positions in the ministry came to be known as simony. The word comes from the name of this man who tried to buy a share in the apostolic ministry.

20 Peter answered: "May your money perish with you, because you thought you could buy the gift of God with money! 21 You have no part or share in this ministry, because your heart is not right before God. 22 Repent of this wickedness and pray to the Lord. Perhaps he will forgive you for having such a thought in your heart. 23 For I see that you are full of bitterness and captive to sin."

24 Then Simon answered, "Pray to the Lord for me so that nothing you have said may happen to me."

We were told that Simon himself believed. Now his heart was not right with God, and Peter cursed his conniving unbelief: "May your money perish with you." That was a very harsh saying, but it was a necessary call to repentance.

The Holy Spirit is God's gift, not to be bought or in any way earned. Simon's desire to *use* the Holy Spirit to enhance his power and popularity was blasphemous. God will not be used any more than he will be deceived.

To imagine that a gift can be bought is to turn grace into a business transaction. And then it is no longer grace. Simon could not have a part or share in the ministry of the apostles because it was a ministry of grace, and he did not understand at all what grace is.

The bitterness in Simon of which Peter spoke was not anger or hatred toward the apostles. It was the bitterness of unbelief which God will not "stomach," which he will "spit out."

Why did Peter say, "*Perhaps* he will forgive you"? There is never a question of the Lord's willingness to forgive. The only uncertainty was whether Simon would repent.

Simon's request for the apostles' intercession reminds us of Pharaoh, who asked Moses to pray the Lord to withdraw the plague of thunder and hail (Exodus 9:28). Each asked the Lord's spokesman to pray on his behalf. We are not told that either of them prayed on his own behalf. Did Simon, like Pharaoh, harden his heart, or did he repent? Luke does not say. Second-century Christian writers referred to him as the father of all heresies.

25When they had testified and proclaimed the word of the Lord, Peter and John returned to Jerusalem, preaching the gospel in many Samaritan villages.

The apostles had begun to preach the gospel to non-Jews, using the opportunity of the return trip to Jerusalem to do so. God was keeping the promise he had made through Joel, the prophecy which Peter quoted on Pentecost:

> " 'In the last days,' God says,
> 'I will pour out my Spirit on all people' "
> (Acts 2:17; cp. Joel 2:28).

26Now an angel of the Lord said to Philip, "Go south to the road — the desert road — that goes down from Jerusalem to Gaza." 27So he started out, and on this way he met an Ethiopian eunuch, an important official in charge of all the treasury of Candace, queen of the Ethiopians. This man had gone to Jerusalem to worship, 28and on his way home was sitting in his chariot reading the book of Isaiah the prophet. 29The Spirit told Philip, "Go to that chariot and stay near it."

The Lord's messenger directed Philip to leave Samaria with its many people and go where the population was much more sparse. In fact, Philip was being sent to evangelize just one man.

The Ethiopian was not from the area we know as Ethiopia today. "Ethiopian" simply means that he was a black man. He was from the kingdom of Nubia, which was located on the upper Nile River between Aswan (in modern Egypt) and Khartoum (in the Sudan). Candace was the official title of all Nubian queens, just as Pharaoh was the title of Egyptian kings.

A eunuch could not be a full-fledged convert to the faith of Israel (see Deuteronomy 23:1), but this man was a God-fearing Gentile believer. He had made a pilgrimage to Jerusalem, probably for one of the Jewish religious feasts.

30 Then Philip ran up to the chariot and heard the man reading Isaiah the Prophet. "Do you understand what you are reading?" Philip asked.

31 "How can I," he said, "unless someone explains it to me?" So he invited Philip to come up and sit with him.

Philip heard the man reading, because it was customary to read aloud. He recognized the words as being a portion of Isaiah's prophecy.

32 The eunuch was reading this passage of Scripture:

> **"He was led like a sheep to the slaughter,**
> **and as a lamb before the shearer is silent,**
> **so he did not open his mouth.**
> **33 In his humiliation he was deprived of justice.**
> **Who can speak of his descendants?**
> **For his life was taken from the earth."**

34 The eunuch asked Philip, "Tell me, please, who is the prophet talking about, himself or someone else?" 35 Then Philip began with

that very passage of Scripture and told him the good news about Jesus.

The eunuch was reading from Isaiah, who is sometimes called the great evangelist of the Old Testament. He was reading that portion which deals with the Suffering Servant of the Lord (Isaiah 53:7,8). It prophetically describes our Savior's suffering and death. The Lamb of God, the substitute for sinners, went without complaint to suffer injustice and execution. The wording of the quotation is that of the Septuagint, the Greek translation of the Old Testament.

Philip could tell the good news of Jesus on the basis of this passage because that is what the passage is about. Before Christians began to preach Jesus as the fulfillment of all Scripture, the Jews understood the passage to refer to the Messiah who was to come. Later those who rejected Jesus incorrectly interpreted it as referring to the people of Israel.

[36] As they traveled along the road, they came to some water and the eunuch said, "Look, here is water. Why shouldn't I be baptized?" [38] And he gave orders to stop the chariot. Then both Philip and the eunuch went down into the water and Philip baptized him. [39] When they came up out of the water, the Spirit of the Lord suddenly took Philip away, and the eunuch did not see him again, but went on his way rejoicing.

Philip's instruction must have included reference to baptism. Perhaps the eunuch recalled the passage just before the portion he had been reading: "So will he sprinkle many nations" (Isaiah 52:15). In any case, he in whom faith had been awakened by the good news about Jesus asked to be baptized.

A footnote in the NIV indicates that late manuscripts (eighth century) included these words as verse 37: "Philip said, 'If you believe with all your heart, you may.' The eunuch answered, 'I believe that Jesus Christ is the Son of God.'" There is nothing wrong about these words, but they probably come from a baptismal service rather than from the pen of Luke.

That there was water on that desert road is not mysterious or, necessarily, miraculous. There are springs, pools, even occasional streams in desert areas in Judea. We do not know whether Philip poured water on the man or immersed him. It would depend on the depth of the water. Since *both* Philip and the eunuch "went down into the water" and "came up out of the water" we cannot conclude on the basis of those words that it was immersion — unless Philip was also immersed. What matters in baptism is not how much water is applied or to how much of a person's body it is applied. What matters is that water is used and the word is spoken.

The eunuch was no longer excluded from full fellowship with the people of God. Another non-Jew was added to the company of believers. We do not know from Scripture or from history whether other believers were gathered by his testimony to the Savior after he returned home.

⁴⁰Philip, however, appeared at Azotus and traveled about, preaching the gospel in all the towns until he reached Caesarea.

Azotus was the Old Testament Philistine city of Ashdod, about 20 miles north of Gaza.

Caesarea, on the Mediterranean coast about 55 miles northwest of Jerusalem, is about midway between modern Tel Aviv and Haifa. It was the residence of the Roman governor. Philip seems to have settled there, for the next time we hear of him (Acts 21:8), twenty years after the events we have just read about, he was living in Caesarea.

The Conversion of Saul

9 Meanwhile, Saul was still breathing out murderous threats against the Lord's disciples. He went to the high priest ²and asked him for letters to the synagogues in Damascus, so that if he found any there who belonged to the Way, whether men or women, he might take them as prisoners to Jerusalem.

"The Way" was another designation for believers. It reminds us that Jesus is the Way to the Father (John 14:6) and that the Christian life is a special way of life.

Saul was not satisfied to scatter the Jerusalem believers (8:3,4). He was determined to destroy the church everywhere. Damascus is about 150 miles northeast of Jerusalem. It had a large Jewish population and thus would have been a natural place for persecuted Jewish believers in Jesus to seek refuge. The fugitive believers had preached the word there as they did everywhere they went (8:4).

The Roman government allowed the Sanhedrin to exercise jurisdiction over Jews living outside of Palestine. Saul's intention was to bring those who belonged to the Way to Jerusalem as captives, to be tried by the Sanhedrin. For that purpose he asked for credentials that would give him the authority to do so.

He planned to go to the synagogues because that was where Jewish followers of Jesus would be worshiping. They were Jews who believed that their Messiah had come. They would not stop worshiping with their fellow Jews until it became clear that they (and Jesus' name) were no longer welcome there.

³As he neared Damascus on his journey, suddenly a light from heaven flashed around him. ⁴He fell to the ground and heard a voice say to him, "Saul, Saul, why do you persecute me?"
⁵"Who are you, Lord?" Saul asked.

"I am Jesus whom you are persecuting," he replied. ⁶"Now get up and go into the city, and you will be told what you must do."

We learn from Acts 26:13 that it was about noon. As brilliant as the noonday sun was, an even greater light flashed around Saul. "From heaven" means more here than "from the sky." It means "from the dwelling place of God." Saul was overwhelmed by it and fell to the ground.

He learned that day that in persecuting those who belonged to the Way he had been persecuting another. The voice asked, "Why do you persecute *me*?" "Saul, Saul," like "Martha, Martha," and "Jerusalem, Jerusalem" was really an expression of loving concern on the Lord's part.

The light of God's glory and the voice made Saul realize that he was in the presence of the Lord. His question and the Lord's answer convinced him that Jesus, whom he had been persecuting, is the Lord who came into the world as a servant to save sinners.

From that moment on Saul was under the orders of the Lord. The first order was to go into Damascus and wait for further instructions.

The Pharisee was brought down, his proud self-righteousness shattered. Ever afterward Saul was a man who knew himself to be the chief of sinners and knew Jesus to be the Savior of sinners. More than a hundred times in his letters Paul the apostle used the word "grace." That word was so important in his vocabulary because of what the Lord did for him when he was Saul the Pharisee.

⁷The men traveling with Saul stood there speechless; they heard the sound but did not see anyone. ⁸Saul got up from the ground, but when he opened his eyes he could see nothing. So they led him by the hand into Damascus. ⁹For three days he was blind, and did not eat or drink anything.

Saul's companions were probably Levite guards who came along to arrest and bring back captive believers. They knew that something supernatural had occurred. They heard the sound of a voice but did not understand what Jesus said.

They led the helpless man into the city. His blindness continued, and for a period of three days he acted like a very sick man. He was crushed by the knowledge that what he had thought was a great service to God was in fact a persecution of God's only Son.

[10]In Damascus there was a disciple named Ananias. The Lord called to him in a vision, "Ananias!"

"Yes, Lord," he answered.

[11]The Lord told him, "Go to the house of Judas on Straight Street and ask for a man from Tarsus named Saul, for he is praying. [12]In a vision he has seen a man named Ananias come and place his hands on him to restore his sight."

Saul had been right in thinking that disciples of Jesus would be found in Damascus. Now one of them was going to find him. This is the second Ananias we have met. His name, which means "The Lord is gracious," fits him better than it fit Sapphira's husband.

Saul, too, had had a vision, the Lord told Ananias. From the report of Saul's vision the humble believer learned what his responsibility to Saul would be.

Straight Street was the main east-west thoroughfare of Damascus. The Romans made a kind of promenade out of it, with large porches at either end. It was called Straight Street because nearly all the other streets in the city were crooked.

[13]"Lord," Ananias answered, "I have heard many reports about this man and all the harm he has done to your saints in Jerusalem.

¹⁴**And he has come here with authority from the chief priests to arrest all who call on your name."**

¹⁵**But the Lord said to Ananias, "Go! This man is my chosen instrument to carry my name before the Gentiles and their kings and before the people of Israel.** ¹⁶**I will show him how much he must suffer for my name."**

Ananias knew Saul's reputation, and it was hard for him to understand why the Lord would want to help that persecutor of the people. The man's reputation had preceded him to Damascus. Ananias knew why Saul had come to the city. We are not told that Ananias was afraid, but he certainly was puzzled.

Luke records many different names that were used for the believers. Here Ananias used the term "saints." The word means those whom God has set apart as his redeemed people, set apart to serve him.

The Lord repeated the command to go and place his hands on Saul to restore his sight. Then he graciously told Ananias what he had in mind for Saul. Amazing grace! A Pharisee who had persecuted Jews for believing in Jesus would carry Jesus' name to Gentiles. He who had believed that salvation is in doing the works of the law would teach that salvation is by faith in Christ alone. The Friend of publicans and sinners would use a fanatical Pharisee as his chosen instrument.

Saul did carry Jesus' name to Gentiles, Gentile rulers and his own people. Much of the book of Acts tells the story. He would witness to Jesus' salvation before governors and kings, including Caesar himself.

Just because of the name of salvation Saul would suffer. That is a paradox, but those who do not believe the gospel will from time to time strike out against the messengers of the gospel. Paul himself provides a partial list of what he endured for Jesus' name in 2 Corinthians 11:23-28.

¹⁷Then Ananias went to the house and entered it. **Placing his hands on Saul, he said, "Brother Saul, the Lord — Jesus, who appeared to you on the road as you were coming here — has sent me so that you may see again and be filled with the Holy Spirit."** ¹⁸**Immediately, something like scales fell from Saul's eyes, and he could see again. He got up and was baptized,** ¹⁹**and after taking some food, he regained his strength.**

Saul spent several days with the disciples in Damascus.

Ananias was not an apostle. However, he too was God's instrument. The Lord gave him an assignment which he carried out, and through him the man who would be the greatest of missionaries was healed in body and spirit.

"Brother Saul" was an expression of forgiveness and of fellowship. Ananias was welcoming him into the communion of saints. Saul received the same welcome and support from the other disciples.

The laying on of hands by Ananias was the outward means by which the Lord restored Saul's sight. The scales were like fish scales, and that is all we can say about Saul's condition. Since his sight was restored, we should not conclude, as some have, that he had weak eyes for the rest of his life.

How was Saul filled with the Spirit? After he could see again, he got up and was baptized. The Spirit and baptism belong together. The Spirit was imparted to Saul in baptism, as he was to the new believers on Pentecost and always is.

Jesus had appeared to Saul. That equipped him to be an eyewitness to the fact of the Lord's resurrection. That made him an apostle in the special sense of one who has seen the risen Christ and is sent to proclaim his name. That made him the equal of the other apostles.

²⁰At once he began to preach in the synagogues that Jesus is the Son of God. ²¹All those who heard him were astonished and

asked, "Isn't he the man who raised havoc in Jerusalem among those who call on this name? And hasn't he come here to take them as prisoners to the chief priests?" ²²Yet Saul grew more and more powerful and baffled the Jews living in Damascus by proving that Jesus is the Christ.

The Son of God had appeared to Saul on the road. He had identified himself as Jesus. Paul believed that and, filled with the Holy Spirit, did not delay preaching it. Paul's message was that he who is from eternity God, who was active in the creation of the universe, had come in the person of Jesus to be the world's Redeemer.

Saul was to carry Jesus' name before the people of Israel as well as to the Gentiles. He began his public work in the place where there would be people who waited for the Messiah. There would also be God-fearing Gentiles, who came to hear the Scriptures and to pray. He began his public preaching in the synagogue, and that was very often his first stop on his world mission tours.

The way in which God had turned this persecutor of Jesus' followers into a preacher of Jesus' name caused astonishment. Perhaps some had difficulty taking him seriously.

Paul was not discouraged by their skepticism. The zeal and energy and talent that had gone into the business of destroying the church were now used in the service of the Lord of the church. Saul grew more confident and convincing in his preaching. He demonstrated that Jesus is the Christ, comparing the Scriptures of the Jews with the facts of Jesus' history. But we are not told that any believers were added to the church from among the Jews who heard this. They were baffled, thrown into consternation, because they could not disprove what Saul was saying. Yet, they did not believe it.

23After many days had gone by, the Jews conspired to kill him, 24but Saul learned of their plan. Day and night they kept close watch on the city gates in order to kill him. 25But his followers took him by night and lowered him in a basket through an opening in the wall.

The many days were three years, and part of that time was spent in Arabia (Galatians 1:17,18). At the time the Arab Nabateans, with their capital in Petra, controlled an area that included Damascus. Saul would not have had to go very far to be in "Arabia."

When he returned to Damascus, his countrymen in that city tried to kill him. Evidently, they got official assistance for their plan, for in 2 Corinthians 11:32 Paul mentions that the governor under Aretas, the Nabatean king, issued orders for his arrest. That *may* also indicate that Saul did mission work in the Arabian kingdom and so incurred official wrath.

26When he came to Jerusalem, he tried to join the disciples, but they were all afraid of him, not believing that he really was a disciple. 27But Barnabas took him and brought him to the apostles. He told them how Saul on his journey had seen the Lord and that the Lord had spoken to him, and how in Damascus he had preached fearlessly in the name of Jesus. 28So Saul stayed with them and moved about freely in Jerusalem, speaking boldly in the name of the Lord. 29He talked and debated with the Grecian Jews, but they tried to kill him. 30When the brothers learned of this, they took him down to Caesarea and sent him off to Tarsus.

Saul had left Jerusalem as a persecutor of the church. It is not surprising that when he returned the disciples were afraid of him. They thought he was just pretending to be a Christian in order to do more damage to the community of believers.

Barnabas remedied that by introducing Saul to the apostles. The only apostles whom Saul met at this time were Peter and James, the Lord's brother (Galatians 1:19). Barnabas vouched for Saul and reported on the latter's experiences and activities in Damascus. He made the point that Saul qualified as a witness to the risen Christ, since he had seen and spoken with Jesus on the road to Damascus. He made the further point that Saul had received the Spirit, who enabled him to speak boldly in the name of the Lord. The fact that Paul stayed with the apostles indicates that they accepted him as a Christian and a fellow apostle.

Saul spent two weeks getting acquainted with Peter (Galatians 1:18). James, the Lord's brother, was not one of the original Twelve. He was, however, an apostle in the sense that he had seen the risen Lord (1 Corinthians 15:7). He was the leader of the Jerusalem church.

Saul's bold preaching and his debates with Jews resulted in an attempt to kill him, just as it had happened in Damascus. The Grecian Jews, especially, would regard him as a traitor. He had made common cause with them against Stephen, and now he was preaching in the name of Jesus.

The brothers took him to the port of Caesarea, from where he could take a ship or make his way overland to his home town, Tarsus. It would be fourteen years before he returned to Jerusalem (Galatians 2:1). We know that he continued his work during that time, because the churches in Judea heard the report: "The man who formerly persecuted us is now preaching the faith he once tried to destroy" (Galatians 1:23).

Luke has used yet another name for the believers, "brothers." Believers are part of a family that goes beyond blood relationship, that is joined by faith in Christ.

[31] Then the church throughout Judea, Galilee and Samaria enjoyed a time of peace. It was strengthened; and encouraged by the Holy Spirit, it grew in numbers, living in the fear of the Lord.

Saul had been the fanatical leader of the first persecution of the church. After his conversion there was a period of peace. During that time God gave internal strengthening and external growth. The lifestyle of the believers was motivated and marked by reverence for the Lord. The Holy Spirit brought all this about through the means he always uses, the word of God.

The church had been one community of believers in Jerusalem. Now it included communities of believers in Judea, Samaria and Galilee as well.

Salvation for the Gentiles

Peter's Work in Lydda and Joppa

[32] As Peter traveled about the country, he went to visit the saints in Lydda. [33] There he found a man names Aeneas, a paralytic who had been bedridden for eight years. [34] "Aeneas," Peter said to him, "Jesus Christ heals you. Get up and take care of your mat." Immediately Aeneas got up. [35] All those who lived in Lydda and Sharon saw him and turned to the Lord.

As Peter and John had visited the church which grew up in Samaria, so Peter alone now visited the new believers in the areas of Judea. Lydda was on the road between Jerusalem and the Mediterranean coast, about 27 miles northwest of Jerusalem and about 11 miles southeast of the port of Joppa. The modern city Lod, which was the Old Testament name for the place, is the site of Israel's Ben Gurion International Airport.

Philip had passed through the area that includes Lydda on his way from Azotus to Caesarea. He preached the gospel in all the towns enroute to Caesarea (8:40). His preaching had borne fruit.

107

Peter was visiting the saints in Lydda, so it is possible that Aeneas was a believer. However, Luke simply refers to him as "a man," not as a disciple or believer or brother.

Peter's words indicated that the healing was taking place right then. And so it was. "*Immediately* Aeneas got up." As a paralytic he had not been able to take care of his own sleeping mat or to walk. Now he could do both.

Not only in Lydda but in Sharon people saw the healed man and turned to the Lord. Sharon is the great fertile plain which runs along the Mediterranean coast from south of modern Haifa to modern Jaffa. If Luke's report that "all those who lived in . . . Sharon saw him and turned to the Lord" is to be understood in an absolute sense, it may be that Sharon here does not refer to the region but to a village near Lydda. A village by that name is referred to in an Egyptian papyrus.

All the inhabitants of a town (Lydda) and a village (Sharon) could see the healed Aeneas and turn to the Lord. It is less likely that literally all the inhabitants of the Sharon Plain did so. However, Luke may be using the word "all" merely to express the thought that there was a widespread and general response to Aeneas's healing.

[36]In Joppa there was a disciple named Tabitha (which, when translated, is Dorcas), who was always doing good and helping the poor. [37]About that time she became sick and died, and her body was washed and placed in an upstairs room. [38]Lydda was near Joppa; so when the disciples heard that Peter was in Lydda, they sent two men to him and urged him, "Please come at once!"

[39]Peter went with them, and when he arrived he was taken upstairs to the room. All the widows stood around him, crying and showing him the robes and other clothing that Dorcas had made while she was still with them.

Joppa was the most important port of southern Palestine, located at the southern end of the Plain of Sharon. It is about 38 miles from Jerusalem, about 11 miles from Lydda. Today it is called Jaffa or Yafo and is a suburb of Tel Aviv.

Tabitha's name in English would be "Gazelle." Her faith expressed itself in practical works of love. The Dorcas societies or guilds in some congregations today do the kind of work which she did, sewing for those in need of clothing. She may have been a widow herself, since no mention is made of her husband.

When she died, her body was respectfully treated according to Jewish custom. Messengers were sent to Peter at Lydda. The saints in Joppa knew that he would want to be informed. Perhaps they hoped that he would be able to do even more than offer comfort.

The widows showed Peter the seamstress work that Dorcas had done. In this way they impressed on him how important that woman had been for the church at Joppa. Could he possibly do something to remedy their great loss?

⁴⁰Peter sent them all out of the room; then he got down on his knees and prayed. Turning toward the dead woman, he said, "Tabitha, get up." She opened her eyes, and seeing Peter she sat up. ⁴¹He took her by the hand and helped her to her feet. Then he called the believers and the widows and presented her to them alive.

Peter knew that Jesus had power to raise the dead. He had been there when Jairus's daughter was raised (Mark 5:37-42), when the young man of Nain was restored to his widowed mother (Luke 7:11-17), and when Lazarus came forth after four days in the grave (John 11:1-44). He also knew that Jesus had not raised up all the people who died during his ministry.

What was Jesus' will now? Peter sent everyone out of the room so that he could be alone to pray. He asked the Lord Jesus, if it was his will, to use his divine power to raise this woman whose work was so important to so many of her fellow believers.

Jesus heard Peter's prayer and restored Dorcas to life. Peter invited Dorcas's fellow believers to come in and see what God had done.

[42] This became known all over Joppa, and many people believed in the Lord.

As always, the miracle was a sign pointing to the power of Christ and the truth of his gospel. It had its results in the conversion of many people.

[43] Peter stayed in Joppa for some time with a tanner named Simon.

Peter would have work to do in Joppa, evangelizing and teaching in the city where such a miracle took place. He stayed for some time. His host was a tanner, a man who processed animal hides to turn them into leather.

Tanners were looked down upon by the Jews because they handled the skins of dead animals, and that made them ceremonially unclean, but Peter did not for that reason refuse to stay with him.

A very important event for the spread of the gospel took place on the roof of this man's house. It would set in motion a powerful demonstration that salvation is for the Gentiles and not only for Israel and converts to Judaism.

The Conversion of Cornelius and Its Aftermath

10 At Caesarea there was a man named Cornelius, a centurion in what was known as the Italian Regiment. [2] He and all

his family were devout and God-fearing; he gave generously to those in need and prayed to God regularly.

Caesarea was the seat of the Roman governor, at this time still Pontius Pilate, and the headquarters of the Roman occupation forces in Palestine. The Roman legion was made up of about 6,000 men. It was divided into ten regiments (cohorts) of about 600 men each. A centurion commanded 100 men, about one-sixth of a cohort.

Cornelius and his family were "proselytes (converts) of the gate." That is, their religious faith and practice were Jewish. Only, the men had not submitted to circumcision to become "proselytes of the law" or "proselytes of righteousness." "Family" really means "household" here and would include servants and slaves, not only wife and children.

³One day at about three in the afternoon he had a vision. He distinctly saw an angel of God, who came to him and said, "Cornelius!"

⁴Cornelius stared at him in fear. "What is it, Lord?" he asked.

The angel answered, "Your prayers and gifts to the poor have come up as a memorial offering before God. ⁵Now send men to Joppa to bring back a man named Simon who is called Peter. ⁶He is staying with Simon the tanner, whose house is by the sea."

⁷When the angel who spoke to him had gone, Cornelius called two of his servants and a devout soldier who was one of his attendants. ⁸He told them everything that had happened and sent them to Joppa.

Three in the afternoon was a time of prayer for the Jews, and the proselyte Cornelius was praying (v. 30). The vision was not a dream; one of God's messenger spirits actually appeared to the centurion.

Cornelius recognized that the person who had appeared to him was more than human. He was afraid in the presence of the holy one, and he addressed the angel as "Lord." The angel immediately made it clear that he was not God but that he had a message from God.

The message was that God had accepted the centurion's prayers and alms as a sacrifice pleasing to him. It was pleasing to him because those works had come from a believing heart.

Cornelius acted on the angel's instructions at once. He sent three loyal messenger's to Joppa, about 30 miles down the Mediterranean coast from Caesarea.

⁹About noon the following day as they were on their journey and approaching the city, Peter went up on the roof to pray. ¹⁰He became hungry and wanted something to eat, and while the meal was being prepared, he fell into a trance. ¹¹He saw heaven opened and something like a large sheet being let down to earth by its four corners. ¹²It contained all kinds of four-footed animals, as well as reptiles of the earth and birds of the air.

The Lord prepared the apostle for the visit of Cornelius's messengers. According to the interpretation of the Old Testament ceremonial regulations which all Jews followed, Peter would have had to rebuff these messengers and refuse the invitation of a man who was not a Jew. Before their arrival, therefore, God educated Peter with respect to the ceremonies and how Gentiles were to be regarded by Jewish believers.

Houses in the Mediterranean world still generally have flat roofs, which provide additional living space. A temporary canopy offers protection from the sun and a degree of privacy for relaxation or, as in Peter's case, prayer.

The expression "all kinds" informs us that there were also ceremonially unclean animals and birds mingled with those that were fit to eat under Jewish food laws. The dietary prescriptions of Leviticus 11 list the forbidden foods and prohibit the mixing of clean and unclean food in the same cooking utensils.

13Then a voice told him, "Get up, Peter. Kill and eat."

14"Surely not, Lord!" Peter replied. "I have never eaten anything impure or unclean."

15The voice spoke to him a second time, "Do not call anything impure that God has made clean."

16This happened three times, and immediately the sheet was taken back to heaven.

It was Jesus who addressed Peter and told him to eat food which was prohibited in the regulations of Leviticus 11. Peter recognized that it was Jesus and addressed him as "Lord." But he was not immediately ready to do the Lord's bidding, for never in his life had he eaten forbidden foods.

What Jesus was teaching Peter about food was going to apply to people. From the Jewish point of view the messengers who were coming to Joppa and the centurion who had sent them were unclean, for they were Gentiles, not living according to the ceremonial laws of Israel. But if Jesus himself accepted them by declaring them clean, then they were clean. Neither Peter nor anyone else was to regard them as unclean.

Three times came the command, "Kill and eat." Three times Peter objected. Three times Jesus set aside his objection. There could be no question that the Lord intended to do away with the restrictions of the Old Testament.

Surely we who are freed by Christ from the burdens of the Old Testament laws have no reason to regard any nationality, race or social class as "unclean" or unfit for fellowship with the church.

17While Peter was wondering about the meaning of the vision, the men sent by Cornelius found out where Simon's house was

and stopped at the gate. [18]They called out asking if Simon who was known as Peter was staying there.

[19]While Peter was still thinking about the vision, the Spirit said to him, "Simon, three men are looking for you. [20]So get up and go downstairs. Do not hesitate to go with them, for I have sent them."

While Peter was still pondering what the vision meant and what he should do in response to it, the men arrived. The Spirit instructed him to act on the Lord's words, not to treat those men as "unclean." Now he was not to "kill and eat" those animals, but to go with those Gentile messengers.

[21]Peter went down and said to the men, "I'm the one you're looking for. Why have you come?"

[22]The men replied, "We have come from Cornelius the centurion. He is a righteous and God-fearing man, who is respected by all the Jewish people. A holy angel told him to have you come to his house so that he could hear what you have to say." [23]Then Peter invited the men into the house to be his guests.

The next day Peter started out with them, and some of the brothers from Joppa went along. [24]The following day he arrived in Caesarea. Cornelius was expecting them and had called together his relatives and close friends. [25]As Peter entered the house, Cornelius met him and fell at his feet in reverence.

Peter began to apply what he had learned through the vision. He invited the Gentile messengers to be his guests. Obedient to the Spirit's direction, he went with them to Caesarea. He entered the Gentile centurion's house, again ignoring the ceremonial distinction between clean and unclean.

Peter wanted fellow believers from Joppa to witness and learn from the visit with Cornelius. He took six of them along (see 11:12). Cornelius wanted his relatives and close friends to hear what message from God Simon Peter would have.

The Jew entered the Gentile's house. The Roman centurion greeted the Jew with the deepest humility and respect.

²⁶But Peter made him get up. "Stand up," he said, "I am only a man myself."

²⁷Talking with him, Peter went inside and found a large gathering of people. ²⁸He said to them: "You are well aware that it is against our law for a Jew to associate with a Gentile or visit him. But God has shown me that I should not call any man impure or unclean. ²⁹So when I was sent for, I came without raising any objection. May I ask why you sent for me?"

Cornelius fell at Peter's feet in reverence, mistaking him for an angel or even a divine being. Peter was the Lord's apostle, sent by him to deliver a message. He did not want the man to be confused on that point.

He also assured the group that he would not be dealing with them as inferiors, that God had taught him not to think of them in that way. The angel had told Cornelius to invite Peter, and the Lord had told Peter how to treat Cornelius. But Peter needed to inquire now, "May I ask why you sent for me?"

Cornelius's answer was to recount the story of his vision:

³⁰Cornelius answered: "Four days ago I was in my house praying at this hour, at three in the afternoon. Suddenly a man in shining clothes stood before me ³¹and said, 'Cornelius, God has heard your prayer and remembered your gifts to the poor. ³²Send to Joppa for Simon who is called Peter. He is a guest in the home of Simon the tanner, who lives by the sea.' ³³So I sent for you immediately, and it was good of you to come. Now we are all here in the presence of God to listen to everything the Lord has commanded you to tell us."

Cornelius used the Jewish way of reckoning days. On day one he had the vision and sent his emissaries. On day two the two servants and the soldier arrived in Joppa and were hospitably received by Peter. On day three the three messengers and the six brothers set out for Caesarea with Peter. On the fourth day they arrived at Cornelius's house. We would say "three days ago," but the Jews counted four.

What the centurion had seen was an angel. What he thought he was seeing was "a man in shining clothes," which was the appearance the angel presented.

All of Cornelius's actions and words showed that he realized that God had great things in store for him. He was convinced that when Peter began to speak it would be with a message from God and that all present should receive it as such. It was an ideal congregation which God had prepared for Peter. The people gathered there were ready to hear.

34Then Peter began to speak: "I now realize how true it is that God does not show favoritism 35but accepts men from every nation who fear him and do what is right."

God accepts believers regardless of their nationality. Peter had understood that from Scripture (Deuteronomy 10:17; 2 Chronicles 19:7) perhaps, but now he was grasping its practical significance.

36"You know the message God sent to the people of Israel, telling the good news of peace through Jesus Christ, who is Lord of all. 37You know what has happened throughout Judea, beginning in Galilee after the baptism that John preached — 38how God anointed Jesus of Nazareth with the Holy Spirit and power, and how he went around doing good and healing all who were under the power of the devil, because God was with him.

39"We are witnesses of everything he did in the country of the Jews and in Jerusalem. They killed him by hanging him on a tree,

[40]but God raised him from the dead on the third day and caused him to be seen. [41]He was not seen by all the people, but by witnesses whom God had already chosen — by us who ate and drank with him after he rose from the dead. [42]He commanded us to preach to the people and to testify that he is the one whom God appointed as judge of the living and the dead. [43]All the prophets testify about him that everyone who believes in him receives forgiveness of sins through his name."

God sent his message to the people of Israel first. The message was the good news that through Jesus there is peace with God and, since he is Lord of all, peace between Jew and Gentile. As a proselyte of the gate, Cornelius was waiting for Israel's Redeemer to come. He needed to hear that the Redeemer *had* come, and that was Peter's message to him and his household and his guests.

Peter's hearers were familiar with what had happened to Jesus of Nazareth. The one whose coming John had foretold was himself baptized by John. "And as he was praying, heaven was opened and the Holy Spirit descended on him in bodily form like a dove. And a voice came from heaven: 'You are my Son, whom I love; with you I am well pleased'" (Luke 3:21,22). That God anointed him with the Spirit meant that he was the Messiah.

Jesus identified himself as the Messiah promised by Isaiah when he declared,

> "The Spirit of the Lord is on me,
> because he has anointed me
> to preach good news to the poor.
> He has sent me to proclaim freedom for the prisoners
> and recovery of sight for the blind,
> to release the oppressed,
> to proclaim the year of the Lord's favor"
>
> (Luke 4:18,19: see Isaiah 61:1,2)

117

These were things Peter's hearers were aware of. They were the historic facts of Jesus' ministry. As he always did, the apostle then continued with his testimony to the things which he and other disciples had witnessed: the Jews had killed Jesus, but God raised him from the dead. The good news for sinful human beings is that "God raised him from the dead." Without that fact all of Jesus' work and his suffering would have been useless.

Verse 41 is Peter's summary of the forty days after Jesus' resurrection. It also answers the question, "Why didn't he appear to everyone?" Peter says that the risen Lord appeared to "witnesses whom God had already chosen." Those who had rejected Jesus during his ministry, who had refused to believe that his teaching and his works were from God, would not have believed even if they had seen him alive from the dead.

He who came as Savior of all will come again as judge of all. Peter's words in this sermon are a beautiful summary of the gospel. They remind us of the Second Article of the creeds.

Jesus' name is the revelation of who he is and what he has done. It is the gospel in a nutshell. Those who hear that name and believe in him receive the forgiveness of sins. That is true of Jew and Gentile alike, of "everyone who believes in him."

There is specific prophecy which speaks of forgiveness through Messiah's name. We read, for example, in Isaiah 53:5,6:

> "But he was pierced for our transgressions,
>   he was crushed for our iniquities;
>   the punishment that brought us peace was upon him,
>   and by his wounds we are healed.
> We all, like sheep, have gone astray,
>   each of us has turned to his own way;

and the LORD has laid on him
    the iniquity of us all."

However, every prophecy which spoke of God's forgiveness
was a testimony to Jesus, because he is God come in the flesh
and through him forgiveness was to be won.

**⁴⁴While Peter was still speaking these words, the Holy Spirit
came on all who heard the message. ⁴⁵The circumcised believers
who had come with Peter were astonished that the gift of the Holy
Spirit had been poured out even on the Gentiles. ⁴⁶For they heard
them speaking in tongues and praising God.**

The gospel which Peter was preaching had its intended
powerful effect. He may have wanted to say more, but the
Holy Spirit did not need more. Those who heard the message were converted by it. That is, the Holy Spirit came on
them. More than that, he gave special evidence of his presence: they spoke in tongues.

Those who had received the gift of the Holy Spirit on
Pentecost had been Jews. Those who had received the Holy
Spirit in Joppa were Jews. Those six brothers, the circumcised believers who had come with Peter from Joppa, were
astonished that now Gentiles were receiving the Holy Spirit. That meant that salvation was for the Gentiles and that
they did not have to become Jews first by submitting to
circumcision and all the other legal requirements of Moses'
code.

**Then Peter said, ⁴⁷"Can anyone keep these people from being
baptized with water? They have received the Holy Spirit just as we
have." ⁴⁸So he ordered that they be baptized in the name of Jesus
Christ. Then they asked Peter to stay with them for a few days.**

The gift of the Holy Spirit and the water of baptism
belong together. Peter's question was a recognition of that

119

fact and no one objected to what he proposed. There could be no objection.

Obviously, it was not necessary for these Gentile believers to become Jews before they could become part of the fellowship of believers in Jesus. God had made that clear to Peter through the vision on the roof at Joppa, and now he had made it clear to all present in Cornelius's house at Caesarea.

Peter ordered that they be baptized, and it goes without saying that he accepted their hospitality. Both acts demonstrated that he regarded them as full-fledged disciples of Christ and part of his holy people. In view of God's clear revelation he could not refuse without disobeying the divine will.

In connection with the revelation of Jesus Christ and by his authority they were baptized. That's what it means that they were baptized "in the name of Jesus Christ."

11 **The apostles and the brothers throughout Judea heard that the Gentiles also had received the word of God. ²So when Peter went up to Jerusalem, the circumcised believers criticized him ³and said, "You went into the house of uncircumcised men and ate with them."**

When the news that Gentiles had been converted spread, the Jewish believers in Jerusalem did not react with immediate joy and praise to God. In their criticism of Peter they did not speak of the fact that Cornelius and the others had heard God's word and believed it, or that they had received the Holy Spirit and had been baptized. Instead, they concentrated on Peter's "unlawful" contact with those Gentiles. They noted that he had received Gentile guests at the house of Simon the Tanner. He had also been a guest of Cornelius in the Gentile centurion's house. Both of these actions violated ceremonial law. Obviously they were not convinced

that the Gentiles could be part of God's family without first
becoming Jews.

**⁴Peter began and explained everything to them precisely as it
had happened: ⁵"I was in the city of Joppa praying, and in a trance
I saw a vision. I saw something like a large sheet being let down
from heaven by its four corners, and it came down to where I was.
⁶I looked into it and saw four-footed animals of the earth, wild
beasts, reptiles, and birds of the air. ⁷Then I heard a voice telling
me, 'Get up, Peter. Kill and eat.'**

**⁸"I replied, 'Surely not, Lord! Nothing impure or unclean has
ever entered my mouth.'**

**⁹"The voice spoke from heaven a second time, 'Do not call
anything impure that God has made clean.' ¹⁰This happened three
times, and then it was all pulled up to heaven again.**

**¹¹"Right then three men who had been sent to me from Caesa-
rea stopped at the house where I was staying. ¹²The Spirit told me
to have no hesitation about going with them. These six brothers
also went with me, and we entered the man's house. ¹³He told us
how he had seen an angel appear in his house and say, 'Send to
Joppa for Simon who is called Peter. ¹⁴He will bring you a
message through which you and all your household will be saved.'**

**¹⁵"As I began to speak, the Holy Spirit came on them as he had
come on us at the beginning."**

Peter's defense was simply to recount in detail what had
happened to prompt him to act as he had. The six brothers
were with him as witnesses to what had taken place in
Cornelius's house, and that suggests that Peter had gone up
to Jerusalem expecting to answer criticism.

Verse 14 is not a direct quotation of the angel's words to
Cornelius (10:6,32). It is Peter's interpretation of why the
angel instructed Cornelius to send for the apostle.

**¹⁶"Then I remembered what the Lord had said, 'John baptized with
water, but you will be baptized with the Holy Spirit.' ¹⁷So if God**

gave them the same gift as he gave us, who believed in the Lord Jesus Christ, who was I to think that I could oppose God!"

Peter had remembered Jesus' promise made before his ascension (1:5). That promise had been fulfilled on Pentecost for Jewish believers. Peter had realized that it was being fulfilled for the Gentile believers at Caesarea. To refuse baptism to them, to insist that they must first conform to the ceremonial law, would have been to oppose God. Peter had started to do that when he argued about the unclean animals in the vision. He dared not oppose God when God so clearly revealed his will by sending his Spirit to Cornelius and the assembly in his house.

[18] When they heard this, they had no further objections and praised God, saying, "So then, God has even granted the Gentiles repentance unto life."

The Jewish believers who had begun by criticizing Peter ended by praising God. They accepted and agreed with the principle which God had demonstrated: salvation is by faith in Jesus alone and not in living the Jewish life. Unfortunately, not all other Jewish believers always accepted that principle, as we shall learn in chapter 15 and as Paul's letter to the Galatians also makes clear.

The Mission Church in Antioch

[19] Now those who had been scattered by the persecution in connection with Stephen traveled as far as Phoenicia, Cyprus and Antioch, telling the message only to Jews.

We have read in 8:4 that "those who had been scattered preached the word wherever they went." Here we see that they went beyond Judea, Samaria and Galilee. We also learn that they told the message of salvation, but only to Jews.

Between 8:4 and the present verse we have read of the gospel work among the Samaritans, with the Ethiopian eunuch and in the house of Cornelius. All of these were Gentiles. We also read the story of Saul's conversion and learned that he was to be the Lord's apostle to the Gentiles.

Now Luke is ready to tell us about work among Gentiles outside of Palestine. Especially, he will begin the record of Saul's work. Saul had not been idle in the years since his conversion, but neither Luke nor anyone else provides us with details from those years. We know that Saul was in Syria and Cilicia (Galatians 1:21) and that he seems to have preached during the time he was there (Galatians 1:23).

Phoenicia was north of Palestine, a long narrow country along the northeast coast of the Mediterranean Sea. Today it is called Lebanon.

Cyprus is the large island in the northeastern Mediterranean, shared today by Turks and Greeks. It is in the angle between the coasts of modern Turkey and Syria. Antioch was the third city of the empire, after Rome and Alexandria, about one-half million in population. It was the capital of the Roman province of Syria and had a large Jewish population. Even though it was 300 miles from Jerusalem, it would have been a natural place for persecuted Christians to find refuge. The city was on the Orontes River, about sixteen miles from the port of Seleucia.

[20]Some of them, however, men from Cyprus and Cyrene, went to Antioch and began to speak to Greeks also, telling them the good news about the Lord Jesus. [21]The Lord's hand was with them, and a great number of people believed and turned to the Lord.

Among the scattered Jerusalem Christians were some whose homes had originally been on the island of Cyprus. Others from the same group had their roots in Cyrene in Libya. They began to share the gospel with non-Jews.

Without the Lord's hand there can be no results in mission work. "The Lord's hand was with them." He blessed this work and there were many converts. The great commission (Matthew 28:18-20) was being carried out as they made disciples of "the nations," that is, Gentiles.

22News of this reached the ears of the church at Jerusalem, and they sent Barnabas to Antioch. 23When he arrived and saw the evidence of the grace of God, he was glad and encouraged them all to remain true to the Lord with all their hearts. 24He was a good man, full of the Holy Spirit and faith, and a great number of people were brought to the Lord.

Just as Peter and John had been sent to visit and oversee the work of Philip in Samaria (8:14), so Barnabas was sent to supervise the evangelism work at Antioch. For the Jerusalem church, the fact that "God has granted even the Gentiles repentance unto life" (11:18) was an established fact for which they praised God. Barnabas's assignment was to make sure that the Gentile believers at Antioch would be properly instructed, so that the unity of the church would be preserved.

We have met the "Son of Encouragement" as a generous contributor to the welfare fund of the Jerusalem congregation (4:36,37). Barnabas was encouraged by what God had accomplished through the gospel testimony of the believers from Cyprus and Cyrene. He encouraged all the believers to be wholehearted in their devotion to the Savior.

"He was a good man" says that he was practical and effective in his work at Antioch. The gifts which the Spirit gave him and the faith with which God had filled him were used by the Lord to bring a great number of people to Jesus.

25Then Barnabas went to Tarsus to look for Saul, 26and when he found him, he brought him to Antioch. So for a whole year

Barnabas and Saul met with the church and taught great numbers of people. The disciples were called Christians first at Antioch.

It had been Barnabas who vouched for Saul at Jerusalem and introduced him to the apostles. He knew that Saul had preached fearlessly in Damascus and spoken boldly in Jerusalem (9:27,28). He knew that Saul had been called by the Lord to preach to the Gentiles. Seven or eight years had passed since the brothers in Jerusalem took Saul down to Caesarea and sent him off to Tarsus. To get Paul to help him with the huge task in Antioch was a logical and practical thing to do.

Luke makes a point of mentioning that Saul worked with Barnabas for a whole year. In the future Saul's visits to the various cities on his mission tours would usually be more brief. When he did stay longer, as here in Antioch, it was only because the Lord had exceptionally large tasks for him to carry out. That was the case here in Antioch, for Barnabas and Saul "met with the church and taught great numbers of people." Not only evangelism of Gentiles but instruction of believers is implied in Luke's summary of their work. Again, the great commission was being carried out as "the nations" were taught to obey everything which Jesus commanded.

"Christians" means "those who belong to or follow Christ." We do not know who gave them the name. Unbelieving Jews would probably *not* call them "people who belong to Messiah (Christ)." Perhaps the Gentiles gave it to them; perhaps the Christians took the name for themselves. It is certainly an appropriate name for those who "remain true to the Lord with all their hearts" (v. 23). The general public knew them by this name, some with respect and some with derision.

It is apparent that the name Christian made a distinction between Jews and those who believed in Jesus. In Antioch

125

Jews and Christians were not regarded as the same kind of people. The addition of Gentiles to the church forced that distinction to be made.

The Jerusalem Church Preserved in Famine and Persecution

27During this time some prophets came down from Jerusalem to Antioch. 28One of them, named Agabus, stood up and through the Spirit predicted that a severe famine would spread over the entire Roman world. (This happened during the reign of Claudius.)

During the year in which Barnabas and Saul were teaching in Antioch the church there was visited by Agabus and a number of other prophets. This is the first mention of prophets in Acts. The work of a prophet in both the Old Testament and the New was forthtelling (preaching God's word) and foretelling (predicting future events). Not all prophets did the latter. Either ability was a special gift from the Holy Spirit.

Whenever people left the holy city Jerusalem they went "down," even when they were going way up north to Antioch in Syria. Going to Jerusalem was always going "up."

Agabus predicted an empire-wide famine. Claudius ruled as emperor from A.D. 41 to 54, and there were many famines in various parts of the empire during his reign. The Jewish historian Josephus wrote of a particularly bad famine which struck Palestine in A.D. 46. That could have been the famine Agabus predicted, *if* we assume that the relief funds which the Antioch congregation sent to Judea were sent *before* the famine actually struck (v. 30).

29The disciples, each according to his ability, decided to provide help for the brothers living in Judea. 30This they did, sending their gift to the elders by Barnabas and Saul.

The "disciples" were the believers in Antioch. Each one gave proportionately to raise a famine relief fund for their fellow believers in the Jewish homeland. In this way they expressed their love for the Lord and their fellowship with the Jewish believers.

They chose Barnabas and Saul to deliver the gift to the elders of the Jerusalem church. This is the first mention of elders in Acts. The term suggests that older men had been chosen for leadership in the congregation. If not all of them were old in years, then still they had demonstrated a maturity which made their fellow believers trust them to lead.

12 **It was about this time that King Herod arrested some who belonged to the church, intending to persecute them. ²He had James, the brother of John, put to death with the sword.**

This King Herod is Herod Agrippa I. His grandfather, Herod the Great, was the king who had the infants of Bethlehem slaughtered in an attempt to kill the King of the Jews, Jesus. His uncle, Herod Antipas, was the man who beheaded John the Baptist and who wanted Jesus to do a miracle at his trial.

Herod Agrippa was Rome's "puppet" ruler in the province of Judea (including Galilee, Samaria and Perea as well as Judea) from A.D. 41 to 44. His treatment of the church of Christ was in the family tradition.

The first martyr of the Twelve, as far as Scripture informs us, was James the Son of Zebedee, brother of the Apostle John. James was probably beheaded as John the Baptist had been, although he may have been run through with the sword. This was not a legal execution but an example of a tyrant demonstrating his tyranny.

³When he saw that this pleased the Jews, he proceeded to seize Peter also. This happened during the Feast of Unleavened Bread.

⁴After arresting him, he put him in prison, handing him over to be guarded by four squads of four soldiers each. Herod intended to bring him out for public trial after the Passover.

Herod was willing to shed more blood in order to curry the favor of the Jews, most of whom did not recognize him as their legitimate king. What better way to win their approval than by putting to death an "enemy" of their religion? Jerusalem would be crowded with pilgrims at Passover time and religious sentiment would be running high.

The Feast of Unleavened Bread was the week that followed the Passover itself. Passover was really the 24-hour period that began with an evening meal to commemorate the deliverance of Israel from Egypt. For a week after the Passover the Jews continued to eat bread that had not been leavened. It was during that week that Herod arrested Peter, and it was after that week that he intended to stage the public trial. Luke is using the two terms, Passover and Feast of Unleavened Bread, as synonyms. That was common usage in the first century A.D. Did Herod remember that the trial of Jesus had occurred at the same time of the year?

Each squad of soldiers customarily stood a three-hour watch. Thus the four squads provided the required number of guards for a twelve-hour period.

⁵So Peter was kept in prison, but the church was earnestly praying to God for him.
⁶The night before Herod was to bring him to trial, Peter was sleeping between two soldiers, bound with two chains, and sentries stood guard at the entrance.

Since it had been the king and not the Sanhedrin who arrested Peter, he was probably not kept in the temple precincts as he and the other apostles had been on an earlier occasion (5:18). The Romans had built the Antonia Tower, a stronghold at the northwestern corner of the temple compound, and it is likely that Peter was imprisoned there.

The church did what the church and individual Christians always do in time of trouble. They prayed earnestly for a fellow believer. They did not know whether it would be God's will to free Peter as he had before (5:19), but they asked the Lord to be with him.

Two soldiers had Peter between them. It was Roman practice to attach each of the prisoner's two chains to each of two guards. Not only were there two more guards from the squad standing watch, but other soldiers were stationed as sentries. Security was tight.

7Suddenly an angel of the Lord appeared and a light shone in the cell. He struck Peter on the side and woke him up. "Quick, get up!" he said, and the chains fell off Peter's wrists.

8Then the angel said to him, "Put on your clothes and sandals." and Peter did so. "Wrap your cloak around you and follow me," the angel told him. 9Peter followed him out of the prison, but he had no idea that what the angel was doing was really happening; he thought he was seeing a vision. 10They passed the first and second guards and came to the iron gate leading to the city. It opened for them by itself, and they went through it. When they had walked the length of one street, suddenly the angel left him.

11Then Peter came to himself and said, "Now I know without a doubt that the Lord sent his angel and rescued me from Herod's clutches and from everything the Jewish people were anticipating."

Peter was not spending the night in worry about the next day's trial or what would happen after that. He lived by the Lord's promises and committed himself into the Lord's hands. He slept soundly, so soundly that he did not realize that the angel's rescue was actually taking place.

One gate of the Antonia Fortress led into the temple area, the other into the city. The iron gate to the city "opened for them by itself." God had heard the prayers of the church. His answer was to miraculously deliver Peter in such a way that the guards were not even aware of what was happening.

When Peter finally realized that he was not seeing a vision but had actually been rescued, he acknowledged the miracle. Herod and the Jewish people would be disappointed in their desire to put him to death.

12When this had dawned on him, he went to the house of Mary the mother of John, also called Mark, where many people had gathered and were praying. 13Peter knocked at the outer entrance, and a servant girl named Rhoda came to answer the door. 14When she recognized Peter's voice, she was so overjoyed she ran back without opening it and exclaimed, "Peter is at the door!"

15"You're out of your mind," they told her. When she kept insisting that it was so, they said, "It must be his angel."

16But Peter kept on knocking, and when they opened the door and saw him, they were astonished. 17Peter motioned for them to be quiet and described how the Lord had brought him out of prison. "Tell James and the brothers about this," he said, and then he left for another place.

In verse 12 Luke introduces a person about whom he will have more to tell us later, John Mark. His mother was known and remembered in the church as one who had opened her home to believers who gathered there to pray. Hospitality is frequently acknowledged in Acts and in the Bible as a whole.

By "his angel" the people meant Peter's guardian angel. Some Jews believed that a person's guardian angel could make himself visible and that when he did he would look like that person.

James was not one of the Twelve but was the Lord's brother. He became the leader of the church in Jerusalem, and that is why Peter mentioned him by name, singling him out.

"He left for another place" means that Peter left the city, not simply that he left Mary's house. The Lord had delivered his servant so that his work could continue. It would continue in another place, a place where Peter would not be immediately rearrested.

¹⁸In the morning, there was no small commotion among the soldiers as to what had become of Peter. ¹⁹After Herod had a thorough search made for him and did not find him, he cross-examined the guards and ordered that they be executed.

The great commotion among the soldiers was not only due to the fact that they were bewildered by Peter's disappearance. They were also terrified because when a prisoner escaped, the soldiers customarily received the punishment which was intended for the prisoner. And so it turned out. Peter was not to be found and the guards were executed.

Then Herod went from Judea to Caesarea and stayed there a while. ²⁰He had been quarreling with the people of Tyre and Sidon; they now joined together and sought an audience with him. Having secured the support of Blastus, a trusted personal servant of the king, they asked for peace, because they depended on the king's country for their food supply.

Luke takes the opportunity to tell us how God punished this persecutor of his church. Caesarea was a part of Judea, but the Jews regarded it as a Roman rather than a Jewish city. Herod the Great had built it in honor of Caesar Augustus. That is why Luke distinguishes it from Judea.

Peter

There was no Roman governor at that time, and so Herod Agrippa used the city as his capital. Being on the Mediterranean shore, it was cooler in summer than Jerusalem. There may have been other reasons, having to do with his relations with the Jews, that made him prefer Caesarea.

Tyre and Sidon were two Roman free cities in Phoenicia. They had depended on Galilee for grain and olive oil since the time of King Solomon (1 Kings 5:11; Ezekiel 27:17). When there was a quarrel between those cities and King Herod, their food supply was endangered. They tried to mend the breach with the help of Blastus, probably bribing that official to intercede on their behalf.

[21]On the appointed day Herod, wearing his royal robes, sat on his throne and delivered a public address to the people. [22]They shouted, "This is the voice of a god, not of a man."

The Jewish historian Josephus writes that the appointed day was a day of celebration in honor of the Emperor Claudius. If it was, then it would seem that Herod intended to use the occasion also to impress the representatives of Tyre and Sidon.

While he was addressing the people of Caesarea in his splendid royal robes, the cry went up, "This is the voice of a god, not of a man." No doubt the representatives of Tyre and Sidon joined in — or even instigated — this blasphemous flattery in order to regain Herod's good will.

[23]Immediately, because Herod did not give praise to God, an angel of the Lord struck him down, and he was eaten by worms and died.

By not disowning the blasphemous shout of the crowd Herod did not give praise to God. The Lord sent his messenger to punish him at once. Intestinal worms consumed his digestive tract and he died.

133

24But the word of God continued to increase and spread.

The threat of famine and the outbreak of persecution did not stifle the church or stop the gospel's spread. On the contrary, the word was preached ever more widely and effectively.

The Lord preserved the church at Jerusalem from famine by moving the hearts of the Antioch Christians to provide relief funds. Most often he provides for his church through human agents.

He preserved the Jerusalem church from persecution through supernatural means. He can still act in that way on behalf of his church if and when it pleases him.

25When Barnabas and Saul had finished their mission, they returned from Jerusalem, taking with them John, also called Mark.

It might seem that Luke has been telling us that Herod Agrippa's persecution and his death all took place while Barnabas and Saul were in Jerusalem. That was not the case. Luke simply wants us to know about the persecution, which probably took place before Barnabas and Saul brought the relief funds to that city.

Now he returns to the story of Barnabas and Saul. He informs us that John Mark, whom he introduced in verse 12, went back to Antioch with them. We shall read much more about all three of them in the second half of Luke's history, which begins in chapter 13.

PART II
PAUL AND HIS COMPANIONS WITNESS
IN ASIA MINOR AND EUROPE

ACTS 13 — 21:16

Paul's First Mission Tour: Asia Minor

The Commissioning

13 **In the church at Antioch there were prophets and teachers: Barnabas, Simeon called Niger, Lucius of Cyrene, Manaen (who had been brought up with Herod the tetrarch) and Saul.**

Since Luke does not indicate which of these men were prophets and which were teachers, we may assume that all five of them performed both functions. They preached and they taught. They served throughout the city, wherever there were groupings of Christians. All five were Jews by birth.

Barnabas and Saul we have met. Niger means "black" and Simeon was probably a dark-complexioned man, perhaps of African ancestry.

Manaen had been brought up with Herod Antipas, the tyrant who murdered John the Baptist. When Judea had been divided into four governmental units, Herod Antipas ruled Galilee and Perea. That was why Pontius Pilate turned Jesus of Nazareth, a Galilean, over to him for trial.

We learned in 11:20 that men from Cyrene were part of the group who came to Antioch after Stephen's death and spoke to the Greeks about Jesus. Lucius was most likely one of those men. He is not to be confused with Luke, the author of *Acts*.

2 While they were worshiping the Lord and fasting, the Holy Spirit said, "Set apart for me Barnabas and Saul for the work to which I have called them." 3 So after they had fasted and prayed, they placed their hands on them and sent them off.

From here to the end of his history, Luke's major focus will be on Saul (Paul) and his ministry. The account begins about A.D. 47.

It is not clear who was worshiping and fasting, the congregation or the five men just mentioned. We do not know just how the Holy Spirit made his will known. It is clear that it was God's will that Barnabas and Saul be released from their ministry in Antioch to preach among the Gentiles.

Again, it is not clear who placed their hands on Barnabas and Saul after fasting and praying. It may have been the other three prophets and teachers. They may have included other leaders of the Antioch church. We can see how the entire congregation might fast and pray before this commissioning but not how they could all lay hands on the two men whom the Holy Spirit had chosen.

The service was not an ordination but a commissioning. These two men were already active in the public ministry of the church. Now God had called them to a specific assignment and the laying on of hands in blessing signified that.

"Sent them off" could be translated more literally as "released them." The church released Barnabas and Saul from their ministry in Antioch so that they could undertake another ministry.

This commissioning was not what made Saul an apostle. The risen Lord made him an apostle by revealing himself to Saul on the road to Damascus. The risen Lord announced that Saul would be his apostle when he sent Ananias to baptize him: "This man is my chosen instrument to carry my name before the Gentiles and their kings and before the people of Israel. I will show him how much he must suffer for my name" (9:15).

On Cyprus

⁴The two of them, sent on their way by the Holy Spirit, went down to Seleucia and sailed from there to Cyprus. ⁵When they arrived at Salamis, they proclaimed the word of God in the Jewish synagogues. John was with them as their helper.

The missionaries were sent forth by the Holy Spirit. The church had been his agent for commissioning them, but *he* had called them for this work.

Seleucia was Antioch's port city. From there they sailed to Barnabas's homeland, Cyprus, the island in the angle beween Asia Minor and Syria. Our word copper comes from Kupros, Cyprus; the island was an important source of copper in the Middle East. Cyprus was a province of the Roman empire, controlled by the Senate of Rome, administered by a proconsul.

They landed on the east coast of the island at Salamis. Salamis was the principal city of Cyprus and seat of government for the eastern half of the island. It was near the site of the modern city of Famagusta.

We are not sure what John's work as "helper" was. The term had been used for a synagogue attendant who took care of the less important affairs of the congregation. Some scholars think John was along to teach children the good news about Jesus. This was the man who was also called Mark, Mary's son (12:12) and Barnabas's cousin (Colossians 4:10).

At Salamis Saul began his pattern of proclaiming God's word in the synagogue first. He had a responsibility to Israel, and there were Gentile proselytes of the gate, "God-fearers," there as well. What the results of the preaching in Salamis were Luke does not tell us. When results were immediate and dramatic, Luke usually recorded them. We are sure that God's word had its effect there, accomplishing what God wanted it to accomplish. The outcome of mission preaching is not always immediately evident and may not be evident for many years. The seed of the word is planted, and God gives the increase in his time and according to his will.

⁶They traveled through the whole island until they came to Paphos. There they met a Jewish sorcerer and false prophet named Bar-Jesus, ⁷who was an attendant of the proconsul, Sergius Paulus. The proconsul, an intelligent man, sent for Barnabas and Saul because he wanted to hear the word of God.

Paphos was about 94 miles from Salamis, across the island on the west coast. It is not likely that Barnabas and Saul went directly across the island through the mountains. More likely, they followed the coast to the south and around to Paphos. Here was the proconsul's residence, the seat of Roman government for this province.

Evidently the missionaries met the proconsul's attendant before they met the proconsul. Bar-Jesus means "Son of Joshua" and it was not an unusual name. He had or pretended to have supernatural abilities, but he definitely did not speak for God; he was a *false* prophet.

Sergius Paulus was not a man like Cornelius the centurion, "devout and God-fearing," generous in giving and regular in prayer (10:2), but he was an intelligent man who had the good sense to send for Barnabas and Saul for the purpose of hearing God's word.

⁸But Elymas the sorcerer (for that is what his name means) opposed them and tried to turn the proconsul from the faith.

⁹Then Saul, who was also called Paul, filled with the Holy Spirit, looked straight at Elymas and said, ¹⁰"You are a child of the devil and an enemy of everything that is right! You are full of all kinds of deceit and trickery. Will you never stop perverting the right ways of the Lord? ¹¹Now the hand of the Lord is against you. You are going to be blind, and for a time you will be unable to see the light of the sun."

"Elymas" was Bar-Jesus' nickname, meaning sorcerer. His position with Sergius Paulus was threatened by the proconsul's willingness to hear the word. If his master heard and believed the gospel, he would no longer want a sorcerer and false prophet as an attendant. Elymas did his worst to deprive Sergius Paulus of the saving truth.

Saul's words of rebuke came from a man filled with the Holy Spirit. His cutting and biting condemnation was intended to show the sorcerer his sinful condition. They were like Jesus' words to the Pharisees: "You belong to your father, the devil, and you want to carry out your father's desire" (John 8:44). The expression means, "You are the opposite of a child of God; you have the qualities of the devil."

God's right way is to save people by the preaching of the gospel. Elymas was perverting God's way by trying to turn the proconsul from salvation. Paul would not have been doing Elymas a favor by softening his rebuke.

Elymas was not the first man who had to be led by the hand when God put an end to his wickedness by blinding him for a time. Remember the persecutor on the road to Damascus? Here was a warning and an opportunity for the sorcerer to repent. Unless he did repent, eternal punishment was in store for him.

For the first time Luke informs us that Saul the Jew had a Roman name as well: Paul. It was the custom of Greek-speaking Jews in the empire to give a child two names, one Hebrew and the other Greek or Latin. From here to the end of the book, the author will use the name of Paul the Roman citizen. Some say that Luke does this because Paul's work among the Gentiles really began with preaching to Sergius Paulus.

Immediately mist and darkness came over him, and he groped about, seeking someone to lead him by the hand. [12]When the proconsul saw what had happened, he believed, for he was amazed at the teaching about the Lord.

The groping blindness of Elymas was a sign which pointed to the truth of the word of God which Paul had spoken. Sergius Paulus believed *when* he saw what happened; he believed *because of* the teaching about the Lord.

Luke does not report on further work or successes in Paphos. It would be speculation to say more than Scripture tells us.

In Pisidian Antioch

[13]From Paphos, Paul and his companions sailed to Perga in Pamphylia, where John left them to return to Jerusalem. [14]From Perga they went on to Pisidian Antioch.

When their work in Paphos was finished, the missionaries went to the mainland of Asia Minor. Pamphylia was a Roman province, a long and narrow region between the Mediterranean and the Taurus mountains. They landed at the port of Perga, which was three miles up the Cestrus River from the coast and five miles from the city of Perga. Perga was the capital of the province.

Until now we have read of "Barnabas and Saul." From now on, on Gentile mission fields, it will be "Paul and

Barnabas." Paul became the leader, and so we read that "Paul and his companions" sailed to Perga.

John Mark the helper left at this point. Luke does not tell us why. Acts 15:38 suggests that Paul did not approve of Mark's return to Jerusalem, for Paul refused to take him along on another mission tour.

Luke does not indicate that any gospel work was done in Perga at this time. Some years later Paul wrote to the churches of southern Galatia: "As you know, it was because of an illness that I first preached the gospel to you" (Galatians 4:13). This suggests that Paul had to leave the lowlands of Pamphylia to get to the higher altitudes of the province of Galatia and that for that reason the stay in Perga was very brief. Paul and Barnabas did preach the word in Perga on their way home after this first mission tour (14:25).

Because of Paul's illness, perhaps malaria, he and Barnabas went on to Antioch. They had come from Antioch in Syria. Pisidian Antioch was a smaller city, also named after the Syrian king who had been one of the successors to Alexander the Great in the fourth century B.C. Pisidian Antioch was the administrative center for the southern part of the Roman province of Galatia. It was also an important trade center and a city where retired Roman soldiers settled. It was about 110 miles from Perga.

On the Sabbath they entered the synagogue and sat down. [15]After the reading from the Law and the Prophets, the synagogue rulers sent word to them, saying, "Brothers, if you have a message of encouragement for the people, please speak."

It was the function of the synagogue rulers to control the order of worship and to decide who would read the Scriptures or speak. There were no pastors who preached on a regular basis. The rulers realized that they had guests in the congregation that day, perhaps knew who the guests were, surmised that the guests had something to say and invited them to do so. "Brothers" here means fellow Jews, not fellow believers in Jesus.

16Standing up, Paul motioned with his hand and said: "Men of Israel and you Gentiles who worship God, listen to me! 17The God of the people of Israel chose our fathers; he made the people prosper during their stay in Egypt. With mighty power he led them out of that country 18and endured their conduct forty years in the desert. 19He overthrew seven nations in Canaan and gave their land to his people as their inheritance. 20All this took about 450 years.

Paul accepted the invitation to speak, signaled for silence and began to preach. There were Gentile proselytes of the gate among the hearers.

Some scholars think that this is only a summary of Paul's address, since it would take only three to five minutes to preach verses 16 to 41. Perhaps. However, Paul said everything that needed to be said, and there was no reason why he would have to preach for twenty minutes.

The apostle began by briefly recalling Israel's history from the patriarchs to King David. Israel's God graciously chose the sons of Jacob and blessed them when they were resident aliens in Egypt, even when they were persecuted by Pharaoh. He graciously delivered them from slavery and patiently put up with their murmuring and acts of rebellion during the forty years of wilderness wandering.

When they entered the Promised land, God continued to act on their behalf. The seven nations in Canaan whom the Lord overthrew are listed in Deuteronomy 7:1-3. They were Hittites, Girgashites, Amorites, Canaanites, Perizzites, Hivites and Jebusites. Chapters 14 to 21 of the book of *Joshua* tell how the land was distributed among all the tribes of Israel.

The 450 years include the 400 years in Egypt, forty years in the desert and ten years in Canaan to the time the land was divided.

"After this, God gave them judges until the time of Samuel the prophet. [21]Then the people asked for a king, and he gave them Saul son of Kish, of the tribe of Benjamin, who ruled forty years. [22]After removing Saul, he made David their king. He testified concerning him: 'I have found David son of Jesse a man after my own heart; he will do everything I want him to do.' [23]From this man's descendants God has brought to Israel the Savior Jesus, as he promised."

Israel had not annihilated all the heathen nations in the Promised Land as God commanded. As a result there were frequent raids and conflicts. During those perilous times God gave his people a series of judges. These were not people who tried cases in courts of law. They were spiritually and physically gifted men and women who helped Israel overcome their various enemies. Again and again, in situations which the Israelites brought on themselves by disobedience and idolatry, the Lord acted on their behalf.

The last of the judges was also the first prophet since Moses. Samuel exercised wise and able leadership, but Israel wanted to be like other nations. They wanted a king.

God gave them Saul, who disobeyed the Lord in many ways during his reign. Early in Saul's rule the Lord indicated that David, the seventh son of Jesse, would be Saul's successor. Samuel anointed him at the Lord's command.

Taking his language from several places in Scripture (1 Samuel 13:14; 16:12,13; Psalm 89:20; Isaiah 44:28), Paul compressed the story of David into a single "quotation." The Jews regarded David's reign as the highpoint of their history. In a sense it was, but they must not overlook what God promised David and how God kept that promise.

143

God promised, "When your days are over and you rest with your fathers, I will raise up your offspring to succeed you, who will come from your own body, and I will establish his kingdom. He is the one who will build a house for my Name, and I will establish the throne of his kingdom forever" (2 Samuel 7:12,13). That promise was fulfilled in Solomon and the other kings of Judah, but only in part.

That line of kings descended from David came to an end when the Kingdom of Judah was taken off to captivity in Babylon. However, God promised:

> "A shoot will come up from
> the stump of Jesse [David's father];
> from his roots a Branch will bear fruit" (Isaiah 11:1).

Jesus, the Son of Mary, descended from David, is the fulfillment of those promises and of all God's promises of salvation.

[24]"Before the coming of Jesus, John preached repentance and baptism to all the people of Israel. [25]As John was completing his work, he said: 'Who do you think I am? I am not that one. No, but he is coming after me, whose sandals I am not worthy to untie.'

[26]"Brothers, children of Abraham, and you God-fearing Gentiles, it is to us that this message of salvation has been sent."

John was the last of the prophets and the first preacher of the baptism of repentance and remission of sins. As Jesus' forerunner, preparing the people for Jesus' ministry, he addressed his message of repentance to all Jews.

John "confessed freely, 'I am not the Christ' " (John 1:20). He did not preach himself but one greater than himself. God had given him a great role to play in the history of salvation, but he acknowledged that he was not worthy to do the most menial service of the lowliest slave for Jesus (Luke 3:16).

The message which John preached and which Paul was preaching is not only *about* salvation. It is the gospel that brings salvation and gives salvation because it has the power to create faith in people's hearts. Paul was calling both Jews and Gentiles to faith. The message of salvation is for all.

27"The people of Jerusalem and their rulers did not recognize Jesus, yet in condemning him they fulfilled the words of the prophets that are read every Sabbath. 28Though they found no proper ground for a death sentence, they asked Pilate to have him executed. 29When they had carried out all that was written about him, they took him down from the tree and laid him in a tomb."

As Peter did on Pentecost and on other occasions, Paul showed how God's gracious purpose was carried out through the evil actions of the Jews who rejected and condemned Jesus. They fulfilled the very Scriptures which were read in all the synagogues every Sabbath Day.

"They," that is the Sanhedrin acting for the people, carried out all that was written about him. Then "they," the same leaders, took him down for burial by getting permission from Pilate and allowing Joseph of Arimathea and Nicodemus to have the body.

In the verses 17 to 25 Paul had spoken of what God did in the history of Israel in order to carry out his plan of salvation. In verses 26 to 29 he spoke of what Israel, in ignorant unbelief, did to the Savior whom God had sent. In verses 30 to 39 Paul continued the history of God's saving work.

30"But God raised him from the dead, 31and for many days he was seen by those who had traveled with him from Galilee to Jerusalem. They are now his witnesses to our people.

32"We tell you the good news: What God promised our fathers 33he has fulfilled for us, their children, by raising Jesus from the dead.

The crucified Savior did not stay dead. He would not have been the Savior then. God raised him and during forty days his disciples saw him. This is the seventh time in Acts that the central message of the apostles, "God raised him from the dead," is recorded. This is the seventh time the apostles are cited as witnesses.

The Scriptures which were read every Sabbath were fulfilled when God raised up Jesus. God sent him. God acknowledged him at his baptism. God equipped him for his ministry. God accepted his perfect life and his innocent death. God certified that by raising him from the dead.

With the expressions "our fathers" and "us, their children" Paul made clear that he included Gentile believers as recipients of the good news. The God-fearing Gentiles regarded Israel's ancestors as their spiritual fathers. The good news is good news for all.

"As it is written in the second Psalm:
  'You are my Son;
    today I have become your Father.'"

By quoting Psalm 2:7 Paul was saying the same thing he later wrote in Romans 1:4: that Jesus Christ our Lord "was declared with power to be the Son of God by his resurrection from the dead." He is God's Son from eternity, who came and took on our human nature. God acknowledged him as his Son by raising him from the dead.

[34]"The fact that God raised him from the dead, never to decay, is stated in these words:
  'I will give you the holy and sure blessings
    promised to David.'"

Paul quoted Isaiah 55:3 to show that the promises made to David would be fulfilled in the Messiah. He was quoting

Mary Magdalene and the Holy Women at the Tomb

147

the Septuagint, the Greek translation of the Old Testament. Our NIV text at Isaiah 55:3 has the same meaning, but it does not use exactly the same words because it is translated directly from the Hebrew original. In this case, Paul found the Septuagint wording more suitable for making his point.

35"So it is stated elsewhere:

'You will not let your Holy One see decay.'

36"For when David had served God's purpose in his own generation, he fell asleep; he was buried with his ancestors and his body decayed. 37But the one whom God raised from the dead did not see decay."

Verse 35 is another quotation from the Greek translation. It is Psalm 16:10, which Peter had also quoted on Pentecost (2:27). Paul used it for the same purpose in the same way.

Paul's point has been that God's promises to David were not fulfilled to David personally but to David's Son. David's Son, Jesus has been acknowledged as God's Son, has received the blessings promised to David, and has been raised from the dead. David served God's purpose only in his own generation, and then he died. David's Son lives to serve God's purpose in all generations.

What conclusion were they to draw from this? Paul told them in the beautiful gospel summary of verse 38 and 39:

38"Therefore, my brothers, I want you to know that through Jesus the forgiveness of sins is proclaimed to you. 39Through him everyone who believes is justified from everything you could not be justified from by the law of Moses."

"My brothers" includes all of Paul's hearers, Jew and Gentile, male and female. Really, it includes all who ever read or hear these words.

Because of what Jesus did, it is possible to say to everyone, "Your sins are forgiven." Because of what he did, everyone who believes the word of forgiveness is acquitted, declared innocent, cleared of every charge. The believer *is* justified already.

The law of Moses could not acquit, declare innocent, or clear sinners of a single charge against them. It could not justify, but only press charges, demonstrate our guilt and condemn us.

A few years later Paul wrote to the Christians in Galatia: "[We] know that a man is not justified by observing the law, but by faith in Jesus Christ" (Galatians 2:16).

40"Take care that what the prophets have said does not happen to you:

> **41"Look, you scoffers, wonder and perish,**
> **for I am going to do something in your days**
> **that you would never believe,**
> **even if someone told you.' "**

All this God has done through Christ. What would Paul's hearers do? Paul concluded with a solemn warning, quoting from Habakkuk 1:5 according to the Septuagint. Habakkuk had warned the people of Judah about the invasion of the Babylonians, with all the death and misery that would bring. Paul adapted the prophet's words to speak of God's final judgment on those who scoff at the good news about Christ.

God had done "something" in their days. He had sent his Son, offered him as the sacrifice for sins, raised him up and forgiven sins through him.

"Someone," Paul, was telling them this.

Would they be scoffers and perish and never believe? Or would they accept the good news and trust Jesus for their

149

salvation? The gospel confronts everyone who hears it with this question.

[42] As Paul and Barnabas were leaving the synagogue, the people invited them to speak further about these things on the next Sabbath. [43] When the congregation was dismissed, many of the Jews and devout converts to Judaism followed Paul and Barnabas, who talked with them and urged them to continue in the grace of God.

[44] On the next Sabbath almost the whole city gathered to hear the word of the Lord.

The synagogue congregation, in general, wanted to hear more a week later. But many of Paul's hearers, Jews and converts, did not want to wait a week for the next Sabbath service. They followed Paul and Barnabas, who urged them to keep on trusting God's grace in Christ Jesus.

A week later the synagogue had a "standing room only" crowd. Not only Jews and converts to Judaism and proselytes of the gate, but other inhabitants of Antioch as well, gathered to hear the Lord's message.

[45] When the Jews saw the crowds, they were filled with jealousy and talked abusively against what Paul was saying.

[46] Then Paul and Barnabas answered them boldly: "We had to speak the word of God to you first. Since you reject it and do not consider yourselves worthy of eternal life, we now turn to the Gentiles. [47] For this is what the Lord has commanded us:

'I have made you a light for the Gentiles,
that you may bring salvation to the ends
of the earth.' "

It was not so much that the Jews were jealous of Paul's popularity. They were jealous for what they thought was God's honor. They believed that Paul was wrong to say that no one can be justified by the law of Moses, but only by

Christ. They thought that this dishonored God as the giver of the Law. Paul had thought and spoken and acted that way, too, before his conversion. Then he had learned that God is honored when people accept his Son as the fulfillment of the law and the Savior of sinners.

God had done something and someone had told them about it. They would not believe. The gospel had been brought to them first as the people through whom God provided salvation for the world. *God* was willing to give them eternal life. *They* decided that they were not worthy of that gracious gift. They rejected it. God's offer of mercy is always sincere, but it is possible to resist his grace.

Now Paul and Barnabas would turn to the Gentiles with the gospel. It was not that they would never preach to Jews anywhere ever again. However, they would not preach to those Jews in that city again. Gentiles believing and Jews rejecting would be a recurring event during the rest of Paul's ministry.

Paul quoted Isaiah 49:6 from the Septuagint. The first part of that verse helps us understand the application Paul made to his hearers. The Lord addresses his Servant, the Messiah:

> "It is too small a thing for you to be my servant
> to restore the tribes of Jacob
> and bring back those of Israel I have kept."

The Lord's Servant was to do that and it was an important part of his work to restore and rescue God's remnant among the Jewish people. But he would not be limited to so "small" a service:

> "I will also make you a light for the Gentiles,
> that you may bring my salvation to the ends of the earth"
> [the NIV rendering of the Hebrew text at Isaiah 49:6].

151

Simeon, singing in the temple with the infant Jesus in his arms, knew that these words applied to the baby, that he is the Servant of the Lord: "a light for revelation to the Gentiles" (Luke 2:32). Paul realized that these words also apply to those who serve the Servant, and so he said: "This is what the Lord has commanded *us*."

The good news is for the Jews, but not only for them.

48 When the Gentiles heard this, they were glad and honored the word of the Lord; and all who were appointed for eternal life believed.

49 The word of the Lord spread through the whole region.

The Gentiles rejoiced to hear that redemption was for them. They did not have to become Jews first in order to be God's children.

Jews and Gentiles, "all who were appointed for eternal life believed." They became believers by God's doing, not because of their attitude or decision. No one but God could make such an appointment. The Jews who rejected the gospel and abused the preachers, on the other hand, did *not* do that because God appointed them to be unbelievers. God has never done that. They themselves counted themselves out.

More and more people in the region around Antioch had the opportunity to hear the good news.

50 But the Jews incited the God-fearing women of high standing and the leading men of the city. They stirred up persecution against Paul and Barnabas, and expelled them from their region.
51 So they shook the dust from their feet in protest against them and went to Iconium.

The prominent women were proselytes, the kind of people who were often happy to hear and believe the gospel. Not this time. The leading men were not necessarily the city officials. They were leaders in commerce and civic affairs. Both groups would be influential in getting the government officials to persecute and expel two traveling preachers who were upsetting the leading Jews of the community. The Jews used them for that purpose. Not mob action but legal means were used to oust Paul and Barnabas from Antioch and its environs.

To shake off the dust from the feet was a Jewish way of declaring: "I have no further responsibility toward you." Jesus said, "But when you enter a town and are not welcomed, go into its streets and say, 'Even the dust of your town that sticks to our feet we wipe off against you' " (Luke 10:10,11).

Iconium was eighty miles southeast of Antioch, a four or five day walk. (See map on page 293.) It was an important city in the central plain of Galatia.

52 And the disciples were filled with joy and with the Holy Spirit.

The preachers were driven out of town but the believers remained. Theirs was a joyous faith, and their lives were controlled by the Holy Spirit. On the way back to Antioch in Syria after their first mission tour, Paul and Barnabas would stop to strengthen and encourage the disciples at Pisidian Antioch (14:22).

In Iconium

Events in Iconium followed a pattern similar to what had happened in Pisidian Antioch.

14 At Iconium Paul and Barnabas went as usual into the Jewish synagogue. There they spoke so effectively that a great number of Jews and Gentiles believed.

Paul

"A great number" could include several hundred people. This was not the result of a single visit to the synagogue. The work in Iconium continued for a considerable time. The Gentiles included people who were not proselytes. What made the preaching of Paul and Barnabas so effective was the power of the gospel and the Holy Spirit, who works through the gospel.

2But the Jews who refused to believe stirred up the Gentiles and poisoned their minds against the brothers. 3Paul and Barnabas spent considerable time there, speaking boldly for the Lord, who confirmed the message of his grace by enabling them to do miraculous signs and wonders.

The missionaries' response to the destructive opposition of the Jews was to spend more time and speak more boldly for the Lord. They could speak boldly because their faith and their message were based on him and his salvation. The Lord enabled them to do miracles which pointed to the truth of the message. Hebrew 2:4 tells us, "God also testified to [this salvation] by signs, wonders and various miracles, and gifts of the Holy Spirit distributed according to his will."

4The people of the city were divided; some sided with the Jews, others with the apostles.

Here for the first time in *Acts* Paul and Barnabas are called "apostles." The Twelve were apostles, men who had been with Jesus during his ministry, who had seen him alive from the dead and who testified to his resurrection. Paul was an apostle who saw the risen Christ on the road outside Damascus, and the Lord called him to be a witness to the resurrection.

In what sense was Barnabas an apostle? Since he is coupled with Paul here, he must have qualified by seeing the risen Savior during those forty days between Easter and the Lord's ascension. There was one occasion when Jesus was seen by more than five hundred disciples; Barnabas was very likely one of those witnesses. Some scholars think that he was one of the two with whom Jesus walked and talked on the road to Emmaus.

It is clear from Luke's use of the word that he did not limit the number of apostles to twelve.

⁵There was a plot afoot among the Gentiles and Jews, together with their leaders, to mistreat them and stone them. ⁶But they found out about it and fled to the Lycaonian cities of Lystra and Derbe and to the surrounding country, ⁷where they continued to preach the good news.

This was not legal action as in Antioch, but mob action. They actually made the attempt to mistreat and stone the apostles.

Someone warned Paul and Barnabas, and the plot misfired on this occasion. Some of the same people would try again at another time and place, with somewhat more success (14:19).

Jesus had instructed his disciples, "When you are persecuted in one place, flee to another"(Matthew 10:23). The work of evangelizing Iconium was done and the apostles fled.

They turned a desperate emergency into an opportunity. They kept on preaching the gospel, but in a new area. Lycaonia was a region within the province of Galatia. Lystra was about eighteen miles southwest of Iconium. The location of Derbe is uncertain since it no longer exists. It is probably beyond Lystra, since it was visited after Lystra. (See map on page 293.)

In Lystra and Derbe

⁸In Lystra there sat a man crippled in his feet, who was lame from birth and had never walked. ⁹He listened to Paul as he was

speaking. Paul looked directly at him, saw that he had faith to be healed [10]and called out, "Stand up on your feet!" At that, the man jumped up and began to walk.

The man's condition seemed hopeless. The Holy Spirit, who did not move and direct the apostles to heal every illness, had his reasons for moving Paul to act and speak as he did here.

The man's faith did not accomplish this healing or contribute to it. Faith accepted what God was doing.

[11]When the crowd saw what Paul had done, they shouted in the Lycaonian language, "The gods have come down to us in human form!" [12]Barnabas they called Zeus, and Paul they called Hermes because he was the chief speaker. [13]The priest of Zeus, whose temple was just outside the city, brought bulls and wreaths to the city gates because he and the crowd wanted to offer sacrifices to them.

The Lycaonian people were like many other conquered races in at least one respect. They learned the language of their conquerors, but among themselves, and especially when they were excited, they spoke in their native tongue.

The healing of the crippled man so impressed them that they were ready to worship Paul and Barnabas as divine. The gods of pagan mythology had come to earth in many forms, including the human. What they shouted simply agreed with their beliefs.

Zeus was the chief god of the Greek collection of gods. That they called Barnabas "Zeus" might indicate that his appearance was more impressive than Paul's. But they may have called him that because they expected Zeus and Hermes to appear together and they had already decided that Paul was Hermes, the chief messenger of the gods. That judgment was based on the fact that Paul was the chief speaker of the two.

The Lycaonians expected Zeus and Hermes to appear together because of a local legend. The story was that an elderly couple, Philemon and Baucis, had entertained the two gods without recognizing who they were, whereas the townspeople had rejected them. The people of Lystra did not want to repeat that mistake. And so the priest and the people were ready to offer sacrifices to Barnabas and Paul. Zeus was the protector of their city, and they must not offend him by failing to recognize him.

¹⁴But when the apostles Barnabas and Paul heard of this, they tore their clothes and rushed into the crowd, shouting: ¹⁵"Men, why are you doing this? We too are only men, human like you. We are bringing you good news, telling you to turn from these worthless things to the living God, who made heaven and earth and sea and everything in them. ¹⁶In the past, he let all nations go their own way. ¹⁷Yet he has not left himself without testimony: He has shown kindness by giving you rain from heaven and crops in their seasons; he provides you with plenty of food and fills your hearts with joy." ¹⁸Even with these words, they had difficulty keeping the crowd from sacrificing to them.

The apostles tore their clothes to express their disapproval of what the pagan priest and the crowds were doing. The heathen may not have understood that their actions were blasphemous, but Barnabas and Paul wanted to reject their sacrifices in the most vivid way.

The apostles were messengers, not gods. Their message was the good news. They called on the people to repent, that is, to turn from idols and idolatry to worship the Creator of the universe.

The living God had not immediately punished the idolatry of those nations which worshiped false gods. Ultimately he will destroy every idolatrous people and punish every unbeliever. He bides his time, letting a nation's corruption run its course.

Through thousands of years he preserved the various Gentile nations by regulating the seasons and granting the harvests. This was to be a testimony to his kindness and his power. The Gentiles' response had been to make gods for themselves. Even that day at Lystra it was difficult to turn them from the superstitious act they intended to perform.

¹⁹Then some Jews came from Antioch and Iconium and won the crowd over. They stoned Paul and dragged him outside the city, thinking he was dead.

Those Jews who came from that distance must have really hated Paul and his message. They turned a crowd which had brought bulls and wreaths for sacrifice into a lynch mob. It was an ugly scene and the apostle suffered a terrible battering. He was left for the carrion birds and animals to dispose of.

²⁰But after the disciples had gathered around him, he got up and went back into the city. The next day he and Barnabas left for Derbe.
²¹They preached the good news in that city and won a large number of disciples.

Years later, as a prisoner of Rome, Paul wrote to Timothy: "You . . . know . . . what kinds of things happened to me in Antioch, Iconium and Lystra, the persecution I endured. Yet the Lord rescued me from all of them" (2 Timothy 3:10,11). The enemies of Christ did their best to kill Paul. They left him for dead. The Lord still had a great deal of work for his servant to do, and he preserved his life.

It is remarkable that Paul survived a stoning and more remarkable that he was able to travel the next day. It is most remarkable that his brutal treatment and brush with death did not deter him from continuing to preach the gospel. The Lord gave a generous harvest of disciples in Derbe.

Return to Syrian Antioch

Then they returned to Lystra, Iconium and Antioch, [22]strengthening the disciples and encouraging them to remain true to the faith. "We must go through many hardships to enter the kingdom of God," they said.

It is interesting that Paul did not say we must surmount and triumph over many hardships. He said "we must go through" them. The life of a Christian is not one grand victory procession. It will look that way at the end, but the cross comes before the crown. These thoughts strengthened and encouraged the disciples. How? By reminding them, as they remind us, that hardships do not mean God has forsaken or forgotten us. They are a sign that we are entering his kingdom.

The kingdom of God does not mean only heaven and eternity. It is God's gracious rule in our lives here on earth and hereafter in eternal life.

The apostles were retracing their steps. In spite of opposition and persecution at each of these three cities, they returned to strengthen and encourage the disciples.

[23]Paul and Barnabas appointed elders for them in each church and, with prayer and fasting, committed them to the Lord in whom they had put their trust.

So that the churches' worship and work could continue in an orderly way, the apostles appointed men who were respected for their mature judgment. The elders' responsibility in those churches almost certainly went farther than that of the seven "deacons" in the Jerusalem church. The church always needs preaching and teaching.

Paul and Barnabas left those churches in the confidence that he who created faith in the disciples would preserve them in faith. We have read before (13:2,3) that the church's leaders combined prayer and fasting. They were no longer under any Old Testament regulations, and Jesus had not commanded fasting. However, these Jewish believers knew from experience that fasting helped them concentrate when they prayed.

24After going through Pisidia, they came into Pamphylia, 25and when they had preached the word in Perga, they went down to Attalia.

26From Attalia they sailed back to Antioch, where they had been committed to the grace of God for the work they had now completed.

On this return trip they spent more time at Perga (13:13) and preached the word there. Attalia was the main seaport of Pamphylia, and they sailed from there to Antioch in Syria. Antioch had committed them to God's grace for this first mission tour in Gentile lands. By his grace they had completed it and returned to home base.

27On arriving there, they gathered the church together and reported all that God had done through them and how he had opened the door of faith to the Gentiles. 28And they stayed there a long time with the disciples.

The church is always interested in what its missionaries have done. Paul and Barnabas did not boast of their achievements but reported what God had done *through* them. They especially emphasized that Gentiles had entered the kingdom of God by faith in Jesus, without first becoming Jews.

"A long time" probably means several months. It may mean as much as a year.

161

The Council at Jerusalem

15 Some men came down from Judea to Antioch and were teaching the brothers: "Unless you are circumcised according to the custom taught by Moses, you cannot be saved."

These men were not representing the churches of Judea and Jerusalem. Their position was not that of the apostles. The question of whether Gentiles must conform with the law of Moses had been settled in the case of Cornelius. The Holy Spirit had settled it by coming to the Gentile centurion and his household just as he had come to the Jewish believers (11:15-18).

God had "opened the door of faith to the Gentiles" (14:27). These unnamed characters from Judea were trying to close that door and require the Gentiles to enter through the door of Judaism. For that reason they are usually referred to as "Judaizers."

In effect they were saying, "There is something you must do to be saved." They did not deny that Jesus is Christ, that he died for all and that God raised him from the dead. They believed that he was their Savior. But they did not understand that Christ's salvation is received by faith alone. They did not realize that if there is something I must do to be saved, then my salvation is no longer accomplished by Christ alone.

2This brought Paul and Barnabas into sharp dispute and debate with them. So Paul and Barnabas were appointed, along with some other believers, to go up to Jerusalem to see the apostles and elders about this question.

This issue would divide the church if it were not resolved. Worse, it would cast doubt on the gospel of salvation which Paul and Barnabas had preached, which the Holy Spirit had attested at the conversion of Cornelius. Worst of all, it directed people away from Christ's work to a work of their own, circumcision.

The church at Antioch was not appealing to the leaders at Jerusalem for a ruling to which they would then submit. They knew the truth and they knew that they were saved. They wanted to know the position of the church in Jerusalem, wanted to know that there was agreement in the gospel, wanted to know whether what "some men" said was really being taught or tolerated in Judea.

They sent a delegation to consult. Among the other believers was Titus, as we learn from Galatians 2:3. Verses 1 to 10 of Galatians 2 are Paul's account of the council which he and Barnabas, with others, attended.

³The church sent them on their way, and as they traveled through Phoenicia and Samaria, they told how the Gentiles had been converted. This news made all the brothers very glad.

We learned in 11:19 that some of the believers who were scattered by the first persecution settled in Phoenicia and witnessed there. Luke does not provide any details, but there were groups of believers who could rejoice with Paul and Barnabas over the successful mission among the Gentiles. The apostles told them in detail about the conversion of many heathen.

The Greek word for "sent them on their way" makes it clear that the church in Antioch helped its representatives with food, money and travel arrangements for their trip to Jerusalem.

⁴When they came to Jerusalem, they were welcomed by the church and the apostles and elders, to whom they reported everything God had done through them.

⁵Then some of the believers who belonged to the party of the Pharisees stood up and said, "The Gentiles must be circumcised and required to obey the law of Moses."

The delegation was cordially received, and the missionaries gave a full report on the journey to Cyprus and Asia Minor. They were careful to give all glory to God.

Then the Judaizers raised the issue that had made this meeting necessary. These men were Pharisees, known for their strict adherence to all the details of the law of Moses and to the traditions which surrounded it. They believed that Jesus is the Messiah, the Savior. Unfortunately, they also believed that the Gentiles must convert to Judaism in order to be saved. In Paul's account of what happened at this council he writes: "Some false brothers had infiltrated our ranks to spy on the freedom we have in Christ Jesus and to make us slaves" (Galatians 2:4).

The Judaizers in the Jerusalem church were consistent. They not only demanded circumcision; they demanded compliance with the entire law of Moses. Now the matter must be discussed and the issue resolved.

⁶The apostles and elders met to consider this question.

While the whole church was still assembled, the leaders held a caucus. We do not know how many of the apostles were present. They came and went in their work of evangelizing and were not always in the city. That is why the church had its resident elders to take care of the day-to-day work of the congregation.

⁷After much discussion, Peter got up and addressed them: "Brothers, you know that some time ago God made a choice among you that the Gentiles might hear from my lips the message of the gospel and believe. ⁸God, who knows the heart, showed

that he accepted them by giving the Holy Spirit to them, just as he did to us. ⁹He made no distinction between us and them, for he purified their hearts by faith."

Peter reminded his hearers of the conversion of Cornelius (Acts 10 and 11). The vision at Joppa and the baptism of Cornelius with his household had occurred about ten years ago. He reminded them that at that time *God* decided the issue of how Gentiles were to come into the church. God settled the matter and set the church's policy by giving the Gentiles the Holy Spirit just as he had given the Jewish believers the Holy Spirit on Pentecost.

God knew the hearts of the centurion and his household. That is, he knew they were believers. He himself had made them believers. He accepted them and demonstrated that by giving them his Spirit.

What had God done? He had accepted them by giving the Holy Spirit. He had purified their hearts. He had done this by giving them faith. These were not separate events, extended over a period of time while Cornelius and the others completed some requirements like being circumcised or fulfilling the requirements of the ceremonial law. All these things occurred simultaneously in one great gracious act of God.

What did that prove? It proved that God made no distinction between Gentile believers in Christ and Jewish believers in Christ. God had not required the Gentiles to *do* something before they could be saved. He had declared them clean, and the Judaizers must not regard them as unclean.

¹⁰"Now then, why do you try to test God by putting on the necks of the disciples a yoke that neither we nor our fathers have been able to bear?"

The Pharisees with their demands were going against God's revealed will. They were second-guessing him.

Whether they realized it or not, they were trying God's patience and provoking his anger, "testing" him.

Yokes are placed on beasts of burden so that they can pull a load. Peter was saying, "Our Israelite forefathers could not pull the load of the law. We have not been able to pull such a load ourselves." Peter realized that, if the Gentiles submitted to circumcision and the other demands of the Pharisees, they would be subjecting themselves to the entire law with all its demands and restrictions. Not long after this Paul wrote to the Christians of Galatia: "I declare to every man who lets himself be circumcised that he is obligated to obey the whole law" (Galatians 5:3).

No man, except the God-man Jesus, ever fulfilled the law. That was true of the ceremonial law and of the moral law with its demand of perfect love for God and man. More than anything else, the law was there to show people that they needed a Savior.

11"No! We believe it is through the grace of our Lord Jesus that we are saved, just as they are."

Let us not make such demands of others when we ourselves have not lived up to them.

To whom does the word "they" refer? It may refer to the Gentiles, and then Peter was saying what he said in verse 9: "He made no distinction between us and them." It may, however, refer to "our fathers." Then Peter would be making the point that Old Testament believers were also saved by the grace of the Lord Jesus, for whom they waited in hope. It is like the thought expressed by Jesus: "Your father Abraham rejoiced at the thought of seeing my day; he saw it and was glad" (John 8:56). See the great list of Old Testament believers in Hebrews 11 who lived by faith in the one to come.

Again, it is possible to translate this verse, "No! Through the grace of our Lord Jesus we believe that we are saved, just as they are (or "were," if it refers to the forefathers)." That would remind Peter's listeners and us that even our faith is God's gracious gift and not something we have generated or accomplished. "For it is by grace you have been saved, through faith — and this not from yourselves, it is the gift of God — not by works, so that no one can boast" (Ephesians 2:8,9).

12The whole assembly became silent as they listened to Barnabas and Paul telling about the miraculous signs and wonders God had done among the Gentiles through them.

Now, as part of the discussion and in opposition to the Judaizers, Barnabas and Paul reported what God had done among the Gentiles on the mission field. If God had done these things for the Gentiles without their being circumcised, how could the Judaizers demand that they be circumcised?

Here Luke mentions Barnabas before Paul. The church in Jerusalem had known Barnabas for a long time, and they had only good memories of him. It is likely that he did more talking as the mission journey was described because so much of what had happened had happened through Paul. It could have been embarrassing for Paul to relate the story.

13When they finished, James spoke up: "Brothers, listen to me. 14Simon has described to us how God at first showed his concern by taking from the Gentiles a people for himself. 15The words of the prophets are in agreement with this, as it is written:

> **16" 'After this I will return**
> **and rebuild David's fallen tent.**
> **Its ruins I will rebuild,**
> **and I will restore it,**

> ¹⁷that the remnant of men may seek the Lord,
>   and all the Gentiles who bear my name,
>   says the Lord, who does these things'
> ¹⁸   that have been known for ages."

The speaker was James the Lord's brother, the presiding officer of the church in Jerusalem and the chairman of this council.

James acknowledged that what Peter had described was accurate and that it was to the point. God's people were no longer made up of Jews only. Now his people came from all nations. God had taken heathen and made them his people.

To what God had been doing James added the authority of what God had prophesied many years before through Amos (9:11,12). The quotation adapts the Greek translation of the Old Testament text.

The first part of the prophecy was fulfilled in the Jewish Christians. They were the restored Tent of Meeting (tabernacle) of David. They were the rebuilt house of God.

The second part of the prophecy confirms the point that Peter and the delegates from Antioch were making. Gentiles were bearing the name of the Lord. That is, they were becoming his people. It was the Lord who was doing these things.

Verse 18 is James' comment and not part of the quotation. He was saying, "These are not new ideas. The Lord announced them through the prophets long ago."

> ¹⁹"It is my judgment, therefore, that we should not make it difficult for the Gentiles who are turning to God. ²⁰Instead we should write to them, telling them to abstain from food polluted by idols, from sexual immorality, from the meat of strangled animals and from blood."

168

Nothing should be required that would hinder the Gentiles' conversion. James was not rendering this judgment on his own authority. The Holy Spirit had made it clear that the Gentiles did not have to Judaize. He had done so in the case of Cornelius. The success which he gave to the mission in Asia Minor also testified to it. The apostles and elders and the whole church could only concur with God's decision. James proposed that they do so.

The message which James proposed be sent to Antioch and to Gentiles everywhere would not attach any conditions to their salvation. It would not place any obstacles in the way of their becoming full-fledged members of God's family. It was intended, rather, to encourage them to avoid things that would make it difficult for Jews to share a meal with them or express full fellowship with them in other ways.

Leviticus 17:1-9 prohibited the sacrifice of animals to "goat idols" or demons. James and the Jerusalem church were not afraid that Gentile believers would do that. But they knew that in the Gentile world the meat sacrificed to idols was sold in the market. For Gentile believers to eat such meat would make it difficult for Jewish Christians to have table fellowship with them.

Leviticus 17:10-14 prescribed the way in which the Jews were to slaughter animals for food. It was to be done in such a way that all blood was drained from the animal. To wring the neck of a chicken, for example, would not be a proper way to kill a bird for food. When the congregation gathered for a common meal before celebrating the Lord's Supper, Jews would want to know that the meat that was served was kosher.

In proposing that they tell the Gentiles to abstain from sexual immorality James was not saying that the Jerusalem believers tell them not to commit adultery and fornication. The apostles always spent time teaching their converts and certainly taught them the moral law. Leviticus 18 dealt with particular kinds of sexual relationships. The Gentiles were to avoid sexual relationships and marriages which their laws and customs might permit but which the law of Moses forbade. Such conduct would gravely endanger the fellowship between Jewish and Gentile believers.

James proposed that with regard to these things which were especially offensive to Jews and of which some Gentiles might be ignorant they tell the Gentiles: "You do well to avoid these things." As to the demand concerning circumcision, the answer was "No." Paul writes in Galatians 2:3, "Not even Titus, who was with me, was compelled to be circumcised, even though he was a Greek."

[21]"For Moses has been preached in every city from the earliest times and is read in the synagogues on every Sabbath."

James's point here was that many Gentiles were already familiar with these Jewish laws and others could learn them. For the sake of maintaining the fellowship with Jewish Christians they ought to observe them. This was not a compromise which would require that *some* law other than circumcision be observed. It was an injunction not to jeopardize the bond, the fellowship between believers of Jewish upbringing and those of Gentile background.

[22]Then the apostles and elders, with the whole church, decided to choose some of their own men and send them to Antioch with Paul and Barnabas. They chose Judas (called Barsabbas) and Silas, two men who were leaders among the brothers.

James's judgment was the judgment of the whole church. We must assume that the Judaizers also agreed with it after Peter, Paul, Barnabas and James had presented their arguments.

Representatives of the Jerusalem church would accompany Paul and Barnabas to present a joint report on the findings of the council to the church at Antioch. Judas may have been a brother of Joseph Barsabbas, who had been a candidate to replace Judas Iscariot (1:23). More likely, his second name meant that he was born on a Saturday: "son of the Sabbath." We will hear more of Silas, who became one of Paul's coworkers in the Gentile mission.

23 With them they sent the following letter:
The apostles and elders, your brothers,
To the Gentile believers in Antioch, Syria and Cilicia:
Greetings.
24 We have heard that some went out from us without our authorization and disturbed you, troubling your minds by what they said. 25 So we all agreed to choose some men and send them to you with our dear friends Barnabas and Paul — 26 men who have risked their lives for the name of our Lord Jesus Christ. 27 Therefore we are sending Judas and Silas to confirm by word of mouth what we are writing. 28 It seemed good to the Holy Spirit and to us not to burden you with anything beyond the following requirements: 29 You are to abstain from food offered to idols, from blood, from the meat of strangled animals and from sexual immorality. You will do well to avoid these things.
Farewell.

The senders' names appeared first, as was the custom. The senders recognized that brotherhood existed between the Gentile addressees and themselves, and so they used an expression which they would once have reserved for Jews: "your brothers."

Cilicia adjoined Syria and was part of the administrative province of Syria. Antioch was the center of Christian activity for both regions. The letter was to be shared by the

Antioch church with the churches throughout Syria and Cilicia.

The letter began by making clear that those men who had come down from Judea had not represented the position of the Jerusalem church. Their disturbing legalism was not the teaching or practice of the apostles and elders. In commending Paul and Barnabas as dear friends who had risked their lives for the Savior's name the letter endorsed their teaching as the teaching of the whole church.

Verse 27 reminds us that written messages can be misunderstood. Letters cannot answer questions about themselves. Judas and Silas could confirm and interpret the message if any explanation was needed.

The requirements laid out in verses 28 and 29 were not to be understood as a condition of the Gentiles' (or the Jews') salvation. It was not, "Believe in Jesus and do these things and you will be saved." They were an evangelical admonition not to endanger the brotherhood.

The Holy Spirit made it clear in the case of Cornelius and on the Gentile mission fields that Gentiles did not have to become Jews in order to be people of God. The Holy Spirit made it clear in the Amos prophecy about David's fallen tent that the Gentiles were to be saved as Gentiles, not Jews. The church in Jerusalem, like the church at all times in all places, could only agree with what the Spirit has revealed.

[30] The men were sent off and went down to Antioch, where they gathered the church together and delivered the letter. [31] The people read it and were glad for its encouraging message. [32] Judas and Silas, who themselves were prophets, said much to encourage and strengthen the brothers.

The people of God in Antioch received the letter and rejoiced in it. Judas and Silas added their spoken encouragement to the encouragement of the written message. By their words they performed an important function of all prophets, giving encouragement and strength to the saints.

[33] After spending some time there, they were sent off by the brothers with the blessing of peace to return to those who had sent them.

The blessing of peace was an expression of fellowship. The footnote in the NIV reports that some manuscripts of the New Testament add as verse 34: "but Silas decided to remain there." Whatever the reason for such an addition, it would contradict the plain statement of verse 33.

[35] But Paul and Barnabas remained in Antioch, where they and many others taught and preached the word of the Lord.

A great crisis, more dangerous for the church than any persecution, had been resolved. The false doctrine of the Judaizers had been repudiated. The truth of salvation for all by faith alone without law works had been reaffirmed. The fellowship between Jewish and Gentile believers had been preserved.

Now the church and its servants could get back to the work of telling the good news everywhere. Paul and Barnabas had many coworkers in Antioch. The church needed many teachers and preachers because it was growing.

Paul's Second Mission Tour: Europe

Strengthening the Churches in Asia Minor

[36] Some time later Paul said to Barnabas, "Let us go back and visit the brothers in all the towns where we preached the word of the Lord and see how they are doing."

After a few months of teaching and preaching in Antioch Paul proposed that he and Barnabas visit the believers in the towns of Cyprus and southern Asia Minor. Paul intended this to be a pastoral visit, and it was, but we will see that it turned into a great mission tour as well.

[37]Barnabas wanted to take John, also called Mark, with them, [38]but Paul did not think it wise to take him, because he had deserted them in Pamphylia and had not continued with them in the work. [39]They had such a sharp disagreement that they parted company. Barnabas took Mark and sailed for Cyprus, [40]but Paul chose Silas and left, commended by the brothers to the grace of the Lord.

John Mark had not been the helper he was supposed to be on the first mission tour, deserting the missionaries at Perga in Pamphylia (13:13). Paul was not ready to trust him as a helper on this trip.

Two men who had worked together closely and successfully for years disagreed to the extent their partnership was broken up. From this point on, neither Barnabas nor Mark is a part of Luke's history.

We know that their gospel work continued, though. We also know that Paul thought highly of both of them, in spite of this falling-out over a practical matter. Paul later acknowledged that Barnabas worked to support himself while serving as a missionary (1 Corinthians 9:6). Mark was part of Paul's group when the latter was imprisoned at Rome the first time (Colossians 4:10; Philemon 24). Paul asked the Christians at Colosse to welcome Mark (Colossians 4:10). Near the end of his life, during his second imprisonment, Paul asked that Mark be brought to him to help with the ministry (2 Timothy 4:11).

Barnabas gave his cousin Mark a second chance by taking him along on the visit to Cyprus. Mark later worked with Peter (1 Peter 5:13) and became the author of the second Gospel. Without criticizing Paul for his refusal to take Mark along on the visit to the young churches of Asia Minor, we can commend Barnabas for salvaging an important worker for Christ's kingdom. Especially, we can thank God, who found use for a man who once failed to do his duty.

Silas had returned to Jerusalem after delivering that church's letter to Antioch (15:22-33). Now he was back in Antioch and became Paul's coworker, taking the place of Barnabas. Paul and he left with the approval of the Antioch congregation, which relied on the Lord to direct and protect them.

⁴¹He went through Syria and Cilicia, strengthening the churches.

Since Barnabas and Mark had gone to Cyprus, there was no need for Paul to visit the churches there. He called on the churches of his home area, where he had spent about eight years after his conversion and before Barnabas called on him to work in Antioch (11:25,26; Galatians 1:21). He strengthened the churches in the way churches are always strengthened, by instructing them in God's word.

16 He came to Derbe and then to Lystra, where a disciple named Timothy lived, whose mother was a Jewess and a believer, but whose father was a Greek. ²The brothers at Lystra and Iconium spoke well of him.

Traveling by land, Paul visited the two towns which had been his last stops on the initial tour (14:6-19). At Lystra lived a young believer who was the child of a mixed marriage. We know that he was quite young because about fifteen years later Paul could still refer to his youth (1 Timothy 4:12). The Jewish mother, Eunice, and Timothy's grandmother, Lois, are mentioned in Paul's Second Letter to Timothy, 1:5. From them the boy had learned the Scriptures (2 Timothy 3:14,15).

The brothers at Lystra and Iconium gave Timothy a good character reference. Some year later Paul gave Timothy this

175

high commendation: "I have no one else like him, who takes a genuine interest in your welfare. . . . You know that Timothy has proved himself, because as a son with his father he has served with me in the work of the gospel" (Philippians 2:20,22).

3Paul wanted to take him along on the journey, so he circumcised him because of the Jews who lived in that area, for they all knew that his father was a Greek.

Paul had refused to circumcise Titus, a Gentile, when the pharisaic believers demanded it as necessary for salvation (Galatians 2:3-5; Acts 15:5). Now, so that Timothy's work among the Jews who knew that his father was a Gentile would not be hampered, Paul had him circumcised. The one action was for the gospel's sake, lest anyone get the impression that Gentiles *must* be circumcised. The other was also for the gospel's sake, lest the Jews among whom Timothy would work as a missionary be repelled by him before they ever heard the good news about Jesus.

4As they traveled from town to town, they delivered the decisions reached by the apostles and elders in Jerusalem for the people to obey. 5So the churches were strengthened in the faith and grew daily in numbers.

The decision of the Jerusalem Council, which had been sent to the churches of Antioch, Syria and Cilicia, was now relayed to the churches in Galatia as well. This information, along with Paul's continued instruction, strengthened the faith of the believers and drew others into the fellowship.

The Call to Macedonia

6Paul and his companions traveled throughout the region of Phrygia and Galatia, having been kept by the Holy Spirit from preaching the word in the province of Asia.

The visits to the churches founded on the first mission journey were completed. Now Paul, Silas and Timothy traveled in a northwesterly direction from the province of Galatia, skirting the province of Asia. "Throughout the region" might suggest that they visited all of Phrygia and Galatia. What it means is that they traveled through the border area between the ancient homeland of the Phrygians and that of the Galatians. Whatever gospel work they might have done in this area is not recorded by Luke. It is clear that they did not stay in any one place for any length of time.

How did the Holy Spirit keep them from preaching the word in Asia? It may have been by a direct revelation. It may have been through someone's good advice. Paul and his companions may have interpreted a certain situation as evidence that the Spirit wanted them to pass the province of Asia by.

There were many large and important cities on the coast of the province. They presented an inviting mission field. For his own reasons and in his own way the Spirit kept them from preaching the word in that province at that time.

7When they came to the border of Mysia, they tried to enter Bithynia, but the Spirit of Jesus would not allow them to. 8So they passed by Mysia and went down to Troas.

"The Spirit of Jesus" is another way of saying "the Holy Spirit." The expression reminds us that the Spirit proceeds from the Son as well as from the Father. Just as he had prevented the group from entering Asia, so he would not allow them to enter Bithynia. Again, we do not know how the Spirit communicated his will to them.

Bithynia was a senatorial province on the Black Sea, and Mysia was west of it, in the extreme northwest of Asia Minor. Traveling by way of Mysia and not stopping to preach along

177

the way, the missionaries came to Troas, about ten miles from the site of ancient Troy. Troas was a seaport.

Paul and his troupe had traveled a great distance, from one corner of Asia Minor to the other. The Spirit had kept them from the populous areas of Asia and from Bithynia. Now they were in a remote corner of Asia Minor. What did the Lord have in mind for them?

9During the night Paul had a vision of a man of Macedonia standing and begging him, "Come over to Macedonia and help us."10After Paul had seen the vision, we got ready at once to leave for Macedonia, concluding that God had called us to preach the gospel to them.

Macedonia was that Roman province which covered the area which today includes Yugoslavia. To go to Macedonia meant to take the gospel to the continent of Europe. The only way in which Paul could understand "help us" was as an urgent invitation to preach the gospel there. He and his mission team accepted the vision as a command from the Lord. They acted accordingly. When a clear call for spiritual help comes, what else can God's people do but respond?

For the first time in his account the author writes "we." We do not know just when Luke joined Paul and his companions, but he was with them when they entered Europe to preach the gospel there.

In Philippi

11From Troas we put out to sea and sailed straight for Samothrace, and the next day on to Neapolis. 12From there we traveled to Philippi, a Roman colony and the leading city of that district of Macedonia. And we stayed there several days.

Samothrace is an island in the northern Aegean Sea, a midpoint on the voyage from Troas to Neapolis. Neapolis was the harbor for Philippi, about ten miles south of that city.

Philippi was founded by and named for Philip of Macedon, father of Alexander the Great. Caesar Augustus gave it the status of a Roman colony. That meant it enjoyed the right of self-government. It did not need to pay tribute to Rome. Its citizens enjoyed the same rights and privileges as the citizens of an Italian city. Many of its citizens were retired soldiers of the Roman army.

Philippi was neither the capital nor the largest city of the district. It was, however, the most renowned, because of its location as a kind of "gateway to the East." It was on the Egnatian Way, a 500-mile road that provided a land route between Italy and Asia Minor.

[13]On the Sabbath we went outside the city gate to the river, where we expected to find a place of prayer. We sat down and began to speak to the women who had gathered there. [14]One of those listening was a woman named Lydia, a dealer in purple cloth from the city of Thyatira, who was a worshiper of God. The Lord opened her heart to respond to Paul's message. [15]When she and the members of her household were baptized, she invited us to her home. "If you consider me a believer in the Lord," she said, "come and stay at my house." And she persuaded us.

There was no synagogue at Philippi at which Paul could begin his work, as he usually did. Ten men were needed to form a synagogue, and Philippi had only a small Jewish population. In the story of the gospel work in that city there is a hint that there was anti-Jewish sentiment (vv. 20,21).

There was, however, a place of prayer where Jews met. It was a house or shelter on the bank of the Gangites River. Such places were often erected near water, so that the ceremonial washings prescribed in the Jewish law could be performed. Paul and his companions conversed with the women who had gathered there on the Sabbath. From what happened it is clear that the subject of their conversation was the good news about Jesus.

Lydia was from the province of Lydia, from a city which had been founded by Greeks from Macedonia. Thyatira was known for its production of rich purple cloth. She was a Gentile who worshiped the God of Israel, a proselyte.

The Lord opened her heart to the gospel. She and her household received baptism as a seal of faith. Because Lydia seems to have been the head of a houshold, it is assumed that she was either a widow or unmarried.

She expressed her appreciation for the gift of faith by offering hospitality to those who had brought the gospel to her. Convinced of her sincerity and her honest intentions, the missionaries accepted her invitation. Her home became their headquarters for mission work in Philippi. Her household provided the nucleus of a congregation in that city.

[16]Once when we were going to the place of prayer, we were met by a slave girl who had a spirit by which she predicted the future. She earned a lot of money for her owners by fortune-telling. [17]This girl followed Paul and the rest of us, shouting, "These men are servants of the Most High God, who are telling you the way to be saved." [18]She kept this up for many days. Finally Paul became so troubled that he turned around and said to the spirit, "In the name of Jesus Christ I command you to come out of her!" At that moment the spirit left her.

The spirit which possessed the slave girl was an evil spirit. Fortune-telling is the devil's work, and the devil was using her to turn people's thoughts away from God's will and God's word. The men who owned her exploited her as a rich source of income. That was the devil's work, too.

The girl's shouts were not an attempt to preach the gospel, to help Paul and the other missionaries. It was an attempt to interrupt and embarrass those who preached the gospel. She spoke the truth but in a deceitful way and without trusting the God of truth. This kind of unwelcome testimony had also occurred during Jesus' ministry: "In the synagogue there was a man possessed by a demon, an evil spirit. He cried out at the top of his voice, 'Ha! What do you want with us, Jesus of Nazareth? Have you come to destroy us? I know who you are — the Holy One of God!' Moreover, demons came out of many people, shouting, 'You are the Son of God!' But he rebuked them and would not allow them to speak, because they knew he was the Christ" (Luke 4:33,34,41). Where Jesus and his gospel are, there the devil will use any and every means to stifle the good news and frustrate God's gracious purpose.

Only the Lord Jesus Christ can deliver anyone from the power of the devil. He has done that with his holy precious blood and his innocent suffering and death. It was the power of his name that delivered the slave girl from Satan's grip.

[19]When the owners of the slave girl realized that their hope of making money was gone, they seized Paul and Silas and dragged them into the marketplace to face the authorities. [20]They brought them before the magistrates and said, "These men are Jews, and are throwing our city into an uproar [21]by advocating customs unlawful for us Romans to accept or practice."

When the demon left, so did the slaveowners' hope of making money. They did not rejoice that a human being had been delivered from possession by an evil spirit. They resented the men through whom God had delivered her. They dragged them to the marketplace, where the authorities had their headquarters.

The magistrates were the highest authorities in a colony like Philippi. There were two of them. They judged cases involving crimes against Roman law. The charge was that Paul and Silas were trying to convert Roman citizens to Judaism. The Emperor Claudius had recently expelled all Jews from the city of Rome as troublemakers. Philippi, as a colony of Rome which tried to be like Rome in every way, would not want Jews to come and make trouble there.

The real motive behind the charge was, of course, anger that they had lost their source of income when the slave girl was relieved of the evil spirit.

22 The crowd joined in the attack against Paul and Silas, and the magistrates ordered them to be stripped and beaten. 23 After they had been severely flogged, they were thrown into prison, and the jailer was commanded to guard them carefully. 24 Upon receiving such orders, he put them in the inner cell and fastened their feet in the stocks.

The magistrates could see that the crowd was in an uproar, as the accusers said. They assumed there must be some truth to the charges. They ordered that Paul and Silas be shamed and brutalized. The magistrates did not realize that those two Jews were also Roman citizens, protected by law from such treatment. They violated their civil rights in a very serious way.

There was no trial, only accusation and punishment. No one asked about the Most High God and the way of salvation. No one was interested in justice or salvation. Paul and Silas were flogged on the charge that they were Jews who had tried to make converts.

The jailer, as ordered, put them into the maximum security cell. In the stocks the prisoners' legs were spread wide and they would suffer severe cramps after a short time. That pain would continue until they were released.

²⁵About midnight Paul and Silas were praying and singing hymns to God, and the other prisoners were listening to them. ²⁶Suddenly there was such a violent earthquake that the foundations of the prison were shaken. At once all the prison doors flew open, and everybody's chains came loose. ²⁷The jailer woke up, and when he saw the prison doors open, he drew his sword and was about to kill himself because he thought the prisoners had escaped. ²⁸But Paul shouted, "Don't harm yourself! We are all here!"

It did not seem like the time or place to do mission work, but they praised God and the other prisoners heard them. Under very painful conditions Paul and Silas sang hymns. They could do such things because they trusted the living Lord Jesus and because he gave them the strength.

He answered their prayers. Not only the door of their cell but all the doors of the entire prison flew open.

When prisoners escaped, the jailer or guard had to suffer whatever punishment was due those prisoners. Evidently some of the prisoners in the jail at Philippi were guilty of capital crimes, because the jailer was ready to take his own life rather than be executed by the authorities.

But none of the prisoners had left!

²⁹The jailer called for lights, rushed in and fell trembling before Paul and Silas. ³⁰He then brought them out and asked, "Sirs, what must I do to be saved?"

³¹They replied, "Believe in the Lord Jesus, and you will be saved — you and your household." ³²Then they spoke the word of the Lord to him and to all the others in his house.

The man asked the most important question a human being can ask. He was convinced of his need for salvation. What he knew about his prisoners, what he had learned from their hymns and praises, the earthquake with its results

— these things had stirred his conscience. The answer to his question is the most important information any human being can have. There is only one true answer and the missionaries would provide it.

God does not usually use an earthquake to make people aware of their need for salvation. Sometimes it is a mild heart attack, a slight stroke, a small tumor, a microscopic virus or a minor accident. But when people who have been careless about spiritual things know that they must meet their maker and judge, they often ask the jailer's question.

The answer is not "Do," but "Trust." The answer for the jailer, for each individual in his household, for every human being is the same. Trust the Lord Jesus. He saves. Not, "This is how you must act or think or feel," but, "Believe in the Lord Jesus and you will be saved."

Paul and Silas told the story of Jesus and his salvation to the jailer and his family in more detail.

33At that hour of the night the jailer took them and washed their wounds; then immediately he and all his family were baptized. 34The jailer brought them into his house and set a meal before them; he was filled with joy because he had come to believe in God — he and his whole family.

Like Lydia, the jailer celebrated his coming to faith with hospitality to those who had told him the way of salvation. As Lydia and her household had done, so the jailer and his family received Holy Baptism.

35When it was daylight, the magistrates sent their officers to the jailer with the order: "Release those men." 36The jailer told Paul, "The magistrates have ordered that you and Silas be released. Now you can leave. Go in peace."

The magistrates had no intention of bringing the prisoners to trial. They had intended to teach them a lesson by treating them in such a brutal way. They had hoped that Paul and Silas would then leave town and be no further trouble.

With "go in peace" the jailer was suggesting that they leave quietly. He was simply relaying the orders of the officers.

[37]But Paul said to the officers: "They beat us publicly without a trial, even though we are Roman citizens, and threw us into prison. And now do they want to get rid of us quietly? No! Let them come themselves and escort us out."
[38]The officers reported this to the magistrates, and when they heard that Paul and Silas were Roman citizens, they were alarmed. [39]They came to appease them and escorted them from the prison, requesting them to leave the city.

Paul and Silas were Roman citizens. That made the beating illegal, and since it was a public beating many had witnessed this illegal act. It had been done without a trial, and that compounded the illegality.

Paul was not simply demanding his civil rights or trying to protect his personal dignity. It was important for the future of the church at Philippi that the whole city know that Paul and Silas were innocent of any crime or misdemeanor.

The magistrates themselves could have been severely punished for violating the rights of Roman citizens. That, rather than a sense of justice, accounts for their alarm and the polite way in which they now treated the prisoners.

[40]After Paul and Silas came out of prison, they went to Lydia's house, where they met with the brothers and encouraged them. Then they left.

Paul and Silas did not leave without meeting with the small and young group of believers at Philippi to encourage them. Luke and Timothy remained behind to continue building up the church in that place.

In Thessalonica

17 **When they had passed through Amphipolis and Apollonia, they came to Thessalonica, where there was a Jewish synagogue.**

Paul and Silas traveled on the Egnatian Way until they reached the capital of the whole province, Thessalonica. Amphipolis was about thirty miles southwest of Philippi. The province of Macedonia was divided into three administrative districts, and Amphipolis was capital of the first district. But the apostle and his coworker passed through.

Apollonia was another thirty miles southwest of Amphipolis. Thirty-five miles farther to the west was the capital city of Macedonia, Thessalonica. From here the Lord's message would go out to all of Macedonia and Achaia (Greece). The Thessalonian Christians would become a model to all the believers in Macedonia and Achaia, and even beyond (1 Thessalonians 1:7,8).

[2] As his custom was, Paul went into the synagogue, and on three Sabbath days he reasoned with them from the Scriptures, [3] explaining and proving that the Christ had to suffer and rise from the dead. "This Jesus I am proclaiming to you is the Christ," he said. [4] Some of the Jews were persuaded and joined Paul and Silas, as did a large number of God-fearing Greeks and not a few prominent women.

Paul's method in the synagogue was to take passages from the Old Testament and compare them with the facts of Jesus' life, death and resurrection. He showed that the prophecies about the Messiah speak of his suffering and rising again. He proclaimed that Jesus has fulfilled the prophecies and is therefore the Christ (Messiah). The idea of a suffering Messiah was a stumbling block to the Jews, and so it was important to show that he *must* suffer.

This was the method Paul had used in the synagogue at Damascus, immediately after his conversion (9:20-22). It was what Jesus did on the day of his resurrection, on the road to Emmaus (Luke 24:26,27).

Paul's preaching bore fruit. Some, however, resented it:

⁵But the Jews were jealous; so they rounded up some bad characters from the' marketplace, formed a mob and started a riot in the city. They rushed to Jason's house in search of Paul and Silas in order to bring them out to the crowd.

It must be said again that the jealousy of the Jews was not mere envy at the success of Paul. It was also a jealousy for what they regarded as the honor of God. They demonstrated by their actions, of course, that they had a warped notion of God's honor and of how to guard it.

Paul and Silas had evidently been staying at Jason's house. New believers often showed hospitality to the apostles, as we have seen in the case of Lydia and the jailer at Philippi. It seems safe to conclude that Jason was also a beginner in the faith who showed his gratitude to God by helping those who preached God's salvation to him.

⁶But when they did not find them, they dragged Jason and some other brothers before the city officials, shouting: "These men who have caused trouble all over the world have now come here, ⁷and Jason has welcomed them into his house. They are all defying Caesar's decrees, saying that there is another king, one called Jesus." ⁸When they heard this, the crowd and the city officials were thrown into turmoil. ⁹Then they made Jason and the others post bond and let them go.

When the mob could not find Paul and Silas, they settled for Jason and a number of other believers. The accusations were similar to those which the Jews hurled against Jesus: "We have found this man subverting our nation. He opposes payment of taxes to Caesar and claims to be Christ, a king" (Luke 23:2).

False witness, in public court or private conversation, usually involves half-truths and exaggerations. It was true that the apostles were trying to preach the gospel all over the world. It was not true that they had already done so. It was true that there is often trouble where the gospel is preached. It was not true that the apostles caused that trouble. It is true that Jesus is a king, the King of kings, but it is not true that his gracious rule is intended to overthrow governments.

The charges boiled down to an accusation of treason, for which Jason and the others could have been put to death. The gospel of Jesus as the only Lord and Savior is God's power to create faith and give forgiveness. But sometimes it disturbs people's notions of what is right and brings out the worst in them.

The officials must have realized that the charges of treason were false. They simply required Jason to put up a sum of money as a guarantee that he and the others would not cause further trouble. Paul summed up these events and the work done in Thessalonica in his first letter to the church in that city: "You know, brothers, that our visit to you was not a failure. We had previously suffered and been insulted in Philippi, as you know, but with the help of our God we dared to tell you his gospel in spite of strong opposition" (1 Thessalonians 2:1,2).

In Berea

10 As soon as it was night, the brothers sent Paul and Silas away to Berea. On arriving there, they went to the Jewish synagogue.

The Lord had blessed the work of his missionaries in Thessalonica. He brought a strong young church into existence. Further efforts by Paul and Silas were not essential and would result in further trouble for Jason and others. It was time to leave and the church sent them to another city. Berea was in the next district of Macedonia, about fifty-five miles southwest of Thessalonica. It was a bit south of the Egnatian Way, in a mountainous region.

[11]Now the Bereans were of more noble character than the Thessalonians, for they received the message with great eagerness and examined the Scriptures every day to see if what Paul said was true. [12]Many of the Jews believed, as did also a number of prominent Greek women and many Greek men.

In Thessalonica "some of the Jews were persuaded and joined Paul and Silas." Most were not convinced, and they used vicious means to stop the preaching of the gospel.

In Berea the Jews were more receptive, more open to persuasion, more honest in dealing with Scripture. They took their Bibles more seriously, and daily they compared the Scriptures with the good news about Jesus which Paul was preaching. They tested his message. Jesus had said, "These are the Scriptures that testify about me" (John 5:39). Paul's method in the synagogues was to demonstrate that the Scriptures do testify of Jesus. The Bereans were brought to the same conclusion.

The word of God written in the Old Testament and the gospel preached by Paul achieved God's purpose in Berea. Many Jews and many Gentiles believed.

[13]When the Jews in Thessalonica learned that Paul was preaching the word of God at Berea, they went there too, agitating the crowds and stirring them up. [14]The brothers immediately sent Paul to the coast, but Silas and Timothy stayed at Berea. [15]The

men who accompanied Paul brought him to Athens and then left with instructions for Silas and Timothy to join him as soon as possible.

Fifty or sixty miles away, in Thessalonica, the Jews were still jealous. Just as Jews from Iconium and Antioch had come to Lystra and won the crowd over (14:19), so these agitators came to Berea to spoil the Spirit's work.

Paul was the special target of these troublemakers. Before the crowd could be worked up to actual violence, the church sent Paul on the way to Athens. Timothy had remained for a time at Philippi (16:40) and then rejoined Paul and Silas at Berea. Now he and Silas remained behind to continue the work.

Paul and those who accompanied him may have sailed to Athens, or they may have used the coast road to travel by land. His escorts took back the message that he would wait at Athens for Silas and Timothy, expecting them to join him as soon as the situation in the church at Berea would permit them to leave that young church and go on to newer fields.

In Athens

16While Paul was waiting for them in Athens, he was greatly distressed to see that the city was full of idols. 17So he reasoned in the synagogue with the Jews and the God-fearing Greeks, as well as in the marketplace day by day with those who happened to be there.

Athens taught the world the concept of democracy, the rule of the people. It had been the great center of philosophy, the love of wisdom. For its past contributions in politics, art, literature and the world of ideas the city was honored by the Roman Empire. But its glories had dimmed and it was no longer the chief city of Greece.

The love of wisdom had not put a stop to the service of idols. Where the pagan world saw glory, Paul saw shameful idolatry, and he was greatly distressed.

While he waited for Silas and Timothy to join him, he followed his usual practice of visiting the synagogue to discuss the word with the Jews and proselytes there. His distress at the number of idols in the city also moved him to begin conversations in the marketplace, where he would have contact with Gentiles.

The marketplace was not only a place of business. It was also where philosophers and gentlemen of leisure met for conversation and the exchange of ideas.

[18]A group of Epicurean and Stoic philosophers began to dispute with him. Some of them asked, "What is this babbler trying to say?" Others remarked, "He seems to be advocating foreign gods." They said this because Paul was preaching about Jesus and the resurrection.

Epicurus (341-270 B.C.) taught that the gods are not interested in the affairs of men and that there is no afterlife in which we will be called to account. His followers were urged to enjoy life by doing what is wise and right. By the first century A.D. this philosophy had degenerated to hedonism, the love of pleasure: "Eat, drink and be merry, for tomorrow we die."

The Stoic school of philosophy was founded by Zeno (340-265 B.C.). His followers considered it their highest pleasure to do their duty and their highest duty to act reasonably.

Representatives of these two schools of philosophy disputed with Paul over a number of days. Some of the audience referred to him as a babbler, literally a "seedpicker." This uncomplimentary term suggested that Paul was like a bird, picking up seeds of knowledge here and there, but not really knowing much. Others heard the word *anastasis*, resurrection, and thought that Paul was speaking of a goddess. Thus, Jesus and Resurrection were understood to be two foreign deities.

¹⁹Then they took him and brought him to a meeting of the Areopagus, where they said to him, "May we know what this new teaching is that you are presenting? ²⁰You are bringing some strange ideas to our ears, and we want to know what they mean." ²¹(All the Athenians and the foreigners who lived there spent their time doing nothing but talking about and listening to the latest ideas.)

Literally, Areopagus means "Mars Hill." That had once been the meeting place of Athens's Council of Twelve, the highest court. The name Areopagus came to be applied to the council itself. By the first century the group no longer met on the hill, but the name stuck. It was no longer the highest court of Athens, either. It did, however, pass judgment on new philosophies, new religions and foreign gods. Athens was known as a city of ideas where the leisure class, both native-born and foreign, were always ready to hear and discuss something new.

²²Paul then stood up in the meeting of the Areopagus and said: "Men of Athens! I see that in every way you are very religious. ²³For as I walked around and observed your objects of worship, I even found an altar with this inscription: TO AN UNKNOWN GOD. Now what you worship as something unknown I am going to proclaim to you.
²⁴"The God who made the world and everything in it is the Lord of heaven and earth and does not live in temples built by hands. ²⁵And he is not served by human hands, as if he needed anything, because he himself gives all men life and breath and everything else."

Paul saw statues, altars and shrines dedicated to a great number of deities. It had been said that there were more gods than men in Athens. Greeks and others customarily dedicated an altar to unknown gods so that they would not offend some deity by omitting it.

Notice that Paul says "*what* you worship" rather than "*whom* you worship." The altar was dedicated to an unknown, impersonal "something." Paul would make known the living personal God, the creator of the universe and the judge of every human being.

Dominating the landscape of Athens was the Parthenon, whose ruins still stand. It is the temple dedicated to the patron goddess of the city, the virgin Pallas Athene. Paul said, "The creator of the universe does not need anything that human beings might make for him, any dwelling that they might build for him." The giver and preserver of life is not in need of anything man can offer him.

26"From one man he made every nation of men, that they should inhabit the whole earth; and he determined the times set for them and the exact places where they should live. 27God did this so that men would seek him and perhaps reach out for him and find him, though he is not far from each one of us. 28'For in him we live and move and have our being.' And some of your own poets have said, 'We are his offspring.' "

In creating one man, Adam, God created all the descendants of Adam. The nations who cover the earth in all their variety of stature and color and appearance descend from a single ancestor. Their migrations and accomplishments are in his hands. Empires rise and fall according to his will. Civilizations and cultures and the geography and history of nations are ordered by him.

God demonstrated his power and intelligence in creation and in the history of nations so that people would realize that an intelligent and powerful being is in charge of the universe. In God's intention this should make them seek him, reach for him and find him. The people who had built an altar TO AN UNKNOWN GOD had sought but had not found.

The Stoic philosophers agreed with the idea that God is not far from each one of us. In fact, most philosophers of Paul's time were pantheists. They confused the creator with his creation by teaching that everything is god. Paul used their mistaken beliefs as a starting point from which to go on and preach the gospel of the true God.

The first quotation in verse 28 acknowledges that life is from God. It may be from the *Cretica* of the poet Epimenides (about 600 B.C.). The second quotation says essentially the same thing and appears twice in ancient Greek literature. The poet Aratus (315-240 B.C.) from Paul's homeland, Cilicia, wrote it in his *Phaenomenon*. His contemporary, Cleanthes (331-233 B.C.), included it in his *Hymn to Zeus*.

[29]"Therefore since we are God's offspring, we should not think that the divine being is like gold or silver or stone — an image made by man's design and skill. [30]In the past God overlooked such ignorance, but now he commands all people everywhere to repent. [31]For he has set a day when he will judge the world with justice by the man he has appointed. He has given proof of this to all men by raising him from the dead."

Since we come from God, how can God come from us? An image made by man's design and skill is man's creation. How can it be his creator?

Paul told the Athenians what he had told the people at Lystra who wanted to offer sacrifice to him and Barnabas (14:16). God did not immediately punish idolatry in the past. Ignorance was not innocence, but he chose not to destroy the idolaters at once. Now he has revealed himself in Jesus Christ, and he calls on people everywhere to turn from idols to him. With these words Paul was calling his hearers to repentance.

The day will come when every human being must give an account of what he or she has done with the gift of life. God has appointed a man to judge the world with justice. God has given proof of this by raising him from the dead. This proof is intended for all.

Paul did not immediately name this man. He wanted the Athenians to think about who it could be. Between the past times when God overlooked heathen ignorance and the future time when he will judge his world lies *now*, the time for repentance. *Now* is the time to turn from every false god to the living God and to his Son Jesus Christ.

³²When they heard about the resurrection of the dead, some of them sneered, but others said, "We want to hear you again on this subject." ³³At that, Paul left the council. ³⁴A few men became followers of Paul and believed. Among them was Dionysius, a member of the Areopagus, also a woman named Damaris, and a number of others.

It was the day of grace for those people at the Areopagus. While Paul spoke of familiar things about which they agreed, they listened. When he spoke of the resurrection of Christ, they stopped listening. Some dismissed God's message with a sneer. Others, more politely, put an end to Paul's address by vaguely suggesting that perhaps he could finish some other time.

They interrupted God's spokesman, and that day of grace was over. They did not persecute Paul, for they were tolerant of virtually everyone and everything. Tolerance, however, easily becomes indifference. They were indifferent to the eternally important message Paul was trying to share with them.

Only one member of the Council heard and believed the rest of what Paul had to say. The number of others may or may not have included some who heard Paul at the synagogue. There is no further mention in the New Testament of a congregation of believers in Athens.

In Corinth and back to Antioch

18 After this, Paul left Athens and went to Corinth. ²There he met a Jew named Aquila, a native of Pontus, who had recently come from Italy with his wife Priscilla, because Claudius had ordered all the Jews to leave Rome. Paul went to see them, ³and because he was a tentmaker as they were, he stayed and worked with them.

About 45 miles east of Athens lay Corinth, which was the capital of the Roman senatorial province of Achaia (Greece). It is located on the isthmus which joins northern and southern Greece. It was a commercial center and, in a world where sexual immorality was the rule, Corinth was notorious for its sexual immorality.

Paul may have walked from Athens to Corinth on a good Roman road. If not, he sailed from Piraeus, Athens's port, to Corinth's eastern port, Cenchrea.

Aquila's home province, Pontus, was east of Bithynia in northeastern Asia Minor, on the Black Sea. When Emperor Claudius expelled the Jews from Rome in A.D. 49, Aquila and Priscilla were among those who had to leave. Whether they were also Christians at that time we cannot say. Luke introduces Aquila to us as a Jew, not as a brother or disciple. It is possible that Aquila and his wife were Paul's first converts in Corinth.

Claudius's decree was not aware of, or it ignored, any distinction between Jews who were Christians and Jews who were not. The emperor's biographer, Suetonius, writes that Claudius expelled the Jews because of riots caused by "the agitator Chrestus." Historians believe that Suetonius was misspelling Christ's name, that he did not understand who Christ is, and that the riots were the result of conflicts between Jews who believed that Jesus is the Messiah and Jews who did not.

Tentmaking was an important industry in Paul's hometown. It was the custom for Jewish fathers to see that their sons learned a trade, and it seems likely that Paul learned his trade as a young man in Tarsus. He began his stay in Corinth by going to work to earn a living. Later, he would write to the believers in Corinth, "We work hard with our own hands" (1 Corinthians 4:12).

4Every Sabbath he reasoned in the synagogue, trying to persuade Jews and Greeks.

5When Silas and Timothy came from Macedonia, Paul devoted himself exclusively to preaching, testifying to the Jews that Jesus was the Christ.

From 1 Thessalonians 3:1 we gather that Silas and Timothy had joined Paul in Athens, but that then he sent them back to Macedonia because the churches there needed them. Now they joined Paul in Corinth. From the fact that Paul could spend all his time preaching after they arrived we gather that they brought funds from Macedonia to support his gospel work in Corinth.

He told the Jews in the synagogue that the Messiah for whom they had been waiting had come and that Jesus was that Messiah.

6But when the Jews opposed Paul and became abusive, he shook out his clothes in protest and said to them, "Your blood be on

**your own heads! I am clear of my responsibility. From now on I
will go to the Gentiles."**

**⁷Then Paul left the synagogue and went next door to the house
of Titius Justus, a worshiper of God. ⁸Crispus, the synagogue
ruler, and his entire household believed in the Lord; and many of
the Corinthians who heard him believed and were baptized.**

When the Jews rejected Paul's message and blasphemed
the name of Jesus (became abusive), he did and said something like what he had said and done at Pisidian Antioch
(13:45-51). Shaking out his clothes as a gesture of innocence,
he announced that he would take the gospel to the Gentiles.
The guilt for their unbelief was on them for refusing to hear,
not on him for withholding the message.

Titius Justus was a proselyte of the gate, a Gentile who
worshiped Israel's God without being circumcised.

Not all the Jews opposed Paul and blasphemed his Lord.
The ruler of the synagogue and his entire household believed. Over a period of time many Corinthians became
baptized believers.

**⁹One night the Lord spoke to Paul in a vision: "Do not be
afraid; keep on speaking, do not be silent. ¹⁰For I am with you,
and no one is going to attack and harm you, because I have many
people in this city." ¹¹So Paul stayed for a year and a half,
teaching them the word of God.**

Was Paul's work in Corinth completed? Should he leave
before there was a new plot against his life or an outbreak of
persecution against the believers? The risen Savior instructed him not to be afraid. Paul later wrote to the church
in Corinth: "I came to you in weakness and fear, and with
much trembling" (1 Corinthians 2:3).

The Lord had people to gather in Corinth. Paul was his
servant to gather them. Paul's preaching must continue, for

the gospel is the means by which people are gathered. The Lord would be with him in that work.

Paul stayed. The year and a half was most likely the period from autumn of A.D. 51 to spring of 53, the total time of his stay. During this time he also wrote his letter to the Galatians and the two letters to the Thessalonians.

¹²While Gallio was proconsul of Achaia, the Jews made a united attack on Paul and brought him into court. ¹³"This man," they charged, "is persuading the people to worship God in ways contrary to the law."

A proconsul was the head of government in a Roman senatorial province. He ruled for one year. Gallio became proconsul, according to Roman inscriptions, in A.D. 51. He was the brother of Seneca, the Stoic philosopher and author who was the tutor of Nero.

The Jews' religion had legal standing in the empire. They were permitted to worship God according to their religious laws and were not required to participate in the religious rites of the Romans. Their accusation against Paul was that he was making converts to a religion other than Judaism. Their point was that his religion really had no standing in law and that therefore he was violating both Jewish religious law and Roman law.

¹⁴Just as Paul was about to speak, Gallio said to the Jews, "If you Jews were making a complaint about some misdemeanor or serious crime, it would be reasonable for me to listen to you. ¹⁵But since it involves questions about words and names and your own law — settle the matter yourselves. I will not be a judge of such things." ¹⁶So he had them ejected from the court.

Gallio had no interest in or patience for Jewish religious matters, and that was what he correctly considered their charges to be. He believed that they were quibbling about religious technicalities that were beneath his concern. His mention of "names" may be a reference to Paul's testimony "that Jesus was the Christ." Remember Pilate at Jesus' trial: "Take him yourselves and judge him by your own law" (John 18:31).

In the providence of God, the indifferent attitude of powerful men like Gallio made it possible for the gospel to spread with very little opposition from the Roman government. The magistrates at Philippi were not intentionally persecuting Christians. Their actions were intended to brutalize unruly Jews (Paul and Silas), not preachers of the good news about Jesus.

The Jews, who disagreed on many things, had made common cause and presented a united front against Paul. Gallio threw them and their case out of court.

17 Then they all turned on Sosthenes the synagogue ruler and beat him in front of the court. But Gallio showed no concern whatever.

Did the Jews turn on their own synagogue ruler and beat him because he had failed to present a convincing case before Gallio? Some scholars understand verse 17 in that way.

More likely the onlooking Greeks turned on Sosthenes and took out their anti-Jewish feelings on him. They did this in the confidence that the proconsul was not very concerned about protecting Jews from violence. They were not mistaken. Gallio was just as indifferent to the beating of Sosthenes as he was to the Jews' charges against Paul.

One synagogue ruler, Crispus, had already been brought to faith. It is very likely that the synagogue ruler Sosthenes also became a believer. The name was not very common, and there was a man named Sosthenes with Paul when the

apostle wrote his first epistle to the church of God in Corinth
(1 Corinthians 1:1).

**18Paul stayed on in Corinth for some time. Then he left the
brothers and sailed for Syria, accompanied by Priscilla and
Aquila. Before he sailed, he had his hair cut off at Cenchrea
because of a vow he had taken.**

The Jews' failure to incite the Roman proconsul against
him made it possible for Paul to stay on in Corinth. When it
was time to leave for visits in Jerusalem and Antioch of
Syria, his friends Priscilla and Aquila left with him. From
now on Luke will always mention Priscilla first, probably
because she played a more significant role in the gospel work
than her husband did.

Cenchrea was Corinth's port on the Aegean Sea. Here
Paul had his hair cut off to mark the fulfillment of a vow. We
are not told what the vow was in connection with which he
had let his hair grow. It may have been a vow of thanksgiving for God's protection in a city that had seemed hostile to
the gospel. In any case, we see that Paul still followed certain
Jewish customs. That was not for his salvation or because he
believed he had to do it. It was because he was a Jew and he
still expressed his faith by following certain Jewish customs.
According to the custom he would take the hair with him to
Jerusalem and burn it "in the fire that [was] under the
sacrifice of the fellowship offering" (Numbers 6:18).

**19They arrived at Ephesus, where Paul left Priscilla and Aquila.
He himself went into the synagogue and reasoned with the Jews.
20When they asked him to spend more time with them, he declined. 21But as he left, he promised, "I will come back if it is God's
will." Then he set sail from Ephesus. 22When he landed at Caesarea, he went up and greeted the church and then went down to
Antioch.**

Ephesus was located across the Aegean Sea from Corinth. It was the capital of the province of Asia and an important commercial center. The Lord had a special assignment for Priscilla and Aquila here, of which we will read in verses 24 to 26.

At least some of those who heard Paul reasoning in the synagogue at Ephesus were receptive and asked him to stay longer. He declined at that time, but we will see in Chapter 19 that it was God's will for him to return.

"He went up" means that Paul went to Jerusalem to greet the church there. It is possible that he also visited the temple and burned the hair which he had cut off at Cenchrea. "Went down" signifies that he left Jerusalem. He returned to Antioch, to the brothers who had commended him and Silas to the grace of the Lord (15:40).

What had begun as a trip to visit the young congregations founded by Paul and Barnabas became, under God's direction and with his help, the great second missionary journey. The apostle had preached the gospel on the continent of Europe, and the Lord had richly blessed his preaching.

Paul's Third Mission Tour: Asia Minor and Europe

Visits in Asia Minor and Events in Ephesus

23 After spending some time in Antioch, Paul set out from there and traveled from place to place throughout the region of Galatia and Phrygia, strengthening all the disciples.

Once again Paul left Antioch with the intention of visiting and encouraging the believers in the young churches of Asia Minor. The last time he had done that the Lord had led him to Europe by way of Troas. This journey, too, would include more than visits to places where Paul had worked before.

[24]Meanwhile a Jew named Apollos, a native of Alexandria, came to Ephesus. He was a learned man, with a thorough knowledge of the Scriptures. [25]He had been instructed in the way of the Lord, and he spoke with great fervor and taught about Jesus accurately, though he knew only the baptism of John. [26]He began to speak boldly in the synagogue.

Apollos's hometown, Alexandria, is in Egypt, in the Nile delta. It was the second largest city in the empire. From its docks Egypt's grain was shipped to Italy, and Rome was very dependent on it. It had a very large Jewish population, and it was a great center of research and scholarship in Greek literature and art. Apollos's combination of learning and Scripture knowledge was in the tradition of Philo, a Jewish scholar in Alexandria (20 B.C. to A.D. 40). However, he did not follow Philo's methods of interpreting the Bible. Luke says that Apollos's teaching was accurate, and we know that Philo explained away many of the truths of Scripture to make them agree with Greek philosophical ideas. The most popular Greek translation of the Old Testament, the Septuagint, had been produced in Alexandria.

Apollos knew the Old Testament promises concerning the Messiah and the way in which the Lord planned to save Israel and the nations. He knew that Jesus was the fulfillment of those promises, but he did not know the full story of Jesus' suffering and his resurrection. His knowledge of the Savior was really limited to what John had taught about his coming. Just as John had not lived to see the fulfillment of his own prophecies, so Apollos had not yet gotten to know how those prophecies were fulfilled. He was still, in a sense, an Old Testament believer.

When Priscilla and Aquila heard him, they invited him to their home and explained to him the way of God more adequately.

²⁷**When Apollos wanted to go to Achaia, the brothers encouraged him and wrote to the disciples there to welcome him. On arriving, he was a great help to those who by grace had believed. ²⁸For he vigorously refuted the Jews in public debate, proving from the Scriptures that Jesus was the Christ.**

Priscilla and Aquila did Apollos a great kindness in taking him home to tell him the complete story of what Jesus did to save sinners. They did not show up his ignorance in the synagogue but gave him private instruction. They saw his strengths and recognized his weaknesses and determined to help him. They were also doing a great service for the church, because the Lord would use Apollos's great gifts to build up his church.

On the other hand Apollos, a learned man, was not too proud to receive instruction from the tentmaker and his wife. Most likely, Priscilla is mentioned first because she was the more apt teacher of the husband and wife team.

The letter of recommendation which the brothers in Ephesus sent to the disciples in Achaia certified that Apollos was qualified to help in the gospel work in Greece. The disciples would find him reliable and able. And that was how things turned out. Apollos's learning and knowledge of Scripture, along with his new information concerning Jesus, made him a valuable asset to the believers in Achaia. His special work was to demonstrate that the Jesus of history is the Messiah of prophecy, and he did this with vigor.

Incidentally, Luke reminds us in verse 27 that even believing is by God's grace and that believers still need help from God's word to grow in faith. We always need the reminder.

19 **While Apollos was at Corinth, Paul took the road through the interior and arrived at Ephesus. There he found some**

disciples ²and asked them, "Did you receive the Holy Spirit when you believed?"

They answered, "No, we have not even heard that there is a Holy Spirit."

³So Paul asked, "Then what baptism did you receive?"

"John's baptism," they replied.

⁴Paul said, "John's baptism was a baptism of repentance. He told the people to believe in the one coming after him, that is, in Jesus."

After visiting and working in the region of Galatia and Phrygia, Paul took the more northern route across the province of Asia to Ephesus. On his second journey his stop at that city had been very brief. "But as he left, he promised, 'I will come back if it is God's will' " (18:21). God willed it and Paul worked in Ephesus for more than two years.

At Ephesus he was surprised to meet a number of persons who believed what they had heard concerning Jesus but who had never heard of the Holy Spirit. Paul's question, "Did you receive the Holy Spirit when you believed" was simply a friendly inquiry as to whether they had received any special gifts of the Spirit. Their answer betrayed that they knew very little gospel teaching.

Further questioning made clear why they had not received or even heard of the Holy Spirit. Like Apollos, they had only an incomplete knowledge of Jesus' saving work. They had received John's baptism, that is, a baptism which looked forward to Christ's coming rather than a baptism based on what Jesus did. Paul explained to them that John's preaching had pointed to Jesus and that Jesus had come.

They had not really understood what John's message was. Thus, they had participated in a ceremony of washing but they had not really been baptized. That ceremony could not be a true baptism without the revelation, the "name" of

Jesus. That was why they had not received the Holy Spirit.

⁵On hearing this, they were baptized into the name of the Lord Jesus. ⁶When Paul placed his hands on them, the Holy Spirit came on them, and they spoke in tongues and prophesied. ⁷There were about twelve men in all.

When they learned that Jesus was the fulfillment of John's prophecy and when they learned what he had done, they believed. And they were baptized into, or in, Jesus' name. Believing in him, relying on the truth about him, they were made his own people in Holy Baptism.

Paul laid his hands on them as a sign of blessing and fellowship. They who had never heard of the Holy Spirit now received unusual gifts from him. They spoke in tongues, as the Twelve had done on Pentecost (2:4), as Cornelius and his household did at Caesarea (10:44-46). They also prophesied, that is, spoke God's word in plain language.

Faith, baptism and Holy Spirit belong together. The Spirit creates faith and makes baptism a means of grace. Where the means of grace are the Holy Spirit is.

⁸Paul entered the synagogue and spoke boldly there for three months, arguing persuasively about the kingdom of God. ⁹But some of them became obstinate; they refused to believe and publicly maligned the Way. So Paul left them. He took the disciples with him and had discussions daily in the lecture hall of Tyrannus. ¹⁰This went on for two years, so that all the Jews and Greeks who lived in the province of Asia heard the word of the Lord.

It was remarkable that Paul was able to continue his work in the synagogue for as long as three months. In other cities, opposition always arose much sooner. Luke says that the apostle's subject was the kingdom of God, God's gracious rule in the interest of saving people. This was not a new topic; the expression includes all that Paul preached and taught about Jesus as the focus and the fulfillment of God's plan of salvation.

The word of God will eventually cause a division between those who believe it and those who do not. After three months of hearing the word from Paul, some of his hearers hardened themselves against his message. He had taught the Way of salvation, and they began to speak evil of it in an outspoken manner. When God's word is stubbornly rejected, it is time to withdraw from those who claim to have it but will not hear it. Paul and those who were persuaded of the gospel truth left the synagogue.

Tyrannus may have been a lecturer himself, who taught the art of rhetoric or some other subject. He may simply have owned a hall which teachers and philosophers rented for their classes and meetings. There Paul carried on daily instruction, and any synagogue people who wanted to hear could easily find him.

During this time Paul wrote the letter which we call *First Corinthians* to the church at Corinth. Through people coming to hear him and through the work of his assistants the word of the Lord was spread through the whole province. The churches at Colosse, Hierapolis and Laodicea were probably founded at this time.

[11]God did extraordinary miracles through Paul. [12]Handkerchiefs and aprons that had touched him were taken to the sick, and their illnesses were cured and the evil spirits left them.

The miracles were extraordinary because Paul himself was not present to speak or to lay his hands on the sufferers.

The gospel was spreading throughout the province of Asia, and Paul could not be everywhere at once. God, who worked through the words or the touch of the apostle, could also work through the tentmaker's clothing. He did, and that helped the progress of the gospel.

13Some Jews who went around driving out evil spirits tried to invoke the name of the Lord Jesus over those who were demon-possessed. They would say, "In the name of Jesus whom Paul preaches, I command you to come out." 14Seven sons of Sceva, a Jewish chief priest, were doing this.

People who did not trust Jesus as their Savior tried to use his name as a kind of magic incantation. They had seen Paul heal and heard him drive out spirits in Jesus' name. Part of an ancient papyrus document, evidently used by a non-Jewish exorcist reads: "I command you in the name of Jesus the God of the Jews. . . ."

Either Sceva was a member of the priestly family, or "chief priest" was a title he took for himself to add to his prestige. Neither he nor his sons necessarily lived in Ephesus, since people of their type moved from place to place preying on superstitious people.

15The evil spirit answered them, "Jesus I know and Paul I know about, but who are you?" 16Then the man who had the evil spirit jumped on them and overpowered them all. He gave them such a beating that they ran out of the house naked and bleeding.

17When this became known to the Jews and Greeks living in Ephesus, they were all seized with fear, and the name of the Lord Jesus was held in high honor.

An evil spirit in the synagogue at Capernaum had recognized Jesus: "I know who you are — the Holy One of God!" (Luke 4:34). Also at Capernaum "demons came out of many people, shouting, 'You are the Son of God!' " (Luke 4:41). The devil and his angels know and fear the Son of God. This evil spirit knew Jesus and knew about Paul, but he scorned those who were taking Jesus' name in vain by trying to use it for profit. Anyone taking Jesus' name into his mouth for earthly gain or unspiritual purposes ought to realize that even the devils look down on him.

Their plan miscarried, but God used their misuse of his name for his good purposes. Even those who did not trust the Lord Jesus as their Savior had to respect his name. Paul used that name, and extraordinary miracles took place. Sceva's sons used it and an evil spirit beat them up. Such a name must be treated with respect and care, thought the people of Ephesus.

[18]Many of those who believed now came and openly confessed their evil deeds. [19]A number who had practiced sorcery brought their scrolls together and burned them publicly. When they calculated the value of the scrolls, the total came to fifty thousand drachmas.

Among those who were young in the faith there were some who had not completely given up their superstitious practices. Now they publicly acknowledged their wrongdoing. The Greek word for "evil deeds" was sometimes used in the special sense of "magic spells." That meaning seems to fit very well here.

It would have taken 160 workingmen a year of six-day weeks to earn the price of the scrolls which were publicly destroyed.

[20]In this way the word of the Lord spread widely and grew in power.

Paul's teaching and miracles, the driving out of evil spirits and the victory of Jesus' truth over sorcery all made for the widespread and growing influence of the gospel.

21 After all this had happened, Paul decided to go to Jerusalem, passing through Macedonia and Achaia. "After I have been there," he said, "I must visit Rome also." 22 He sent two of his helpers, Timothy and Erastus, to Macedonia, while he stayed in the province of Asia a little longer.

Paul planned to visit the young churches of Macedonia and Greece. Then he wanted to go to Jerusalem. Finally, he was sure that God wanted him to visit Rome.

Part of his purpose in Macedonia and Achaia was to encourage the churches to complete the collection which they were gathering for the needy Christians of Jerusalem and Judea. Part of his purpose in going to Jerusalem was to deliver that collection. Then, he felt, he would be free to go to Rome. We know about the collection for the saints of Judea from references in 1 and 2 Corinthians and Romans.

This is the first mention of Erastus. In Romans 16:23 Paul, writing from Corinth, mentions "Erastus, who is the city's director of public works." If it is the same man, Paul had a very influential helper. The name was quite common, and the same person is not necessarily meant.

Paul's reason for staying a little longer is found in 1 Corinthians 16:8,9: "I will stay on at Ephesus until Pentecost, because a great door for effective work has opened to me, and there are many who oppose me."

23 About that time there arose a great disturbance about the Way. 24 A silversmith named Demetrius, who made silver shrines of Artemis, brought in no little business for the craftsmen. 25 He called them together, along with the workmen in related trades, and said: "Men, you know we receive a good income from this business. 26 And you see and hear how this fellow Paul has convinced and led astray large numbers of people here in Ephesus and in practically the whole province of Asia. He says that man-made gods are no gods at all. 27 There is danger not only that our

trade will lose its good name, but also that the temple of the great goddess Artemis will be discredited, and the goddess herself, who is worshiped throughout the province of Asia and the world, will be robbed of her divine majesty."

One of the seven wonders of the ancient world was the temple of Artemis at Ephesus. It was three times as large as the Parthenon at Athens. Silver models of the temple, with the statue of the goddess inside, were sold to visitors who came to Ephesus out of devotion to Artemis. The people of Asia Minor worshiped Artemis as a fertility goddess, and her temple was served by priestesses who were also prostitutes.

Demetrius rightly regarded the work of Paul in Ephesus and Asia as a threat to his livelihood. Where the true and living God is preached and believed there will be fewer idolaters, fewer people willing to pay costly devotion to false gods. Demetrius's motives and his appeal to the other people involved in the shrine business were a mixture of greed and superstitious religion.

Paul's message in Ephesus must have included the truth which he had expressed before the Areopagus in Athens: "We should not think that the divine being is like gold or silver or stone — an image made by man's design and skill" (17:29). Paul's preaching was more effective than the silversmith wanted it to be, but it had not persuaded Demetrius.

When Demetrius said that Artemis was worshiped throughout the world, he was not stretching the facts by much. In his world, that is, the eastern Mediterranean region, archaeologists have found evidence that the goddess had devotees in thirty or more places besides Ephesus.

28When they heard this, they were furious and began shouting: "Great is Artemis of the Ephesians!" 29Soon the whole city was in

an uproar. The people seized Gaius and Aristarchus, Paul's traveling companions from Macedonia, and rushed as one man into the theater. [30]Paul wanted to appear before the crowd, but the disciples would not let him. [31]Even some of the officials of the province, friends of Paul, sent him a message begging him not to venture into the theater.

In cities such as Ephesus, the large outdoor theaters were used for public meetings as well as for dramas and spectacles. Archaeologists estimate that the theater at Ephesus seated about 26,000.

Gaius was a very common name, and three men named Gaius are mentioned in the New Testament. This is the only mention of the Macedonian Gaius. Aristarchus will be mentioned again in Acts (20:4; 27:2). He was with Paul when the latter was in prison (Colossians 4:10; Philemon 24).

The disciples were sure that Paul's life and the lives of Gaius and Aristarchus would be in danger if he spoke. The mob would only become more violent if they saw and heard the man whose preaching endangered the city's fame as the great center of Artemis worship.

Paul had other friends dissuading him, too, friends in very high places. The officials, known as "asiarchs," were elected from the most influential families of the province. They were supposed to encourage the official religion of Rome. We do not know how they became Paul's friends, but it is difficult to imagine that Paul would ever withhold the gospel from anyone. They may not have been believers, but they were fair-minded men, and they cared enough for justice and for Paul that they did not want him to fall into the hands of a mob.

[32]The assembly was in confusion: Some were shouting one thing, some another. Most of the people did not even know why

they were there. [33]The Jews pushed Alexander to the front, and some of the crowd shouted instructions to him. He motioned for silence in order to make a defense before the people.

The mob's chant, "Great is Artemis of the Ephesians," was intended to intimidate the Jews or anyone who would speak out against the worship of idols. The Jews wanted the mob to know that Paul did not represent them. Since most of the people did not even know why they were there, there was the possibility that the meeting would turn into an anti-Jewish riot. Alexander's speech was not to be a defense of Paul but an assurance that Paul did not speak for the Jews of Ephesus. He never got the opportunity to speak.

[34]But when they realized he was a Jew, they all shouted in unison for about two hours: "Great is Artemis of the Ephesians!"

[35]The city clerk quieted the crowd and said: "Men of Ephesus, doesn't all the world know that the city of Ephesus is the guardian of the temple of the great Artemis and of her image, which fell from heaven? [36]Therefore, since these facts are undeniable, you ought to be quiet and not do anything rash. [37]You have brought these men here, though they have neither robbed temples nor blasphemed our goddess. [38]If, then, Demetrius and his fellow craftsmen have a grievance against anybody, the courts are open and there are proconsuls. They can press charges. [39]If there is anything further you want to bring up, it must be settled in a legal assembly. [40]As it is, we are in danger of being charged with rioting because of today's events. In that case we would not be able to account for this commotion, since there is no reason for it." [41]After he had said this, he dismissed the assembly.

Ephesus was the capital of the province, which was ruled by a Roman proconsul. But local affairs were decided by a people's assembly, and the city clerk was responsible for publishing the decrees of the assembly. He also mediated between the city and the Roman authorities. He was determined to prevent any situation that would make it appear as though Ephesus could not handle local matters.

The image of Artemis did not fall from heaven. What fell from heaven at some time in the city's dim past was probably a meteorite. What sat in the shrine of the temple was a very ugly image, the many-breasted symbol of fertility.

Robbing temples and blaspheming gods were two charges which the Gentiles often raised against the Jews. The city clerk knew that Paul and his companions were not guilty of such actions. He urged that the proper legal channels be followed, if there really was some legitimate grievance. He wanted to be sure that nothing illegal or disorderly was done, lest Ephesus lose the degree of self-rule which it enjoyed. The actions of the mob would be difficult to explain to the Roman authorities.

The master politician addressed them as though they were responsible people and they acted responsibly. They went home, worn out with two hours of shouting and sobered by his warning.

Visits in Macedonia and Greece

20 **When the uproar had ended, Paul sent for the disciples and, after encouraging them, said good-by and set out for Macedonia. ²He traveled through that area, speaking many words of encouragement to the people, and finally arrived in Greece, ³where he stayed three months.**

Paul did not leave on the day of the uproar. He had been planning for some time to leave (19:21), but first he arranged for a gathering of believers at which he spoke words of encouragement and farewell.

He sailed along the coast of Troas, where he hoped to meet Titus and do missionary work (2 Corinthians 2:12,13). When Titus was not to be found at Troas, Paul went northwest across the Aegean to Macedonia. There he visited and encouraged the churches. While he was in Macedonia, probably at Philippi, Titus joined him (2 Corinthians 7:6).

The three months in Greece were spent mostly in Corinth. These were the winter months, when sailing conditions were at their worst. Part of Paul's activity during this time was to compose his great letter to the saints at Rome.

Because the Jews made a plot against him just as he was about to sail for Syria, he decided to go back through Macedonia. 4He was accompanied by Sopater son of Pyrrhus from Berea, Aristarchus and Secundus from Thessalonica, Gaius from Derbe, Timothy also, and Tychicus and Trophimus from the province of Asia. 5These men went on ahead and waited for us at Troas.

Paul intended to leave for Syria, to get to Jerusalem, but the Jews were plotting again, and he decided it would be safer to travel through Macedonia than to board a ship at Cenchrea.

Luke does not mention it, but Paul's seven companions were the official representatives of the Gentile mission in Macedonia and Asia Minor, who would go with him to deliver the collection to Jerusalem (Romans 15:25,26). These men came from the three great Gentile mission fields: the first three from Macedonia, the next two from Galatia, the last two from the province of Asia.

It is clear from the "us" that Luke was with Paul. Perhaps others were, too. Verse 6 suggests that Paul and Luke

215

remained at Philippi to celebrate the Feast of Unleavened Bread, the Passover. Passover was also the anniversary of the Lord's resurrection, and the Jewish Christians who observed Passover were certainly conscious of that.

Events at Troas and Miletus

⁶But we sailed from Philippi after the Feast of Unleavened Bread, and five days later joined the others at Troas, where we stayed seven days.

⁷On the first day of the week we came together to break bread. Paul spoke to the people and, because he intended to leave the next day, kept talking until midnight.

Five days from Neapolis (Philippi's port) to Troas was more than twice as long as Paul's two-day trip in the opposite direction had been (16:11). The winds were not as favorable.

The believers at Troas and the missionaries gathered to break bread. By Jewish reckoning the day began at sundown, and thus the first day of the week began on Saturday evening. But that does not necessarily mean they met that evening. Luke's words can just as well mean that they met anytime before sundown on Sunday. Believers still meet on the first day of the week to remember and celebrate the Lord's resurrection. We do this in freedom, not by the Lord's command.

Breaking bread was the way in which a meal began. The believers ate a meal together and then celebrated the sacrament of Christ's body and blood. All of this action together was called "the Lord's Supper" (1 Corinthians 11:20).

Paul's time with the disciples at Troas was very limited. He wanted to make the most of it, and his address continued till midnight.

8There were many lamps in the upstairs room where we were meeting. 9Seated in a window was a young man named Eutychus, who was sinking into a deep sleep as Paul talked on and on. When he was sound asleep, he fell to the ground from the third story and was picked up dead. 10Paul went down, threw himself on the young man and put his arms around him. "Don't be alarmed," he said. "He's alive!" 11Then he went upstairs again and broke bread and ate. After talking until daylight, he left. 12The people took the young man home alive and were greatly comforted.

The upstairs room was most likely the "penthouse," the room built on the flat roof of the house. The many lamps would tend to make the room hot and stuffy. Even people who are very interested in hearing a message from God's word can grow sleepy under such conditions.

The young man fell a considerable distance. Luke does not say that Eutychus *seemed* to be dead. The young man was dead, lying outside the house. God used Paul's actions to bring him back to life.

After the miracle Paul paused to eat. Others joined him, no doubt, but Luke specifically mentions Paul because he is the central figure in this story. Then he continued talking until morning. The Greek word used for talking here makes it clear that it was conversation and not the formal teaching Paul had been doing when Eutychus fell.

The people had heard the message of God's grace from Paul. They had seen a demonstration of God's power to raise the dead. They took comfort from both.

13We went on ahead to the ship and sailed for Assos, where we were going to take Paul aboard. He had made this arrangement because he was going there on foot. 14When he met us at Assos, we took him aboard and went on to Mitylene. 15The next day we set sail from there and arrived off Kios. The day after that we crossed over to Samos, and on the following day arrived at Miletus.

16Paul had decided to sail past Ephesus to avoid spending time in the province of Asia, for he was in a hurry to reach Jerusalem, if possible, by the day of Pentecost.

Troas was on a peninsula. On the opposite side, the southern side, of the peninsula was Assos. Luke and Paul's other companions sailed the forty miles or so around the peninsula. Paul traveled across by land, a trip of about twenty miles. The trip by ship from Neapolis to Troas had taken five arduous days. The trip around the peninsula was not an easy one. It may be that Paul wanted to avoid more rough sailing when he could. Maybe he had business on the way between Troas and Assos. Perhaps he simply wanted to be alone for a time. We don't really know because Luke doesn't tell us.

It is remarkable that Paul had the energy to walk all day after talking all night. That may be Luke's reason for mentioning this detail.

The ship picked him up at Assos and they proceeded to Mitylene. It was the main town in the island of Lesbos, on its southeast coast.

Kios was another island. They did not land there but anchored offshore overnight. On the third day they made Samos, another island, one of the most important in the Aegean Sea. In crossing to Samos, across Cayster Bay from Kios, they bypassed Ephesus.

The fourth day's sailing brought them to Miletus. They had been "island hopping" and stopping at night, the only safe way at that time to navigate the Aegean along the western coast of Asia Minor. When they reached Miletus, about thirty-five miles south of Ephesus, they were on the mainland of Asia Minor.

Verse 16 tells us why Paul had decided to take a vessel which would sail past Ephesus. Travel time would be lost by the journey itself. In addition, believers in Ephesus and Asia, where he had served for more than two years, would want him to stay for more than a brief visit. The day of Pentecost is fifty days after Easter, and sixteen days had already passed.

17From Miletus, Paul sent to Ephesus for the elders of the church. 18When they arrived, he said to them: "You know how I lived the whole time I was with you, from the first day I came into the province of Asia. 19I served the Lord with great humility and with tears, although I was severely tested by the plots of the Jews. 20You know that I have not hesitated to preach anything that would be helpful to you but have taught you publicly and from house to house. 21I have declared to both Jews and Greeks that they must turn to God in repentance and have faith in our Lord Jesus."

The church at Ephesus was made up of a number of local churches, or congregations. One of these was the church in the house of Aquila and Priscilla (1 Corinthains 16:19).

The elders were the leaders of those churches, men chosen for their mature judgment and spiritual knowledge. They were "overseers" and "shepherds" (v. 28). That can only mean that they carried out the pastoral ministry in those churches.

Paul reviewed his ministry among them, reminding them of what they had observed. What he had done and the manner in which he had conducted his work were to be a positive example to them in their ministry. His work had been marked by humility, not preaching himself but Christ crucified, Jesus as Lord. He did not advance his own interests but the Savior's cause. His ministry had been marked by tears over those who were slow to understand and especially those who refused to believe. He had continued even when the Jews' plots tempted him to discontinue his efforts.

219

"I have not hesitated" is really an understatement. Paul had used every opportunity to preach publicly and to carry on instruction with smaller groups in people's homes. Fatigue, frustration and the enmity of unbelievers might have tempted him to hesitate. He did not.

Repentance and faith in our Lord Jesus are not really two separate things. Faith in our Lord Jesus explains what repentance really is. It is turning from ego and unbelief and sin to trust in Jesus and his righteousness. Verse 21 sums up and condenses the content of the helpful preaching of which Paul spoke in verse 20.

22"And now, compelled by the Spirit, I am going to Jerusalem, not knowing what will happen to me there. 23I only know that in every city the Holy Spirit warns me that prison and hardships are facing me. 24However, I consider my life worth nothing to me, if only I may finish the race and complete the task the Lord Jesus has given me — the task of testifying to the gospel of God's grace."

The Spirit was compelling Paul to go to Jerusalem. He was uncertain what might happen to him there, but the Spirit who was compelling him was also warning him that prison and hardship were facing him.

We are not told how this warning was taking place. At Tyre (21:4) the disciples would urge him not to go to Jerusalem. At Caesarea (21:11) Agabus would prophesy that Paul was going to be handed over to the Gentiles. But these warnings occurred after Paul's words here to the elders of the Ephesian church.

Were there prophecies and urging in cities of Macedonia, Achaia and Asia which Luke has not recorded? Very likely. In all of this, the Spirit who warned Paul was also the Spirit who compelled him to go.

In spite of the dire warnings, Paul was not reluctant to go. On the contrary. He had a race to finish. The race he was running was the task which the Lord Jesus had assigned him, and that task was the whole meaning of his life. To testify that God for Christ's sake does not charge people's sins to them, that he has forgiven them, gave Paul's life purpose and value.

25"Now I know that none of you among whom I have gone about preaching the kingdom will ever see me again. 26Therefore, I declare to you today that I am innocent of the blood of all men. 27For I have not hesitated to proclaim to you the whole will of God."

Paul expressed a personal judgment, based on the warnings he had received about what he faced in Jerusalem. He did not believe he would be free to visit Ephesus and see these leaders again. He was probably wrong in this judgment. A comparison of 1 Timothy 1:3 and 4:13 shows that after his first imprisonment in Rome he intended to visit Ephesus. And 2 Timothy 4:20, written during Paul's final imprisonment, makes clear that he at least visited Miletus.

Paul understood that a preacher must answer to God for the message he preaches or fails to preach. By saying, "I am innocent of the blood of all men," he was saying that no one would go to eternal death because Paul had failed to preach the truth to him.

The whole will of God is that all men "must turn to God in repentance and have faith in our Lord Jesus (v. 21)." All the teaching of the Bible centers in this, and all the true preaching of God's servants does the same. To alter any of God's law or God's gospel is to misrepresent God's will. To say more or to say less than God's word says can make a minister guilty of someone's blood, make him the cause of someone's eternal damnation.

221

28"Keep watch over yourselves and all the flock of which the Holy Spirit has-made you overseers. Be shepherds of the church of God, which he bought with his own blood. 29I know that after I leave, savage wolves will come in among you and will not spare the flock. 30Even from your own number men will arise and distort the truth in order to draw away disciples after them. 31So be on your guard! Remember that for three years I never stopped warning each of you night and day with tears."

Shepherds feed and lead the flock. Pastors feed and lead the church of God. The Holy Spirit had made them overseers, supervisors, for that purpose. He did that through the people who elected them to be elders.

The elders were to guard themselves and the whole flock, or congregation. Paul used the picture of a flock because he was thinking of the Good Shepherd who gave his life for the sheep, the God who "bought the church with his own blood."

That is a striking expression, so striking that some copyists and editors and commentators tried to change it. "God's blood" reminds us that when God became man he did not stop being God. As the God-man he was not two persons but one person. What the Man did God was doing. What belongs to the Man belongs to God. When Jesus' blood was shed, God's blood was shed. When God bought the church he did it with his own blood.

The savage wolves of whom Paul speaks are false prophets of the kind Jesus warned about: "Watch out for false prophets. They come to you in sheep's clothing, but inwardly they are ferocious wolves" (Matthew 7:15). No church anywhere at anytime can be complacent about the possibility of false teachers. Wolves kill sheep. False teachers kill souls. It happened at Ephesus in Paul's lifetime: "As I urged you when I went into Macedonia, stay there in

Ephesus so that you may command certain men not to teach false doctrines any longer nor to devote themselves to myths and endless genealogies. These promote controversies rather than God's work — which is by faith" (1 Timothy 1:3,4).

False prophets do not only come from outside the church. Most dangerous are those who arise from within. They do not oppose the truth in a straightforward way and say that it is false. Rather, they distort it. They use the right words but twist and pervert them. Their intention and purpose is to make people loyal to them and their lies instead of following Christ and his truth.

When the apostle speaks of his tears, this is not a reference to persecution. It reveals how earnestly he struggled to train the elders to present the truth in faithful and clear instruction. Perhaps he sometimes worked himself to exhaustion in trying to prepare them for their work as overseers of the flock. In their work they must never forget his warnings.

[32]"Now I commit you to God and to the word of his grace, which can build you up and give you an inheritance among all those who are sanctified. [33]I have not coveted anyone's silver or gold or clothing. [34]You yourselves know that these hands of mine have supplied my own needs and the needs of my companions. [35]In everything I did, I showed you that by this kind of hard work we must help the weak, remembering the words the Lord Jesus himself said: 'It is more blessed to give than to receive.' "

Who could keep the elders faithful in their work and protect the church from the savage wolves? Only God. How would God do that? Through the word of grace, the Scriptures, which Paul had interpreted to them, and the message of God's grace in Jesus Christ, which he had proclaimed. The word proclaims God's grace, it imparts God's grace and it keeps us in God's grace.

That word would make them grow to Christian maturity and give them a share of the gifts and blessings which God has for his saints. Paul would not be there to help them. God with his word would help them as he had even while Paul was there.

Verse 33 is Paul's statement that he had not done his work with an eye for profit. He had explained to the church at Corinth (writing from Ephesus) why he and his coworkers did not accept a salary, even though they had a right to: "We put up with anything rather than hinder the gospel of Christ. Don't you know that those who work in the temple get their food from the temple, and those who serve at the altar share in what is offered on the altar? In the same way, the Lord has commanded that those who preach the gospel should receive their living from the gospel. But I have not used any of these rights"(1 Corinthians 9:12-15).

With all the gospel work he had done at Ephesus Paul had also worked at his tentmaker's trade in order to support himself and his coworkers. "The weak" here probably means those who are weak in understanding, people who would not realize that they ought to be helping to support those who preach the gospel.

The words of the Lord Jesus himself which Paul quoted are not recorded anywhere in the four Gospels. We know that the Gospel writers did not have to record every last word of his in order to teach us what he has done for us. We know that he spoke the words which Paul quoted here because they are written here.

³⁶When he had said this, he knelt down with all of them and prayed. ³⁷They all wept as they embraced him and kissed him.

[38]What grieved them most was his statement that they would never see his face again. Then they accompanied him to the ship.

As Christian people and ministers of the church they did the only thing that remained to be done. They knelt and took all their concerns for one another to the throne of God's grace. It is still the custom in the Mediterranean world, and many other parts of the world, for people to embrace and to exchange a kiss on the cheek in greeting or farewell.

Journey to Jerusalem

21 After we had torn ourselves away from them, we put out to sea and sailed straight to Cos. The next day we went to Rhodes and from there to Patara. [2]We found a ship crossing over to Phoenicia, went on board and set sail. [3]After sighting Cyprus and passing to the south of it, we sailed on to Syria. We landed at Tyre, where our ship was to unload its cargo.

The parting was painful, but Paul and his companions had to leave, and they did. The first day's sailing was to the island of Cos. From there they sailed to the larger island located off the southwest coast of Asia Minor, Rhodes. Patara was a port city on the mainland, at the southwest-ernmost corner of Asia Minor.

Now the island hopping was at an end. The group boarded a ship which would cross the eastern Mediterra-nean directly to the seacoast of central Syria, that is, to Phoenicia. The voyage would be about 400 miles.

Cyprus is that large island in the angle between Asia Minor and Syria, Barnabas's home and the place where the proconsul Sergius Paulus was converted. It was on their left, "to port," as they sailed past toward Syria. Phoenicia was part of the province of Syria, and Luke uses the name of the province. He had used the historical name in verse 2. The ship's cargo was destined for Tyre.

4Finding the disciples there, we stayed with them seven days. Through the Spirit they urged Paul not to go on to Jerusalem. 5But when our time was up, we left and continued on our way. All the disciples and their wives and children accompanied us out of the city, and there on the beach we knelt to pray. 6After saying good-by to each other, we went aboard the ship, and they returned home.

It was now two weeks until Pentecost. Paul was determined to arrive in Jerusalem for the feast. The disciples at Tyre urged their honored guest not to go.

The Spirit was compelling Paul to go (20:22). The Spirit had warned Paul that prison and hardships awaited him (20:23). The Spirit also informed the disciples at Tyre of what the apostle faced. On the basis of that information they gave Paul mistaken advice, to stay away from Jerusalem. They drew false conclusions from true information, just as people sometimes make false application of God's written word. They meant well, but Paul could not bow to their urging.

When the ship had unloaded its cargo at Tyre, it was time to resume the voyage. The whole congregation accompanied Paul, Luke and the others to the beach. As at Miletus, so here, the company of believers went to their knees, asking God to bless and protect those who were going to Jerusalem, those who were staying at Tyre, and the whole church everywhere.

7We continued our voyage from Tyre and landed at Ptolemais, where we greeted the brothers and stayed with them for a day. 8Leaving the next day, we reached Caesarea and stayed at the house of Philip the evangelist, one of the Seven. 9He had four unmarried daughters who had the gift of prophecy.

Ptolemais was renamed Acre or St. Jean d'Acre during the Crusades. Today it is Acco, in the modern state of Israel.

The southern edge of its natural harbor is formed by the Carmel mountain range, and Haifa is situated there. Acco is on the north side of the bay.

Thirty-five or forty miles down the coast was Caesarea, the Roman capital of Judea. A boat which took cargo from Tyre to Ptolemais would probably have cargo for Caesarea as well. Luke does not say they sailed, but it is likely they did, especially since they made the trip in one day.

Almost twenty-five years before, after the baptism of the Ethiopian eunuch, Philip "appeared at Azotus and traveled about, preaching the gospel in all the towns until he reached Caesarea" (8:40). He was still there, exercising his special gift of telling the good news.

His daughters were also gifted. Recall the prophecy of Joel, which Peter quoted on Pentecost: "Your sons and daughters will prophesy" (2:17; Joel 2:28). Messiah had come. God had poured out his Spirit. Philip's daughters had the gift of being able to explain and apply God's word.

[10]After we had been there a number of days, a prophet named Agabus came down from Judea. [11]Coming over to us, he took Paul's belt, tied his own hands and feet with it and said, "The Holy Spirit says, 'In this way the Jews of Jerusalem will bind the owner of this belt and will hand him over to the Gentiles.' "

Presumably this was the same Agabus who came down from Jerusalem to Antioch to prophesy of famine about fifteen years before (11:28).

The kind of belt which Paul would have worn was a long piece of cloth wrapped around his waist. It could be used for hitching up one's loose outer garment in order to walk or to work. It could also serve as a pocket when it was properly folded and tightened.

Unlike the people of Tyre who warned Paul not to go to Jerusalem, Agabus simply passed on the Holy Spirit's message. As things developed, the Jews would bind Paul in the way they crucified Jesus, by getting the Roman authorities to do it (21:31-33).

¹²When we heard this, we and the people there pleaded with Paul not to go up to Jerusalem. ¹³Then Paul answered, "Why are you weeping and breaking my heart? I'm ready not only to be bound, but also to die in Jerusalem for the name of the Lord Jesus." ¹⁴When he would not be dissuaded, we gave up and said, "The Lord's will be done."

Even Luke and Paul's other travel companions, the delegation from the Gentile churches, joined the people in begging Paul not to walk into a dangerous situation. Paul was by no means callous to their pleas. He was deeply moved by their concern. But the Savior would be served by Paul's going to Jerusalem with the collection from the Gentile churches. That collection was a demonstration that God's salvation is for all nations and that his church is one. And so Paul was ready to go, even to die, if his being bound would lead to that.

"The Lord's will be done" was not simply an expression of resignation on their part. They finally recognized what God's will was, and they resolved to concur with it, to will his will with him.

¹⁵After this, we got ready and went up to Jerusalem. ¹⁶Some of the disciples from Caesarea accompanied us and brought us to the home of Mnason, where we were to stay. He was a man from Cyprus and one of the early disciples.

Paul and his group arrived in time for Pentecost, even after spending a number of days in Caesarea.

An "early" disciple from Cyprus may very well mean a man who was converted on or shortly after the great Pentecost when the Spirit was poured out. Mnason seems to have been a man of means. At least he was a generous man, known to be hospitable, for the disciples from Caesarea knew that Paul's party of nine men was to stay at this man's house.

PART III
PAUL AS PRISONER WITNESSES FROM JERUSALEM TO ROME

ACTS 21:17 — 28:31

Jerusalem: Paul's Arrest and Trial

Paul's Reception

17When we arrived at Jerusalem, the brothers received us warmly. 18The next day Paul and the rest of us went to see James, and all the elders were present. 19Paul greeted them and reported in detail what God had done among the Gentiles through his ministry.

Paul and his companions, bringing the relief collection, arrived in Jerusalem just in time for the Feast of Pentecost. They received a warm welcome, and we may assume that the gift from the Gentile churches was accepted in the spirit in which it was sent, as an expression of love and unity.

James was the Lord's brother, not one of the Twelve. We have met him in chapter 15, presiding over the council which was held in Jerusalem. It appears that none of the Twelve were in Jerusalem at this time, that they were working in various mission fields away from Jerusalem.

A detailed report of the work among the Gentiles would include an account of how and why the collection was gathered. That, too, was something that God had accomplished and for which he had received the credit. Paul's ministry was the instrument, but all the achievements were God's.

²⁰When they heard this, they praised God. Then they said to Paul: "You see, brother, how many thousands of Jews have believed, and all of them are zealous for the law. ²¹They have been informed that you teach all the Jews who live among the Gentiles to turn away from Moses, telling them not to circumcise their children or live according to our customs.

The way "praised" is used in the original language suggests that a service of thanksgiving was held. After Paul's report and after God was praised for what his grace had achieved among the Gentiles, James and the elders had something to say about the gospel's progress among the Jews in the homeland.

There were thousands, perhaps tens of thousands, of Jews in the homeland who believed in Jesus as the Messiah and their Redeemer. As far as their style of living was concerned, they continued to observe the rules and ceremonies of the law of Moses.

These Jewish Christians had heard a rumor which disturbed them. The rumor was that Paul urged Jewish believers in Gentile lands to turn away from the rules and ceremonies of Jewish life. This misinformation did not come from believers but from enemies of the gospel. It is possible that some believing Jews did discontinue their Jewish lifestyle, but not because Paul had told them to do so.

What Paul did teach was that circumcision and living according to the ceremonial law are not necessary for salvation. He had Timothy circumcised, not to make a better or a "complete" Christian of him, but so that the young man could work among the Jews (16:3). As Paul and Silas, with Timothy, visited the churches of Galatia, "they delivered the decisions reached by the apostles and elders in Jerusalem for the people to obey" (16:4).

231

We recall that Paul himself had taken a vow according to Jewish custom (18:18). On the other hand, he refused to have Titus circumcised (Galatians 2:3) when "some of the believers who belonged to the party of the Pharisees stood up and said, 'The Gentiles must be circumcised and required to obey the law of Moses' " (Acts 15:5). In all his actions Paul tried to make clear that no observance of the law was required or could help in saving a person from the guilt and punishment of sin. At the same time he tried to make clear that a person might, out of consideration for the weak and to remove an obstacle to the gospel, observe those laws.

22What shall we do? They will certainly hear that you have come, 23so do what we tell you. There are four men with us who have made a vow. 24Take these men, join in their purification rites and pay their expenses, so that they can have their heads shaved. Then everybody will know that there is no truth in these reports about you, but that you yourself are living in obedience to the law. 25As for the Gentile believers, we have written to them our decision that they should abstain from food sacrificed to idols, from blood, from the meat of strangled animals and from sexual immorality."

26The next day Paul took the men and purified himself along with them. Then he went to the temple to give notice of the date when the days of purification would end and the offering would be made for each of them.

Paul did not have to prove anything to James and the elders, but they believed it was necessary for him to put the rumors to rest. They proposed a way in which Paul could prove that he was not teaching Jews to turn away from their Jewish customs. Four Jewish believers had taken a Nazirite vow, committing themselves to carry out the prescriptions of the Old Testament law regarding such vows (Numbers 6:1-21). Such a vow might be made as a gesture of thanksgiving or in connection with a promise to do some special service to God and man.

By participating in the purificatory rites of these four men, Paul could demonstrate that he was not urging people to forsake their Jewish heritage. He himself would not need to take the vow, but he would assist those who had. This involved considerable expense on his part. It meant going to the temple to arrange for the men's offerings at the end of their days of purification. It included a rite of purification on Paul's part before he could enter the temple after being in Gentile lands.

For the gospel's sake and to avoid anything that would spoil the church's unity, Paul complied. It was an act of loving concern, and it was in keeping with the policy Paul had followed in all his work: "To the Jews I became like a Jew, to win the Jews. To those under the law I became like one under the law (though I myself am not under the law), so as to win those under the law" (1 Corinthians 9:20).

At the same time the decision of the council concerning the Gentile believers and what was asked of them in regard to customs (15:20) was reaffirmed. For Paul to assist the four men with their purification rites was in no way to be understood as in conflict with that decision.

Paul's Arrest

27When the seven days were nearly over, some Jews from the province of Asia saw Paul at the temple. They stirred up the whole crowd and seized him, 28shouting, "Men of Israel, help us! This is the man who teaches all men everywhere against our people and our law and this place. And besides, he has brought Greeks into the temple area and defiled this holy place." 29(They had previously seen Trophimus the Ephesian in the city with Paul and assumed that Paul had brought him into the temple area.)

233

Men who had taken a vow would have their heads shaved on the seventh day after announcing their intention to make the sacrifices which concluded the period of the vow. The day after that they would offer the required sacrifice and burn their hair in the sacrificial fire. Before the time was up, before Paul could finish helping them with the ceremonial obligations, the apostle was charged with sacrilege.

Jews from the province of Asia, from Ephesus or some of the other cities of that province, falsely accused Paul. They had been his bitter enemies in the mission field, and they were infuriated to see him in Jerusalem. Their charges were like those leveled against Stephen more than two decades before (6:13), with one notable addition. They accused Paul of defiling the temple by taking Gentiles into the temple precincts.

The temple area had a court of the Gentiles, but for Gentiles to go beyond a stone barrier in the temple area was an offense punishable by death. Archaeologists have found inscribed stone markers which warned those Gentiles who approached the barrier not to enter the court of Israel.

Trophimus was one of the group who had accompanied Paul in delivering the collection. For him to be in the city was not the same as Paul taking him into the temple. But Paul *had* been seen in the temple area with the four men who had taken a vow. From the presence of Trophimus in the city and the presence of the four men with Paul in the temple the Asian Jews drew a false conclusion.

30The whole city was aroused, and the people came running from all directions. Seizing Paul, they dragged him from the temple, and immediately the gates were shut. 31While they were trying to kill him, news reached the commander of the Roman troops that the whole city of Jerusalem was in an uproar. 32He at once took some officers and soldiers and ran down to the crowd.

When the rioters saw the commander and his soldiers, they stopped beating Paul.

³³The commander came up and arrested him and ordered him to be bound with two chains. Then he asked who he was and what he had done. ³⁴Some in the crowd shouted one thing and some another, and since the commander could not get at the truth because of the uproar, he ordered that Paul be taken into the barracks. ³⁵When Paul reached the steps, the violence of the mob was so great he had to be carried by the soldiers. ³⁶The crowd that followed kept shouting, "Away with him!"

The mob, bent on killing Paul, dragged him from the temple so that their holy place would not be defiled by the shedding of blood. The gates of the inner court were closed so that he could not run back inside for refuge. The mob and the temple police were very concerned about defilement under the ceremonial law, but less concerned about the moral law which forbids murder.

The Roman troops were quartered in the Antonia Tower, which overlooked the temple area from the northwest corner. It had been built there because through the years most disturbances in Jerusalem had begun in the temple area. Since the commander of these troops was a tribune, we can surmise that about 600 soldiers were garrisoned in Jerusalem.

The rioters were battering Paul with the intention of killing him, but they stopped when they saw the representatives of Roman law and order. The quick response of the commander with his officers and men saved Paul's life. But that did not mean Paul would be free to go. Not the leaders of the lynch mob but their intended victim was arrested. Since Paul seemed to be the focus of the violence, the tribune assumed that he had done something wrong.

First he arrested and bound Paul. Then he asked what the crime was. The binding with two chains probably means that Paul was chained between two soldiers. In this way the prophecy of Agabus (21:11) was fulfilled.

The commander could not sort out the conflicting charges against Paul and decided to take him to a safer and more quiet place. "The barracks" refers to the Antonia Tower, which was connected to the temple area by two flights of stairs. So enraged was the mob that even Roman troops had a difficult time protecting their prisoner. "Away with him!" meant "Kill him!"

Paul's Defense

37 As the soldiers were about to take Paul into the barracks, he asked the commander, "May I say something to you?"

"Do you speak Greek?" he replied. 38"Aren't you the Egyptian who started a revolt and led four thousand terrorists out into the desert some time ago?"

39 Paul answered, "I am a Jew, from Tarsus in Cilicia, a citizen of no ordinary city. Please let me speak to the people."

The commander's question was not a request for information. Rather, it expressed his surprise that Paul addressed him in Greek.

The word which the NIV renders as "terrorists" is literally "dagger men." They were extreme Jewish nationalists who were ready to take direct action against Romans or others whom they considered to be enemies of the Jewish people. Their usual method was to assassinate individuals, often stabbing them at festival gatherings and then disappearing into the crowds. They sparked the revolt of A.D. 66, which finally led to the destruction of Jerusalem in A.D. 70.

The Jewish historian Josephus writes that in A.D. 54 an Egyptian led a revolt of 4,000 dagger men (*sicarii*) which the Romans quashed. Hundreds were killed, but the leader escaped. The commander's question was a probing

question, trying to determine why the Jews had turned on
Paul with such murderous fanaticism. Could it be that he
was that Egyptian and that the Jews were taking vengeance
on the man who had led so many of their countrymen to
death while he himself escaped?

Paul's answer stressed that his background and position
were quite different from those of an Egyptian revolutionary. Cilicia was in southeastern Asia Minor. Tarsus was its
capital. "No ordinary city" was an understated way of saying "an important city." Tarsus was famous as a center of
Greek learning. It was a gateway for land travel between
Asia Minor and the rest of Asia and therefore an important
trade center. Paul was a Jew and a citizen of that city, not an
Egyptian fugitive from justice.

**40Having received the commander's permission, Paul stood on
the steps and motioned to the crowd. When they were all silent, he**
22 **said to them in Aramaic:**
1"Brothers and fathers, listen now to my defense."

**2When they heard him speak to them in Aramaic, they became
very quiet.**

**Then Paul said: 3"I am a Jew, born in Tarsus of Cilicia, but
brought up in this city. Under Gamaliel I was thoroughly trained
in the law of our fathers and was just as zealous for God as any of
you are today."**

Paul addressed his contemporaries as "brothers," his
seniors as "fathers," all of them as his countrymen. This was
a respectful way in which to address people who had been
trying to kill him. Paul did it for the gospel's sake, in the
hope of winning his countrymen to faith.

Paul's training as a Pharisee was under the most respected
rabbi of his time, Gamaliel. This was the man who had
advised the Sanhedrin to wait and see whether the apostles'
activity was of human or divine origin (5:34-40). Because of

his own experience as a zealous Pharisee, Paul had written concerning his countrymen: "I can testify about them that they are zealous for God, but their zeal is not based on knowledge" (Romans 10:2). The people whom Paul was addressing that day had certainly demonstrated by their actions that their zeal was not based on knowledge.

4"I persecuted the followers of this Way to their death, arresting both men and women and throwing them into prison, 5as also the high priest and all the council can testify. I even obtained letters from them to their brothers in Damascus, and went there to bring these people as prisoners to Jerusalem to be punished.

6"About noon as I came near Damascus, suddenly a bright light from heaven flashed around me. 7I fell to the ground and heard a voice say to me, 'Saul! Saul! Why do you persecute me?'

8" 'Who are you, Lord?' I asked.

" 'I am Jesus of Nazareth, whom you are persecuting,' he replied. 9My companions saw the light, but they did not understand the voice of him who was speaking to me.

10" 'What shall I do, Lord,?' I asked.

" 'Get up,' the Lord said, 'and go into Damascus. There you will be told all that you have been assigned to do.' "

How misguided his zeal had been Paul showed by recalling the days when he had persecuted the young church. He had gone far beyond holding the cloaks and agreeing with the actions when Stephen was stoned to death. That had happened almost twenty-five years before, but there were still men in the Council (the Sanhedrin) who would remember. The records of the Sanhedrin would also show that this was true. No one could deny that Paul had been an extremely conscientious Jew, even a fanatic.

Paul's account of his conversion included some details which Luke did not include in chapter 9. Two of those details appear in verse 6: the event took place "about noon" and the light was "bright." At the same time Paul did not include every detail in his speech which Luke included in chapter 9.

Acts 9:7 says that Paul's companions heard the sound. Here Paul added the information that they did not understand what they heard. In verse 10 we see that Paul included a detail which is not mentioned by Luke in chapter 9. He had asked that question which a converted believer always asks in some form: "What shall I do, Lord?" A person who recognizes and trusts Jesus as Lord wants to know and do his will.

11"My companions led me by the hand into Damascus, because the brilliance of the light had blinded me.

12"A man named Ananias came to see me. He was a devout observer of the law and highly respected by all the Jews living there. 13He stood beside me and said, 'Brother Saul, receive your sight!' And at that very moment I was able to see him.

14"Then he said: 'The God of our fathers has chosen you to know his will and to see the Righteous One and to hear words from his mouth. 15You will be his witness to all men of what you have seen and heard. 16And now what are you waiting for? Get up, be baptized and wash your sins away, calling on his name.' "

Why had Saul the persecutor become Paul the apostle? How had that super Pharisee come to preach God's salvation to the heathen? It was God's doing according to God's plan. It was by grace alone.

The apostle made the important point that Ananias was a devout observer of the law, not someone who was careless about Jewish teaching and practice. All the Jews living in Damascus held him in high esteem. Would a man of such faith and reputation have anything to do with an enemy of God's people, a despiser of the law, a defiler of the temple? Those were the charges against which Paul was defending himself from the steps of the Antonia Tower.

In verse 14 we see that Paul provided more detail on what Ananias told him in Judas's house on Straight Street (9:17). Ananias's words here are in accord with what the Lord told him about Paul's ministry (9:15).

At Acts 9:18 Luke simply reports that Ananias baptized Paul. Here we learn from Paul what Ananias said at that time. Paul's words remind us, as they informed his hearers, of the meaning and blessing of baptism. It is a washing with water, connected with the word (the name of the Lord), for the washing away of sins. Calling on the name of the Lord is confessing that he is Savior. It is the confession of a person who trusts the word that is spoken in connection with the water.

Joel prophesied: "Everyone who calls on the name of the LORD will be saved" (Joel 2:32). Peter quoted that on Pentecost, and after his sermon, when his hearers asked what they should do, he answered: "Repent and be baptized, every one of you, in the name of Jesus Christ for the forgiveness of your sins" (2:38). Peter was saying to the crowd essentially what Ananias said to Paul. Baptism is a means by which God gives his grace to men. "He saved us through the washing of rebirth and renewal by the Holy Spirit" (Titus 3:5).

17"When I returned to Jerusalem and was praying at the temple, I fell into a trance 18and saw the Lord speaking. 'Quick!' he said to me. 'Leave Jerusalem immediately, because they will not accept your testimony about me.'

19" 'Lord,' I replied, 'These men know that I went from one synagogue to another to imprison and beat those who believe in you. 20And when the blood of your martyr Stephen was shed, I stood there giving my approval and guarding the clothes of those who were killing him.'

21"Then the Lord said to me, 'Go; I will send you far away to the Gentiles.' "

22The crowd listened to Paul until he said this. Then they raised their voices and shouted, "Rid the earth of him! He's not fit to live!"

Did Paul despise the temple? On the contrary; on his first visit to Jerusalem after his conversion he prayed there. His words quoted here provide us with details that Luke did not include at Acts 9:26-30. That is, while Paul was at the temple, in a trance, the Lord appeared to him and commanded him to leave the city.

Paul wondered why it was necessary for him to leave. Wouldn't those Jews who had known him as a persecutor of the Way be willing to listen to his testimony concerning Christ? Wouldn't they at least give him a hearing? No, they tried to kill him (9:29), they would not accept his testimony about Jesus.

The Lord was not moved by Paul's reasoning and commanded him to go. He also told him where and what his mission would be: far from Jerusalem, preaching to the Gentiles.

That was as far as Paul got in his defense before the mob. What incensed them was the idea that the Lord God of Israel would send a zealous Jew to serve Gentiles when the Jews refused to hear. Loudly and shrilly they called for Paul's death.

A Roman Citizen

23As they were shouting and throwing off their cloaks and flinging dust into the air, 24the commander ordered Paul to be taken into the barracks. He directed that he be flogged and questioned in order to find out why the people were shouting at him like this. 25As they stretched him out to flog him, Paul said to the centurion standing there, "Is it legal for you to flog a Roman citizen who hasn't even been found guilty?"

241

Throwing off their cloaks and flinging dust into the air was the mob's way of expressing horror at blasphemy. They believed that what they had heard from Paul's mouth was just that.

The tribune did not understand why the crowd was reacting so violently to what Paul had been saying. He determined to use the method which was commonly used to get the truth from prisoners who were not Roman citizens. There could be no condemnation without a confession, and one way in which to get a confession was to flog and question, to examine under torture.

Paul had been beaten with rods at Philippi, illegally (16:22-24). The instrument of torture the commander at Jerusalem had in mind for Paul's questioning here in the barracks was the scourge. Leather thongs were attached to a handle. At the end of the thongs were pieces of bone or metal. This "cat-o'-nine-tails" not only bruised, it also tore the flesh.

The prisoner would be tied to a whipping post or strapped to a bench. The latter method seems to have been what the "examiners" were doing in Paul's case, since they stretched him out to flog him.

Paul's question to the centurion stopped the proceedings. The answer, of course, was "No." The commander had assumed that he was dealing with an alien who was a subject of the Roman Empire but not a citizen.

26When the centurion heard this, he went to the commander and reported it. "What are you going to do?" he asked. "This man is a Roman citizen."

27The commander went to Paul and asked, "Tell me, are you a Roman citizen?"

"Yes, I am," he answered.

28Then the commander said, "I had to pay a big price for my citizenship."

"But I was born a citizen," Paul replied.

[29]Those who were about to question him withdrew immediately. The commander himself was alarmed when he realized that he had put Paul, a Roman citizen, in chains.

The centurion took the startling news to the commander, and the commander did not wait for Paul to be brought to him. He went to Paul — a sign of his consternation.

Some scholars think that the tribune must have paid a bribe to get his citizenship. But during the reign of Claudius, who was emperor from A.D. 41 to 52, it was possible to buy citizenship. To enter the regular army, even at the lowest rank, it was necessary to be a citizen. To be an officer in the auxiliary army, made up of non-Roman troops, one had to be a citizen. For the sake of his military career and to enjoy the rights of a Roman citizen, the commander had paid a considerable sum.

That Paul was born a Roman citizen meant that his father enjoyed that status, and the family's citizenship may have gone back farther than that generation. It could have come as a reward for services rendered to the state.

The conversation as recorded makes clear that citizenship was highly valued. There was more protection under Roman law for the citizen than for the free alien. The born citizen was considered to be of higher social standing than one who was not born into that status.

The commander had violated Paul's civil rights. He could be punished severely for that, if the prisoner wanted to be vengeful about the matter.

Before the Sanhedrin

[30]The next day, since the commander wanted to find out exactly why Paul was being accused by the Jews, he released him and ordered the chief priests and all the Sanhedrin to assemble. Then he brought Paul and had him stand before them.

243

23 Paul looked straight at the Sanhedrin and said, "My brothers, I have fulfilled my duty to God in all good conscience to this day."

Since the Jews were accusing Paul, the commander wanted the Jews to be specific about their accusations. He directed the Sanhedrin to assemble for a hearing. Technically, he could not give them such an order. Usually the Sadducees, however, were willing to accommodate the Roman authorities. Practically, the Sanhedrin was in no position to refuse if they wanted to satisfy their people by punishing Paul.

"Brothers" meant "fellow countrymen." From the beginning Paul wanted to make clear that he was not a person who spoke against the Jewish people and the Jewish law, a person who would defile the temple. Actually, he only made this beginning, for he was immediately interrupted and never got to finish his defense before this group.

2At this the high priest Ananias ordered those standing near Paul to strike him on the mouth. 3Then Paul said to him, "God will strike you, you whitewashed wall! You sit there to judge me according to the law, yet you yourself violate the law by commanding that I be struck!"

4Those who were standing near Paul said, "You dare to insult God's high priest?"

5Paul replied, "Brothers, I did not realize that he was the high priest; for it is written: 'Do not speak evil about the ruler of your people.' "

Ananias was high priest from about A.D. 47 to 59. His reputation was that of an insolent and violent man. When the revolt against Rome broke out in A.D. 66, he was assassinated by dagger men. Either Paul's address, "My brothers," or Paul's claim that he was a faithful servant of God, or both, enraged him, and he gave the order to slap Paul.

The command was illegal and Paul rebuked him. His words were not so much a curse as a prediction: God would strike the one who gave the order for Paul to be struck. The picture of a "whitewashed wall" signified a person who put up a false front, a hypocrite. For Ananias to violate the law while he sat judging a person according to the law was hypocrisy.

Paul had not thought that the high priest of Israel would order such brutal and illegal action. He wanted to respect his people's highest court and its officer, as the Law of Moses commanded in Exodus 22:28. Obedience to lawful authority is part of the believer's way of life. Paul's words were really a further rebuke: "Surely the high priest does not conduct himself in such a way."

⁶Then Paul, knowing that some of them were Sadducees and the others Pharisees, called out in the Sanhedrin, "My brothers, I am a Pharisee, the son of a Pharisee. I stand on trial because of my hope in the resurrection of the dead." ⁷When he said this, a dispute broke out between the Pharisees and the Sadducees, and the assembly was divided. ⁸(The Sadducees say that there is no resurrection, and that there are neither angels nor spirits, but the Pharisees acknowledge them all.)

The two dominant religious parties in the Sanhedrin were the rationalistic Sadducees and the traditionalist Pharisees. A key point of difference between them was the doctrine of the resurrection. Furthermore, the Pharisees preserved and respected the many traditional rules which had grown up as a "hedge" to "protect" the law. How could members of either party accuse a man of despising the law when he said, "I am a Pharisee"? How could the Pharisees disown a man who confidently expected that God will raise the dead on the last day?

The high priest's action and the Sanhedrin's reaction had made it clear that there would be no fair hearing. Paul had begun to speak and had been rudely interrupted. Since there was to be no just treatment of his case, Paul's words had the desired effect of making it impossible to try him. A divided assembly would never be able to agree on his guilt or innocence, or even on what he should be charged with.

His words were also a summons to the Pharisees to turn from their misalliance with the Sadducees, who had departed entirely from Israel's religion. Let them give Paul a hearing, and he would tell them of him who rose from the dead and who will return to raise all the dead.

⁹There was a great uproar, and some of the teachers of the law who were Pharisees stood up and argued vigorously. "We find nothing wrong with this man," they said. "What if a spirit or an angel has spoken to him?" ¹⁰The dispute became so violent that the commander was afraid Paul would be torn to pieces by them. He ordered the troops to go down and take him away from them by force and bring him into the barracks.

¹¹The following night the Lord stood near Paul and said, "Take courage! As you have testified about me in Jerusalem, so you must also testify in Rome."

The house was divided, and now there were men willing to argue that Paul was not guilty of any crime against Israel or Israel's laws. They even allowed that Paul might not be spreading his own ideas, that he might have received them from God through an angel or a spirit. (They were, perhaps, referring to his account of the events on the road to Damascus and to his vision in the temple, 22:7-10, 17-21). If that was the case, that his teaching really was from God, how could the Sanhedrin condemn him? Their counsel was like that which Gamaliel had given concerning the apostles almost 25 years before (5:38,39).

Once again Roman armed might rescued Paul from violence. This time it was not from a mob but from the highest Jewish authority acting like a mob. The tribune's question was still not answered: what was Paul guilty of, that his own countrymen wanted to tear him to pieces?

Paul had stood before the Sanhedrin as a free man after the commander released him, but now he was again in custody. The risen Lord, the firstfruits of the resurrection in which Paul hoped, came to encourage him. The apostle's career of gospel service was not yet over, not nearly. It was the Lord's will that Paul would also bear witness to him in Rome. Therefore, those Jews in Jerusalem who were bent on his destruction would not succeed.

The Assassination Plot

12The next morning the Jews formed a conspiracy and bound themselves with an oath not to eat or drink until they had killed Paul. 13More than forty men were involved in this plot. 14They went to the chief priests and elders and said, "We have taken a solemn oath not to eat anything until we have killed Paul. 15Now then, you and the Sanhedrin petition the commander to bring him before you on the pretext of wanting more accurate information about his case. We are ready to kill him before he gets here."

Forty men of Israel took God's name in vain by swearing to commit murder. Although Luke does not say so, these conspirators were probably dagger men. Their aim, their method and their oath fit the pattern. It is not likely that men who took such an oath would starve or die of thirst if they failed to do what they had sworn to do, for the rabbis had made it possible for them to be released from such an oath.

It is remarkable that the religious leaders of the people involved themselves in such a plan. They either believed that such actions were a service to God or, as Sadducees who did not believe in a judgment after death, they simply lacked the fear of God.

16But when the son of Paul's sister heard of this plot, he went into the barracks and told Paul.

17Then Paul called one of the centurions and said, "Take this young man to the commander; he has something to tell him." 18So he took him to the commander.

The centurion said, "Paul, the prisoner, sent for me and asked me to bring this young man to you because he has something to tell you."

19The commander took the young man by the hand, drew him aside and asked, "What is it you want to tell me?"

20He said: "The Jews have agreed to ask you to bring Paul before the Sanhedrin tomorrow on the pretext of wanting more accurate information about him. 21Don't give in to them, because more than forty of them are waiting in ambush for him. They have taken an oath not to eat or drink until they have killed him. They are ready now, waiting for your consent to their request."

22The commander dismissed the young man and cautioned him, "Don't tell anyone that you have reported this to me."

23Then he called two of his centurions and ordered them, "Get ready a detachment of two hundred soldiers, seventy horsemen and two hundred spearmen to go to Caesarea at nine tonight. 24Provide mounts for Paul so that he may be taken safely to Governor Felix."

The tribune took the plot seriously, assigning 470 men to guard a Roman citizen. Twice he had seen an undisciplined mob try to kill the prisoner, and only Roman intervention had saved Paul. Now he was contending with a more disciplined group of conspirators. He took every precaution to get this prisoner safely to the administrative headquarters in Caesarea.

Some interpreters think that the word which the NIV renders as "spearmen" refers to 200 pack animals or extra mounts, rather than to armed men. Taking 470 troops away from Jerusalem would considerably weaken the garrison there. Taking 270 would leave more in the city to maintain security. Leaving at 9:00 p.m. was a way of avoiding the hostile attention of the conspirators.

Felix occupied the official position which Pontius Pilate once held. He was governor, or procurator, from A.D. 52 to 60. The Roman historian Tacitus characterized him as a man who "exercised the power of a king with the mind of a slave."

25He wrote a letter as follows:

26Claudius Lysias,

To His Excellency, Governor Felix:

Greetings.

27This man was seized by the Jews and they were about to kill him, but I came with my troops and rescued him, for I had learned that he is a Roman citizen. 28I wanted to know why they were accusing him, so I brought him to their Sanhedrin. 29I found that the accusation had to do with questions about their law, but there was no charge against him that deserved death or imprisonment. 30When I was informed of a plot to be carried out against the man, I sent him to you at once. I also ordered his accusers to present to you their case against him.

Here we learn the tribune's name. The name Claudius suggests that he gained his citizenship during the reign of Claudius or that of his predecessor, Claudius Tiberius. The name Lysias suggests that he was of Greek ancestry.

The form of the letter, with the sender's name first, the addressee second, then the greeting, followed by the message, was typical of the form used for letters in the first century. It is the form which James and the church at Jerusalem used in their letter to the Gentile believers (15:23-29). It is also the form employed by the writers of many of the New Testament epistles.

Claudius Lysias was shading the truth with his explanation of how Paul came to be his prisoner. The first time he and his troops rescued Paul (21:30-33) he had not yet learned that his prisoner was a Roman citizen. He had him bound with chains and later directed that Paul be flogged and questioned (22:24). Only then did he learn through the centurion that Paul was a Roman citizen.

The representative of Roman law had to admit that he did not see any reason why Paul should be punished under Roman law. Like Gallio at Corinth (18:15), he did not think that a religious issue among Jews was something for Roman officials to occupy themselves with.

Paul was in a strange position. He was not charged with any specific crime against Roman law, and yet he was being remanded to a higher Roman authority. Partly to protect him from the Jews, partly to satisfy the Jews, partly to rid himself of a troublesome case which he did not know how to deal with, the tribune was sending Paul to Governor Felix.

31 So the soldiers, carrying out their orders, took Paul with them during the night and brought him as far as Antipatris.

The detachment, with the prisoner, left the city at 9:00 p.m. Antipatris was about forty miles from Jerusalem. The usual march for Roman infantry was twenty-four miles per day. Perhaps moving more quickly than usual in the cool of the night, the group reached their destination before the next day had passed.

Caesarea: Paul's Witness Before Kings and Governors

The Hearing before Governor Felix

32The next day they let the cavalry go on with him, while they returned to the barracks. 33When the cavalry arrived in Caesarea, they delivered the letter to the governor and handed Paul over to him.

The road to Caesarea led away from the center of the Jewish agitation against Paul. The smaller, more mobile, cavalry troop sufficed as an escort for the rest of the trip, about thirty miles to the coast. The infantry returned to Jerusalem.

34The governor read the letter and asked what province he was from. Learning that he was from Cilicia, 35he said, 'I will hear your case when your accusers get here." Then he ordered that Paul be kept under guard in Herod's palace.

Under Roman law Felix had to ask his prisoner from what province he had come. The prisoner could then choose to be tried in his home province or in the province where he had allegedly committed a crime. Felix was a deputy to the legate who governed Syria and Cilicia. Therefore he could claim the right to hear Paul's case no matter which jurisdiction the latter might choose.

The palace which Herod the Great had built at Caesarea was used by the Roman authorities as their official residence and headquarters. Paul was kept there as a prisoner, just as he was kept in the official headquarters in the Antonia Tower at Jerusalem.

24 **Five days later the high priest Ananias went down to Caesarea with some of the elders and a lawyer named Tertullus, and they brought their charges against Paul before the governor. 2When Paul was called in, Tertullus presented his case before Felix: "We have enjoyed a long period of peace under you,**

**and your foresight has brought about reforms in this nation.
[3]Everywhere and in every way, most excellent Felix, we acknowledge this with profound gratitude. [4]But in order not to
weary you further, I would request that you be kind enough to
hear us briefly."**

The elders who went with Ananias were members of the
Sanhedrin. Tertullus was a man who could present the
charges against Paul in a way that accorded with Roman
court procedures. The accusers had to make the case that
Paul was guilty of more than teaching and living contrary to
the Jews' religion. They had to demonstrate that he had
violated Roman law.

Tertullus understood that the standard procedure in addressing a Roman dignitary was to use flattery. There *was*
peace during Felix's rule in the sense that there was no war.
He had crushed the terrorist uprising led by the Egyptian
(21:38). As to reforms under Felix, there is no record. Two
years after this hearing he was called back to Rome and
replaced because of poor performance in office.

Tertullus's use of "we" in his opening words might mean
that he was a Jew with training in the Roman law, but it
could also simply indicate the way in which a lawyer identi-
fies himself with his clients.

Orators tend to promise at the beginning to be brief, even
when they are not. Tertullus really was brief, once he had
finished with the flattery.

**[5]"We have found this man to be a troublemaker, stirring up
riots among the Jews all over the world. He is a ringleader of the
Nazarene sect [6]and even tried to desecrate the temple; so we seized
him. [8]By examining him yourself you will be able to learn the
truth about all these charges we are bringing against him."**

**[9]The Jews joined in the accusation, asserting that these things
were true.**

As in the trials of Jesus and Stephen, the charges amounted to false witness. The Jews had rioted in many of the places where Paul preached, but he had not incited the riots. The word used for "troublemaker" is literally "pestilence." The accusation was that Paul constituted a plague, dangerous to the public welfare. As "ringleader" of a sect, Paul could be charged with advocating an illegal religion, one not allowed under Roman law.

Paul, of course, had not desecrated the temple, nor had he tried to. The accusers knew by now that the charge of the Jews from the province of Asia that Paul had taken a Greek into the court of Israel (21:28) was false. But they were still willing to accuse him of the attempt to do so.

In his charges, Tertullus wanted to make it appear that Paul's actions threatened the "peace" and "reforms" which Felix had brought about. The Jews' reasons for bringing charges were religious, but they wanted to depict Paul as a threat to Roman law and order. Desecrating the temple would have been a violation of Roman law, which protected the religion of the Jews.

The NIV has a footnote here to indicate that some manuscripts of the New Testament read: "So we seized him and wanted to judge him according to our law. 7But the commander, Lysias, came and with the use of much force snatched him from our hands 8and ordered his accusers to come before you." Compare this with 23:10,30 and see how it turns Lysias's rescue of Paul into an injustice against the Jews.

10When the governor motioned for him to speak, Paul replied: "I know that for a number of years you have been a judge over this nation; so I gladly make my defense. 11You can easily verify that no more than twelve days ago I went up to Jerusalem to worship. 12My accusers did not find me arguing with anyone at the temple,

or stirring up a crowd in the synagogues or anywhere else in the city. [13]And they cannot prove to you the charges they are now making against me. [14]However, I admit that I worship the God of our fathers, as a follower of the Way, which they call a sect. I believe everything that agrees with the Law and that is written in the Prophets, [15]and I have the same hope in God as these men, that there will be a resurrection of both the righteous and the wicked. [16]So I strive always to keep my conscience clear before God and man."

Like Tertullus, Paul began his address in a complimentary way, but not with the flattery which Tertullus employed. He simply expressed his gladness at appearing before a judge who knew the Sanhedrin and its tactics, who had dealt with them in the past.

Felix would understand that "no more than twelve days ago" meant that Paul had come to Jerusalem for the Feast of Pentecost. It would be an easy matter to learn what the prisoner had done during that time, especially since he had been in Roman custody for more than half of those twelve days.

Paul categorically denied the charges against him. He asserted that his accusers would not be able to prove them.

He admitted that he was a follower of the Way, but not a ringleader of what Tertullus had called a sect. In his defense Paul stressed the point that he was a religious teacher, that his faith was really the true faith of Old Testament believers, that the disagreement between him and the Jews was not political but religious, and that there really ought not to have been a religious difference between them and him.

In his defense before Felix, before Festus (25:1-12) and before Agrippa (25:13—26:32) Paul tried each time to lead to the message that God raised Jesus from the dead. His accusers never wanted to discuss this fact. Neither could they deny it. Especially the Pharisees could not challenge the resurrection of Jesus without seeming to deny that teaching which set them apart from the Sadducees. Also, Paul's reminder that there will be a resurrection of both the righteous and the wicked was really a call for all who heard him to repent.

Paul then applied this message to himself. He knew that deliberate sin can destroy faith and strove to keep his conscience clear of any sin — against God, his conscience, or other men. He had not desecrated the temple, as he goes on to assert:

[17]**"After an absence of several years, I came to Jerusalem to bring my people gifts for the poor and to present offerings. [18]I was ceremonially clean when they found me in the temple courts doing this. There was no crowd with me, nor was I involved in any disturbance. [19]But there are some Jews from the province of Asia, who ought to be here before you and bring charges if they have anything against me. [20]Or these who are here should state what crime they found in me when I stood before the Sanhedrin — [21]unless it was this one thing I shouted as I stood in their presence: 'It is concerning the resurrection of the dead that I am on trial before you today.' "**

This is the only direct reference in *Acts* to the collection which the Gentile mission churches gathered "for the poor among the saints in Jerusalem" (Romans 15:26). The offerings which he had come to present were probably connected with the vow he had taken, mentioned in 18:18. It was obvious that he had not come to Jerusalem to desecrate the temple or to stir up rebellion against Roman rule. It would also be obvious to Felix after six years in Judea that a man who was bringing offerings to the temple would not be stirring up the crowds while he did it.

If Paul had been guilty of "stirring up riots among the Jews all over the world" (v. 5), then those Jews from Asia who accused him of teaching against Israel and Israel's laws and Israel's temple (21:28) ought to have been present as witnesses in the hearing before Felix. They were not.

What had set off the violent dispute between the Pharisees and Sadducees in the Sanhedrin was Paul's bold confession of the resurrection (23:6,7,10). Preaching the resurrection is a religious statement, not an incitement to rebellion. Any Pharisee in the delegation of elders who stood before Felix could not call that a crime. They would not let the Sadducees call it a crime or the strange doctrine of a strange sect. Once again Paul was demonstrating that the accusations against him were not based on any crime against Israel or Rome.

22Then Felix, who was well acquainted with the Way, adjourned the proceedings. "When Lysias the commander comes," he said, "I will decide your case." 23He ordered the centurion to keep Paul under guard but to give him some freedom and permit his friends to take care of his needs.

Felix knew more about the Way, that is the faith and life of the disciples of Jesus, than might have been expected of a Roman official. His third wife, Drusilla, was Jewish (v. 24). With her help he probably understood both Judaism and Christianity better than most Romans in high official position did.

The governor ordered that Paul be kept under conditions of minimum security, something like house arrest. As far as we know, Lysias never came to Caesarea for the trial. We do know that Felix never did get around to deciding Paul's case.

24Several days later Felix came with his wife Drusilla, who was a Jewess. He sent for Paul and listened to him as he spoke about faith in Christ Jesus. 25As Paul discoursed on righteousness,

self-control and the judgment to come, Felix was afraid and said, "That's enough for now! You may leave. When I find it convenient, I will send for you." [26]At the same time he was hoping that Paul would offer him a bribe, so he sent for him frequently and talked with him.

Felix was willing to hear Paul tell the story of Jesus, but what that story means for life and for eternity he did not want to hear. He was afraid because he had a bad conscience. He put off hearing the whole will of God to a more convenient time. There is no evidence that he ever did find it "convenient" to hear it. The time to hear God's word, law and gospel, is always now, always today.

The motives for Felix's further frequent talks with the apostle were mixed at best. He had perhaps not lost all interest in Paul's message, but he also hoped to receive a bribe. Giving and receiving bribes was not uncommon, either for imprisoning or for releasing people. It was illegal but it was done. Perhaps Paul's mention of the relief gift and offerings (v. 17) gave Felix the notion that Paul, or Paul's friends, had the financial resources which would make a considerable bribe possible.

[27]When two years had passed, Felix was succeeded by Porcius Festus, but because Felix wanted to grant a favor to the Jews, he left Paul in prison.

Time ran out on Felix as far as hearing and believing the gospel were concerned. He was recalled to Rome in A.D. 59 to face charges that he had been inept and remiss in his rule of Judea. Jews from Jerusalem would be his adversaries in the hearings in Rome. Therefore he did the Jews one more favor and left Paul in prison. That was not justice, and it was evidence that he had not repented, in spite of all he had heard from Paul.

Porcius Festus became procurator in A.D. 60 and died in 62. He, too, would have his opportunity to deal justly with Paul. More, he would have opportunity, as Felix had, to hear the gospel and repent.

The Hearing before Governor Festus

25 **Three days after arriving in the province, Festus went up from Caesarea to Jerusalem, ²where the chief priests and the Jewish leaders appeared before him and presented the charges against Paul. ³They urgently requested Festus, as a favor to them, to have Paul transferred to Jerusalem, for they were preparing an ambush to kill him along the way. ⁴Festus answered, "Paul is being held at Caesarea, and I myself am going there soon. ⁵Let some of your leaders come with me and press charges against the man there, if he has done anything wrong."**

The new governor of Judea was eager to visit the political and religious center of his province. He knew that the Jews had been dissatisfied with his predecessor, and he wanted to make a good beginning. He promptly went up to Jerusalem, and the chief priests and leaders of the Jews promptly renewed their case against Paul.

Paul had been sent to Caesarea to foil an assassination plot (23:15). Now another plot was underway, perhaps involving the same people who had earlier vowed to kill Paul. Festus may have known of the plot. He certainly understood that it would be more difficult to conduct a calm and orderly trial in Jerusalem than in Caesarea. He wanted to protect the rights of a Roman citizen. He refused to grant their request.

Festus's words in verse 5 sound like a suggestion or like permission, but they were really a command. Notice that he gave the prisoner the benefit of the doubt: ". . . if he has done anything wrong." If Festus saw the letter which Lysias wrote to Felix (23:26-30), he knew that there had been a plot at that time. He also knew that Lysias did not consider Paul a criminal. Such a letter would be "on file" and would alert the governor not to do the Jews' bidding. Besides, the proper place for a governor to sit as judge was on his seat of judgment, and that was in Caesarea.

⁶After spending eight or ten days with them, he went down to Caesarea, and the next day he convened the court and ordered that Paul be brought before him. ⁷When Paul appeared, the Jews who had come down from Jerusalem stood around him, bringing many serious charges against him, which they could not prove.

⁸Then Paul made his defense: "I have done nothing wrong against the law of the Jews or against the temple or against Caesar."

⁹Festus, wishing to do the Jews a favor, said to Paul, "Are you willing to go up to Jerusalem and stand trial before me there on these charges?"

The "many serious charges" boiled down to doing "wrong against the law of the Jews or against the temple or against Caesar." Essentially, they were the charges which the Jews had earlier lodged with Felix (24:5,6). They had not been able to prove them then and they could not do so now.

As Pontius Pilate did in Jesus' trial and Felix did in Paul's case, so Festus did what he could to curry the favor of those whom he was supposed to rule with impartial justice. Legally, Festus could not require Paul to go to Jerusalem for a trial. But, since the alleged crimes allegedly took place in Jerusalem, he asked Paul whether he would be willing to stand trial in that city.

¹⁰Paul answered: "I am now standing before Caesar's court, where I ought to be tried. I have not done any wrong to the Jews, as you yourself know very well. ¹¹If, however, I am guilty of doing anything deserving death, I do not refuse to die. But if the charges

brought against me by these Jews are not true, no one has the right to hand me over to them. I appeal to Caesar!"

With great dignity and with a polite rebuke for his judge, Paul insisted that he was where a Roman citizen ought to be: before Caesar's court. A judge who knows that the defendant is innocent has one obvious duty, and that is to dismiss the case and free the prisoner. The apostle understood that Festus's request was a device to gain the Jews' favor. He knew that if Festus was not willing to act justly in Caesarea, he would not be able to withstand the pressure of the Sanhedrin in Jerusalem.

Paul was not trying to evade justice, but he would not submit to injustice. For the gospel's sake a preacher of the gospel must not be condemned as a criminal when he is innocent of the charges against him. That would hurt the gospel cause.

On the other hand, if a Roman court would rule in Paul's case that his preaching was not illegal, was within the bounds of legal religious activity, that would give Christianity official recognition as a legally permitted religion. So Paul appealed to the highest earthly judge, the emperor in Rome.

Paul was using the ancient right of a Roman citizen. A person who was condemned in a Roman court could appeal to Caesar and have the case reviewed. In a case which had not been decided, such as Paul's case, the defendant could appeal to Caesar at any point in the proceedings. That would put a stop to the trial and it could not continue except before the imperial court. Caesar, or at least his personal representative, would have to dispose of the case.

At that time Nero was Caesar, emperor from A.D. 54 to 68.

¹²After Festus had conferred with his council, he declared: "You have appealed to Caesar. To Caesar you will go!"

So momentous were Paul's appeal and Felix's decision on the appeal that the governor did not respond until he had conferred with his legal experts. The law said that the appeal must be granted, and so it was. Paul would at last go to Rome, as he had long intended to do (19:21).

In the providence of God the hatred of the Jews and the unjust delaying tactics of the two Roman governors combined to permit Paul to preach the gospel in Rome. Two years before, in the barracks of the Antonia Tower, the Lord had told him: "Take courage! As you have testified about me in Jerusalem, so you must also testify in Rome" (23:11). Now it would happen.

The Hearing before King Agrippa

13 A few days later King Agrippa and Bernice arrived at Caesarea to pay their respects to Festus.

King Agrippa was Herod Agrippa II. He was the son of Herod Agrippa I, who had James put to death with the sword and intended to do the same to Peter (12:1-3). His great uncle was Herod Antipas, who beheaded John the Baptist (Matthew 14:3-12) and tried Jesus (Luke 23:8-12). He was the great-grandson of Herod the Great, who ordered the slaughter of baby boys in and around Bethlehem at the time of Jesus' birth (Matthew 2:16).

Although Agrippa did not rule Judea, he had control over the temple and the right to name the high priest. He controlled certain territories in the north of Galilee and the south of Syria. He had the title "king" under the authority of the Roman government.

It was important that he and Festus get along well, in view of his temple responsibilities, which gave him influence in Jerusalem. Bernice was his sister, but a number of heathen writers of the first century say that she was living with him as his wife.

¹⁴Since they were spending many days there, Festus discussed Paul's case with the king. He said: "There is a man here whom Felix left as a prisoner. ¹⁵When I went to Jerusalem, the chief priests and elders of the Jews brought charges against him and asked that he be condemned.

¹⁶"I told them that it is not the Roman custom to hand over any man before he has had an opportunity to defend himself against their charges. ¹⁷When they came here with me, I did not delay the case, but convened the court the next day and ordered the man to be brought in. ¹⁸When his accusers got up to speak, they did not charge him with any of the crimes I had expected. ¹⁹Instead, they had some points of dispute with him about their own religion and about a dead man named Jesus who Paul claimed was alive. ²⁰I was at a loss how to investigate such matters; so I asked if he would be willing to go to Jerusalem and stand trial there on these charges. ²¹When Paul made his appeal to be held over for the Emperor's decision, I ordered him held until I could send him to Caesar."

What crimes had Festus expected? Treason, sedition, forbidding to pay tribute to Caesar? Gallio (18:14), Lysias (23:29) and now Festus recognized that Jewish religious disputes really had no place in Roman law courts.

Festus was at a loss in trying to investigate and settle the case against Paul, because under Roman law there was no case against Paul. In his desire to get along with the Jewish leaders he had been willing to conduct a trial in Jerusalem. But he would have been no more competent to investigate religious questions in Jerusalem than he was in Caesarea. He had not acted responsibly, and his prisoner finally took the responsibility away from him by appealing to Caesar. In his report to Agrippa, Festus tried to make himself look good, but his performance had not been up to Roman standards of law and order.

²²Then Agrippa said to Festus, "I would like to hear this man myself."

He replied, "Tomorrow you will hear him."

²³The next day Agrippa and Bernice came with great pomp and entered the audience room with the high ranking officers and the leading men of the city. At the command of Festus, Paul was brought in.

Jesus had predicted just such occasions as this for his disciples: "You will be brought before kings and governors, and all on account of my name. This will result in your being witnesses to them. But make up your mind not to worry beforehand how you will defend yourselves. For I will give you words and wisdom that none of your adversaries will be able to resist or contradict" (Luke 21:12-15). A king, the governor of Judea, five Roman tribunes and the leading citizens of Caesarea gathered to see and hear Paul. He would witness to them about his Savior, and they would not be able to contradict him in a reasoned way.

²⁴Festus said: "King Agrippa, and all who are present with us, you see this man! The whole Jewish community has petitioned me about him in Jerusalem and here in Caesarea, shouting that he ought not to live any longer. ²⁵I found he had done nothing deserving of death, but because he made his appeal to the Emperor I decided to send him to Rome. ²⁶But I have nothing definite to write to His Majesty about him. Therefore I have brought him before all of you, and especially before you, King Agrippa, so that as a result of this investigation I may have something to write. ²⁷For I think it is unreasonable to send on a prisoner without specifying the charges against him."

Was Festus exaggerating a bit when he said "the whole Jewish community" wanted Paul's death? Yes and no. The chief priests and Jewish leaders and "the Jews who had come down from Jerusalem" were the representatives of the whole Jewish community. On the other hand, not every last Jew desired Paul's death.

The representative of Roman justice had to admit that there was no reason under Roman law for the prisoner to be held as long as Paul had been held. But now Roman law required that he be sent to Rome because of his appeal. The procurator could neither condemn nor pardon. He could only report what he knew about the case, and he did not understand the case.

Festus could not send Paul to the emperor without specifying charges. He had no idea what charges to specify and he wanted help. Perhaps Agrippa, who tried to live in two worlds — Jewish and Roman — could help.

Where the NIV has "His Majesty" the Greek original has "the Lord." That reminds us that Nero was considered by the Romans to be a divine person. "Caesar is Lord" became a catch phrase of the imperial religion, and it would increasingly cause problems for those who believed and confessed that "Jesus is Lord."

26 **Then Agrippa said to Paul, "You have permission to speak for yourself."**

So Paul motioned with his hand and began his defense: [2]"King Agrippa, I consider myself fortunate to stand before you today as I make my defense against all the accusations of the Jews, [3]and especially so because you are well acquainted with all the Jewish customs and controversies. Therefore, I beg you to listen to me patiently."

Paul understood, as Festus did, that King Agrippa was a man who could help Gentile Roman officials understand Jewish thinking. He would formally defend himself against the Jews' accusations and at the same time seize the opportunity to preach the resurrection. Since he had appealed to Caesar, he did not really have to make a defense, but he would do so for the gospel's sake.

His hand motion was the customary signal which a speaker used to indicate that he wanted to make a formal presentation.

4"The Jews all know the way I have lived ever since I was a child, from the beginning of my life in my own country, and also in Jerusalem. 5They have known me for a long time and can testify, if they are willing, that according to the strictest sect of our religion, I lived as a Pharisee."

Paul was a well-known figure in Jerusalem, and all who knew him knew what his lifestyle had been. In his letter to the Galatians Paul mentions that he outstripped his contemporaries in his zeal for the law of Moses and the traditions which he received from the fathers (Galatians 1:14). In Philippians 3:5,6 he writes: "[I was] circumcised on the eighth day, of the people of Israel, of the tribe of Benjamin, a Hebrew of the Hebrews; in regard to the law, a Pharisee; as for zeal, persecuting the church; as for legalistic righteousness, faultless." No Jew could accuse him of neglect in religious matters. How could they accuse him of trying to desecrate the temple?

6"And now it is because of my hope in what God has promised our fathers that I am on trial today. 7This is the promise our twelve tribes are hoping to see fulfilled as they earnestly serve God day and night. O king, it is because of this hope that the Jews are accusing me. 8Why should any of you consider it incredible that God raises the dead?"

As he had before the Sanhedrin (23:6) and before Felix (24:15), Paul wanted to speak of the hope of the resurrection.

God promised the resurrection in the Old Testament and guaranteed it by raising Jesus from the dead. In speaking of the resurrection there would be opportunity to preach Christ.

How unreasonable for the Jews to persecute Paul for teaching what the twelve tribes of Israel hoped for, what their service to God was all about! Why should King Agrippa or any other Jew consider it incredible that God raised Jesus from the dead? A religion based on the hope of the resurrection of all cannot reject the resurrection of the one!

[9]"I too was convinced that I ought to do all that was possible to oppose the name of Jesus of Nazareth. [10]And that is just what I did in Jerusalem. On the authority of the chief priests I put many of the saints in prison, and when they were put to death, I cast my vote against them. [11]Many a time I went from one synagogue to another to have them punished, and I tried to force them to blaspheme. In my obsession against them, I even went to foreign cities to persecute them."

The name of Jesus is the revelation of who he is and what he has done. Saul of Tarsus wanted to stop that revelation by every possible means. Here is the third account in *Acts* of Paul's persecuting activity and his conversion. Each time it is recorded it makes the point that it was the risen Christ who turned a persecutor into a proclaimer.

Those whom he once persecuted Paul now called "saints," God's holy people. Where had he cast his vote against them so that they suffered capital punishment? It was only the Sanhedrin which could pronounce the death sentence for religious offenses, and only the Romans who could carry out such a sentence. This might suggest that Paul was a member of the Sanhedrin. It is more likely, however, that he cast his vote as a member of an investigating group which made recommendations to the Sanhedrin.

A detail of Saul's raging activity against the saints which has not been mentioned before in *Acts* was that he tried to force believers to blaspheme. Those who would be willing to curse the name of Jesus, and in that way deny him, were spared imprisonment and death. Getting them to do so would be a great victory for one who hated the name of Jesus, greater than putting to death those who would not deny.

12"On one of these journeys I was going to Damascus with the authority and commission of the chief priests. 13About noon, O king, as I was on the road, I saw a light from heaven, brighter than the sun, blazing around me and my companions. 14We all fell to the ground, and I heard a voice saying to me in Aramaic, 'Saul, Saul, why do you persecute me? It is hard for you to kick against the goads.' "

Not at night in the privacy of a room but at noon on the public road the bright light blazed. The light was not simply from or in the sky. It was from heaven, a special brightness signaling the presence of God.

The self-righteous persecutor learned that his activities were only hurting himself and that they were useless. A proverbial saying expressed the foolishness of trying to fight against God. A stick with a sharp point is still used in some countries to control an ox and to get it moving in the right direction. The beast that resists by kicking against the goad only hurts itself.

15"Then I asked, 'Who are you, Lord?'

" 'I am Jesus, whom you are persecuting,' the Lord replied. 16'Now get up and stand on your feet. I have appeared to you to appoint you as a servant and as a witness of what you have seen of me and what I will show you. 17I will rescue you from your own people and from the Gentiles. I am sending you 18to open their

eyes and turn them from darkness to light, and from the power of Satan to God, so that they may receive forgiveness of sins and a place among those who are sanctified by faith in me.' "

The Romans and the Jews in that audience room knew what crucifixion was. There was no doubt that Jesus of Nazareth had died a hard and cruel and certain death. But here was Paul saying that Jesus appeared to him and spoke to him. That was a confirmation that he had arisen. That means that there is a resurrection. The risen Lord called Paul to bear witness to the fact of his resurrection and Paul was doing just that. It was for that that the Jews hated him and were trying to kill him.

The Lord had promised to rescue Paul from the murderous plots of his own countrymen who rejected Jesus and from the attacks of Gentiles. "I am sending you" means the same as "I am making you my apostle."

The apostle's mission was to give unbelievers the light of the gospel, to tell them the good news about Jesus. He was to continue the work which Jesus did in his own ministry and which the Savior established by his perfect life and innocent death, the work foretold by Isaiah:

> "I will keep you and will make you
> to be a covenant for the people
> and a light to the Gentiles,
> to open eyes that are blind,
> to free captives from prison
> and to release from the dungeon
> those who sit in darkness.
> . . . I will lead the blind by ways they
> have not known,
> along unfamiliar paths I will guide them;
> I will turn darkness into light before them"
> (Isaiah 42:6,7,16).

268

The Bible knows nothing of "happy heathen" who live a free life and should be left alone. It does not know of religious people who please God by following "the light that is in them." It knows only of human beings who are in darkness until the gospel light shines on them, who are under Satan's power until the good news about Jesus sets them free to serve God. Gentiles in their lawlessness and Jews who imagined they were keeping God's law were all sinners in need of a Savior.

By faith in the risen Lord those who are turned by the gospel receive the forgiveness of sins, a place among God's saints. In verses 17 and 18 we see that God uses the gospel to save people and that salvation is received by faith.

19"So then, King Agrippa, I was not disobedient to the vision from heaven. 20First to those in Damascus, then to those in Jerusalem and in all Judea, and to the Gentiles also, I preached that they should repent and turn to God and prove their repentance by their deeds. 21That is why the Jews seized me in the temple courts and tried to kill me. 22But I have had God's help to this very day, and so I stand here and testify to small and great alike. I am saying nothing beyond what the prophets and Moses said would happen — 23that the Christ would suffer and, as the first to rise from the dead, would proclaim light to his own people and to the Gentiles."

With God's help, Paul had survived all attacks and conspiracies to that very day, as the Lord promised (v. 17). Here he stood, testifying as the Lord said he would (v. 16).

How could Paul be guilty of a crime for saying that God fulfilled the prophecies which he made through the prophets and Moses? Here at last Paul had his opportunity to make the point that Christ rose from the dead, as the Scriptures foretold. More, he made the point that Christ is only the first, that all will be raised from the dead. For teaching this, the Jews were trying to kill Paul. Just this teaching was what Paul wanted all those powerful people in the audience room at Caesarea to hear.

²⁴At this point Festus interrupted Paul's defense. "You are out of your mind, Paul!" he shouted. "Your great learning is driving you insane."

²⁵"I am not insane, most excellent Festus," Paul replied. "What I am saying is true and reasonable. ²⁶The king is familiar with these things, and I can speak freely to him. I am convinced that none of this has escaped his notice, because it was not done in a corner. ²⁷King Agrippa, do you believe the prophets? I know you do."

Festus heard the call to repentance in Paul's words. If Jesus rose from the dead, then he is the divine judge who will call men to account on the last day. Festus understood that but did not want to believe it or act in accord with that belief. He interrupted. He would not believe, but he could not refute Paul's words. Not quietly, but with a shout, he tried to silence the apostle with a charge of madness.

Paul responded with calm courtesy that his words were true and sane, and then turned again to the king. He assumed that in his heart Agrippa knew very well that the disciples had not stolen and hidden the body of Jesus. All that happened to Jesus, including the fact that he rose from the dead, had been proclaimed openly since the day of Pentecost. It was not a secret reserved for the few but a message to be shared with the many.

If King Agrippa believed the prophets, he could hardly deny the resurrection. If he did not believe the prophets, he could hardly continue as "king of the Jews." What would he answer?

²⁸Then Agrippa said to Paul, "Do you think that in such a short time you can persuade me to be a Christian?"

270

29Paul replied, "Short time or long — I pray God that not only you but all who are listening to me today may become what I am, except for these chains."

Agrippa answered Paul's question with another question. His answer was really to the effect that he did not believe Paul's gospel. He did not believe that Jesus is the fulfillment of the prophecies of the Old Testament. He was rejecting the only Savior he could ever have.

Paul could not persuade Agrippa to be a Christian. Only God can do that. Paul's prayer was that, no matter how long it might take, God would turn the hearts of all who heard him speak that day. He wanted them all to be like him: forgiven sinners and saints of God.

His bondage he did not wish on anyone. He used the word "chains" figuratively, for bondage or imprisonment. A Roman citizen, even a prisoner, could not be chained.

30The king rose, and with him the governor and Bernice and those sitting with them. 31They left the room, and while talking with one another, they said, "This man is not doing anything that deserves death or imprisonment."

32Agrippa said to Festus, "This man could have been set free, if he had not appealed to Caesar."

The hearing was over. Did it help Festus in drafting the charges he would send to Rome concerning this prisoner? Probably not. Paul had preached law and gospel, repentance and faith. He had witnessed to the resurrection. He had not failed to present the Lord's case. His hearers had failed to accept the salvation offered to them.

Privately, the Roman governor and the Jewish king agreed on what they lacked the honesty and courage to say publicly. Nothing in Paul's life, nothing in his teaching, made him guilty of any crime which was punishable by death or imprisonment.

It did not cost Agrippa anything to render this opinion. He did not risk the anger of the Jews by expressing it privately. Paul would have to be sent to Rome as a prisoner because he had appealed to Caesar, and so the Jews would be rid of him. Nothing that Felix or Festus had done in his case suggests that it would have ever been settled if he had not appealed to Caesar.

It seems like a tragedy that a man who could have been set free had to be sent to Rome as a prisoner. But in the providence of God this sad affair would be turned into further opportunities for the spread of the gospel.

Paul's Voyage to Rome

Storm and Shipwreck

27 **When it was decided that we would sail for Italy, Paul and some other prisoners were handed over to a centurion named Julius, who belonged to the Imperial Regiment. [2]We boarded a ship from Adramyttium about to sail for ports along the coast of the province of Asia, and we put out to sea. Aristarchus, a Macedonian from Thessalonica, was with us.**

"Imperial" was an honorary title which was often conferred on a Roman cohort or regiment. A regiment of this type was often made up of soldiers who were not of Roman descent. It normally numbered 600 men.

A centurion commanded one hundred men, but Julius was most likely one of those centurions who served as couriers or as escorts for prisoners. The soldiers who sailed with him were probably fewer than one hundred.

It is evident that Luke was with Paul when the ship sailed, for he begins another "we" section here. The person who decided that the voyage would be made and that the prisoners were to be handed over to the centurion was Governor Festus.

The ship's home port was Adramyttium, in the province of Mysia, in northwestern Asia Minor, on the Aegean Sea, southeast of Troas.

Aristarchus, like Luke, had accompanied Paul to Jerusalem with the relief offering (20:4). He was one of the men who, with Gaius, were rushed into the theater of Ephesus by a raging mob (19:29). In Colossians 4:10, written while Paul was a prisoner in Rome, the apostle refers to Aristarchus as "my fellow prisoner." Luke does not report whether this co-worker of Paul became a prisoner in Rome or while he was in Caesarea.

³The next day we landed at Sidon; and Julius, in kindness to Paul, allowed him to go to his friends so they might provide for his needs. ⁴From there we put out to sea again and passed to the lee of Cyprus because the winds were against us. ⁵When we had sailed across the open sea off the coast of Cilicia and Pamphylia, we landed at Myra in Lycia. ⁶There the centurion found an Alexandrian ship sailing for Italy and put us on board.

The ship was a "coaster," taking cargo and passengers from port to port along the coasts of Judea, Phoenicia, Syria and Asia Minor. Its first stop after leaving Caesarea was at Sidon in Phoenicia, about seventy miles to the north.

The friends whose hospitality Paul enjoyed were disciples, fellow believers.

"The lee of Cyprus," the side of the island protected from the wind, was the eastern coast. The prevailing winds at that time of the year (late August or early September) were from the northwest, making progress to the west very difficult for a sailing vessel. The ship sailed north on the leeward side of the island, heading for Cilicia. Along the coast of Asia Minor an east to west current helped the vessel make headway.

Lycia was the name given to the projection of the southern coast of Asia Minor. The voyage from Caesarea to Myra would have taken about two weeks.

Grain ships from Alexandria in Egypt regularly sailed north to Myra before heading west to Italy and Rome. The centurion transferred his prisoners to one of these ships. A longer but safer way would have been to sail up the Aegean with the coaster and go overland from Macedonia to Rome, on the Egnatian Way. The centurion chose the more direct route which, he hoped, would bring him and his prisoners to Rome much sooner.

⁷We made slow headway for many days and had difficulty arriving off Cnidus. When the wind did not allow us to hold our course, we sailed to the lee of Crete, opposite Salmone. ⁸We moved along the coast with difficulty and came to a place called Fair Havens, near the town of Lasea.

Now the ship was heading into the wind, which made it impossible for the helmsman to hold a course. From Myra to Cnidus was about 170 miles, and it took the ship ten to fifteen days to make that distance. Cnidus was a city on the peninsula of the same name, in the southwestern corner of Asia Minor.

The northwest winds would have driven the ship ashore if they had tried to sail past Crete on the north. Therefore they sailed to the south of Crete, passing Salmone, which was located on a cape at the southeastern corner of the island. Crete is situated south of Greece and Asia Minor, stretching about 160 miles in an east-west direction.

Lasea was about midway along the southern coast of Crete, about five miles from a bay which provided safe harbor: Fair Havens.

⁹Much time had been lost, and sailing had already become dangerous because by now it was after the Fast. So Paul warned them, ¹⁰"Men, I can see that our voyage is going to be disastrous and bring great loss to ship and cargo, and to our own lives also." ¹¹But the centurion, instead of listening to what Paul said, followed the advice of the pilot and of the owner of the ship. ¹²Since the harbor was unsuitable to winter in, the majority decided that we should sail on, hoping to reach Phoenix and winter there. This was a harbor in Crete, facing both southwest and northwest.

The Fast to which Luke refers is the only fast day in the Jewish religious calendar, the Great Day of Atonement (Leviticus 16:29). It is the day before the Jewish New Year, which comes in late September or early October.

In ancient times, not much sailing was done in the Mediterranean after mid-September. Paul's observation about what would happen if they continued the voyage was not a prophecy but a commonsense warning that to continue to Sicily from Crete at that time of year was too dangerous. The possibility of shipwreck must have filled Paul with considerable anxiety, for he had already suffered shipwreck three times. See 2 Corinthians 11:25, which was written before he went to Jerusalem and was arrested.

The centurion took the advice of those who were supposed to know more about sailing than Paul did. For financial reasons many owners of these grain ships preferred to get their cargo to Italy even at some risk rather than wait for the safe shipping season in spring. The owner, who was sailing with them, was willing to take some risk, at least in order to find a better harbor than Fair Havens in which to spend the winter.

Phoenix was another fifty to sixty miles along the coast, and should have been easily reachable.

13When a gentle south wind began to blow, they thought they had obtained what they wanted; so they weighed anchor and sailed along the shore of Crete. 14Before very long, a wind of hurricane force, called the "northeaster," swept down from the island. 15The ship was caught by the storm and could not head into the wind; so we gave way to it and were driven along. 16As we passed to the lee of a small island called Cauda, we were hardly able to make the lifeboat secure. 17When the men had hoisted it aboard, they passed ropes under the ship itself to hold it together. Fearing that they would run aground on the sandbars of Syrtis, they lowered the sea anchor and let the ship be driven along. 18We took such a violent battering from the storm that the next day they began to throw the cargo overboard. 19On the third day, they threw the ship's tackle overboard with their own hands. 20When neither sun nor stars appeared for many days and the storm continued raging, we finally gave up all hope of being saved.

The south wind meant that they would not have to head into the wind to make their way westward. That it was gentle promised that they would not be blown onto the coast.

The "northeaster" originated in the mountains of the island. Heading into the wind is one way of keeping a ship stable in a storm. It may be that they were also trying to return to Fair Havens. The wind was too strong and they simply had to ride with it.

In a northeast wind the lee of Cauda would be the south side of the island, which was about 25 miles off Crete. The lifeboat was usually towed behind a ship. Such a "trailer" would cause problems in a storm, as the wind and waves tended to dash it against the mother vessel.

After the lifeboat was secured, ropes were used to reinforce the ship's timbers, so that the planks would not spring loose and the ship break up. The sandbars of Syrtis were located off the coast of Libya. The northeast winds could drive a vessel that far. To prevent it the crew lowered a sea anchor. This was a large piece of canvas, fashioned into a funnel and lowered into the water behind the ship. There it acted as a drag, slowing the vessel's headlong flight before the winds.

The next day part of the cargo was thrown overboard to prevent the ship's being swamped. The day after that some of the gear of a sailing vessel, such as pulleys and spars, were thrown over the side, perhaps to add to the drag of the sea anchor.

Ancient sailors steered by the sun and stars. When these were hidden for several days during raging storm, it was impossible to navigate intelligently. The situation seemed hopeless.

21 After the men had gone a long time without food, Paul stood up before them and said: "Men, you should have taken my advice not to sail from Crete; then you would have spared yourselves this damage and loss. 22But now I urge you to keep up your courage, because not one of you will be lost; only the ship will be destroyed. 23Last night an angel of the God whose I am and whom I serve stood beside me 24and said, 'Do not be afraid, Paul. You must stand trial before Caesar; and God has graciously given you the lives of all who sail with you.' 25So keep up your courage, men, for I have faith in God that it will happen just as he told me. 26Nevertheless, we must run aground on some island."

The Greek of verse 21, and especially of verse 33, suggests that it was anxiety and seasickness which kept the passengers and crew from eating for a long time. Paul was not trying to make them more miserable by saying, "I told you so," when he reminded them of his advice not to sail from Crete. His reason for the reminder was to get them to heed and believe his words of encouragement.

Paul belonged to God and served him, and God had promised Paul that he would be Jesus' witness in Rome as he had been in Jerusalem (23:11). Now he reaffirmed that promise in a time of grave danger, with the added assurance that he would spare the lives of all aboard. Paul had prayed for all on the ship and God would spare them all. That's what the angel meant by "God has graciously given you the lives of all who sail with you."

Paul's deduction that they would run aground on some island was based on the fact that they were not near the mainland of either Africa or Europe. The condition of the ship was such that they could not reach a mainland port.

[27]On the fourteenth night we were still being driven across the Adriatic Sea, when about midnight the sailors sensed they were approaching land. [28]They took soundings and found that the water was a hundred and twenty feet deep. A short time later they took soundings again and found it was ninety feet deep. [29]Fearing that we would be dashed against the rocks, they dropped four anchors from the stern and prayed for daylight. [30]In an attempt to escape from the ship, the sailors let the lifeboat down into the sea, pretending they were going to lower some anchors from the bow. [31]Then Paul said to the centurion and the soldiers, "Unless these men stay with the ship, you cannot be saved."[32]So the soldiers cut the ropes that held the lifeboat and let it fall away.

Today "Adriatic Sea" refers to the water between Italy and Greece. In ancient times the name was also applied to that part of the Mediterranean which is south of Italy and Greece. In terms of modern geographical usage, we would say that they were still being driven across the Mediterranean.

Sailors sense the approach of land by smell and by the sound of breakers, waves striking rocks or reefs or the shore itself. The soundings confirmed what their noses and ears told them, so they dropped anchor to keep the ship from being driven shoreward in the darkness.

At this point the ship's crew treacherously planned to save themselves by deserting the others. Perhaps Luke, whose language in this entire account of the voyage and the storm demonstrates a good knowledge of sailing, explained to Paul what the sailors were doing. Perhaps Paul understood it by himself. The apostle reminded the military men that, if the sailors were permitted to carry out their intention, no one would be able to bring the ship to the beach. The soldiers took direct action and made it impossible for the sailors to leave.

33Just before dawn Paul urged them all to eat. "For the last fourteen days," he said, "you have been in constant suspense and have gone without food — you haven't eaten anything. 34Now I urge you to take some food. You need it to survive. Not one of you will lose a single hair from his head." 35After he said this, he took some bread and gave thanks to God in front of them all. Then he broke it and began to eat. 36They were all encouraged and ate some food themselves. 37Altogether there were 276 of us on board. 38When they had eaten as much as they wanted, they lightened the ship by throwing the grain into the sea.

It is remarkable how the prisoner, a man of faith, assumed leadership in the crisis, how he took responsibility for the safety and welfare of all aboard the ship. Even in taking some food the prisoner acted the part of a leader. He took his own advice by eating, and he confessed his faith by giving thanks in the presence of all of them.

Lightening the ship would allow it to run faster and farther up the beach before it was finally grounded. The grain was that part of the cargo which had not been thrown overboard earlier.

³⁹When daylight came, they did not recognize the land, but they saw a bay with a sandy beach, where they decided to run the ship aground if they could. ⁴⁰Cutting loose the anchors, they left them in the sea and at the same time untied the ropes that held the rudders. Then they hoisted the foresail to the wind and made for the beach. ⁴¹But the ship struck a sandbar and ran aground. The bow stuck fast and would not move, and the stern was broken to pieces by the pounding of the surf.

The storm had carried the ship well away from the usual shipping lanes, and the land which the crew saw at daybreak was unfamiliar. Now, all the preparations the crew made were carried out to help the ship run as far up on the beach as possible. The anchors which had been lowered to slow the vessel were now cut loose. The rudders were lowered to steer a straight course for the shore. The foresail was raised to catch the wind which, with the waves, would drive them to land.

In reporting the angel's message Paul had said, "Only the ship will be destroyed" (v. 22). The force of the surf broke the stern (the rear) of the vessel to pieces while the bow (front) was caught fast on the sandbar.

⁴²The soldiers planned to kill the prisoners to prevent any of them from swimming away and escaping. ⁴³But the centurion wanted to spare Paul's life and kept them from carrying out their plan. He ordered those who could swim to jump overboard first and get to land. ⁴⁴The rest were to get there on planks or on pieces of the ship. In this way everyone reached land in safety.

The soldiers did not want to pay for escaped prisoners with their own lives or freedom. They intended to do what they knew how to do to prevent any escape. Centurion Julius, who had shown Paul consideration at Sidon (v. 3), now saved the apostle's life and the lives of the other prisoners. Paul was shipwrecked a fourth time (see 2 Corinthians 11:25), but he would live to preach in Rome.

On Malta

28 **Once safely on shore, we found out that the island was called Malta. ²The islanders showed us unusual kindness. They built a fire and welcomed us all because it was raining and cold.**

Malta is the small island about 60 miles to the south of Sicily, about 150 miles southwest of the "toe" of the Italy's "boot." It was part of the Roman province of Sicily. When the ship broke up on the sandbar in the bay, it was about 500 miles west of where the storm first caught it off Crete.

The ship carrying Paul from Caesarea had left in late August or early September. It was now the end of October or the beginning of November. The cold and rain were not pleasant for the islanders, but they came out and did what they could to make the exhausted, shipwrecked group comfortable.

The islanders were descended from Phoenician explorers. Their native language was related to the Aramaic which Paul spoke, and it was possible for them and the apostle to understand each other.

³Paul gathered a pile of brushwood and, as he put it on the fire, a viper, driven out by the heat, fastened itself on his hand. ⁴When the islanders saw the snake hanging from his hand, they said to each other, "This man must be a murderer; for though he escaped from the sea, Justice has not allowed him to live." ⁵But Paul shook the snake off into the fire and suffered no ill effects. ⁶The

people expected him to swell up or suddenly fall over dead, but after waiting a long time and seeing nothing unusual happen to him they changed their minds and said he was a god.

The Maltese natives knew that Paul was a prisoner. When they saw that a poisonous snake had bitten him, they assumed he was a murderer. They based their assumption on their belief that justice would take a life for a life. The capitalization of Justice in the NIV reminds us that the Greek-Roman world regarded justice as a goddess. The sea had not claimed Paul but the viper surely would. These people were neither Jews nor Christians, but they had a sense of right and wrong and of how man is accountable for his actions.

The expected did not happen. We recall Jesus' words: "They will pick up snakes with their hands" (Mark 16:18). Public opinion regarding Paul swung from one mistaken estimate to another. First he was a murderer because a viper bit him, then he was a god because the viper's venom did not affect him. During the three months that followed they would have opportunity to learn that Paul was not a god but that he brought a lifegiving message from the only true God.

[7]There was an estate nearby that belonged to Publius, the chief official of the island. He welcomed us to his home and for three days entertained us hospitably. [8]His father was sick in bed, suffering from fever and dysentery. Paul went in to see him and, after prayer, placed his hands on him and healed him. [9]When this had happened, the rest of the sick on the island came and were cured. [10]They honored us in many ways and when we were ready to sail, they furnished us with the supplies we needed.

The chief officer of the island was the representative of the governor of Sicily. It is not certain whether all 276 men who had been on the ship enjoyed his hospitality, or only Paul and his companions with the ship's owner. There could well have been room for all on an estate, especially since they stayed only three days.

The fever and dysentery could have proved fatal to Publius's father, who must have been a man of advanced age. Just as Peter prayed to know the Lord's will when Tabitha lay dead (9:40), so Paul now sought God's direction. God directed Paul to lay his hands on the sick man, and God healed him. This miracle, like all the miracles of Jesus and his apostles, was to further the cause of the gospel.

God used the circumstances of the storm and shipwreck for his good purpose and brought great blessing to the inhabitants of Malta. They responded with generosity, providing for the needs of Paul and his companions while they were on the island and when they put to sea again.

To Rome

11After three months we put out to sea in a ship that had wintered in the island. It was an Alexandrian ship with the figurehead of the twin gods Castor and Pollux. 12We put in at Syracuse and stayed there three days. 13From there we set sail and arrived at Rhegium. The next day the south wind came up, and on the following day we reached Puteoli. 14There we found some brothers who invited us to spend a week with them.

Assuming that the shipwreck had occurred in late October or early November, Paul and the group around him left Malta in early February. The ancient Greek historian and naturalist, Pliny, says that the sailing season began on February 7.

In Greek mythology Castor and Pollux were the twin sons of Zeus and Leda. There may be a bit of irony in Luke's mention of them, because sailors regarded them as their guardian or patron deities. Those who had been rescued by the God to whom Paul belonged and whom he served would know that a power higher than "the twins" is the ruler of wind and wave.

Syracuse was the leading city of Sicily, on the southeastern coast, about eighty miles from Malta's harbor. From there the vessel tacked for seventy miles, sailing a zig-zag route to catch the winds, and arrived at Rhegium.

Rhegium is located on the "toe" of Italy, the southwestern tip, opposite the Sicilian city of Messina. A south wind enabled the vessel to sail through the straits of Messina and proceed about 190 miles up the coast to Puteoli.

Although it was seventy-five miles from Rome, Puteoli served as the capital city's port for large vessels with heavy cargoes. Ostia, Rome's nearby natural harbor, was not deep enough to serve ships such as an Alexandrian grain vessel.

We cannot be sure why the centurion was willing to stay in Puteoli for a week, enabling Paul, Luke and Aristarchus to enjoy the hospitality of their fellow Christians in that city. One or more of the group may have been sick. Perhaps the centurion Julius had business there.

And so we went to Rome. 15The brothers there had heard that we were coming, and they traveled as far as the Forum of Appius and the Three Taverns to meet us. At the sight of these men Paul thanked God and was encouraged. 16When we got to Rome, Paul was allowed to live by himself, with a soldier to guard him.

At last the centurion with his prisoners, including Paul and his companions, set out for Rome on the famous Appian Way, most likely on foot. A prisoner in a strange land, among heathen, Paul thanked God for the encouraging presence of fellow believers who came out from Rome to greet him. The Forum of Appius was about forty miles from Rome, and one group met Paul and his companions there.

Ten miles closer to Rome, about thirty miles from the capital, a second group met them at the Three Taverns.

On the one hand, the authorities at Rome knew that Paul was not a dangerous criminal or a revolutionary. On the other hand, he had appealed to Caesar and must remain a prisoner until he had his day in court. Therefore he was kept under house arrest, in a residence rented for him for that purpose. This was a much better arrangement than staying in the common prison or the barracks would have been.

Rome: Paul's Ministry as a Prisoner

[17]Three days later he called together the leaders of the Jews. When they had assembled, Paul said to them: "My brothers, although I have done nothing against our people or against the customs of our ancestors, I was arrested in Jerusalem and handed over to the Romans. [18]They examined me and wanted to release me, because I was not guilty of any crime deserving death. [19]But when the Jews objected, I was compelled to appeal to Caesar —not that I had any charge to bring against my own people. [20]For this reason I have asked to see you and talk with you. It is because of the hope of Israel that I am bound with this chain."

The Lord had promised Paul that he would testify in Rome as he had in Jerusalem (23:11). The Lord had brought Paul to Rome in an unexpected and remarkable way. It did not take Paul long to begin his work in that city.

All Jews had been banished from Rome by Emperor Claudius in A.D. 49 (18:2). His edict was no longer in effect and, under Nero, there was once again a Jewish community in the capital. Paul greeted many Jewish believers in his *Epistle to the Romans*, written three years before his arrival in the city.

Now he called the leaders of the Jews together to tell them how it came about that he was in Rome, under Roman

285

custody. As he always did, Paul would also use the occasion to witness to Jesus as the fulfillment of the Old Testament Scriptures. "My brothers" in this context means "my countrymen" rather than "fellow believers in Jesus Christ."

He wanted them to understand that he had not wronged Israel and its religion in any way. It had been an injustice on the part of the Jerusalem Jews to hand him over to the Romans. What Paul said about his innocence and the Romans' desire to release him agreed with the letter of Tribune Claudius Lysias to Governor Felix (23:29). It agreed with Governor Festus's report to King Agrippa (25:25). Festus and Agrippa concurred that Paul could have gone free if he had not appealed to Caesar (26:31,32).

Paul had not appealed to Caesar in order to press charges against his own people, the Jews. He had appealed in order to avoid being handed over to them for punishment. "If the charges brought against me by these Jews are not true, no one has the right to hand me over to them. I appeal to Caesar!" (25:11).

It was not his intention to put his countrymen in a bad legal position. He wanted to show that preaching the gospel was not contrary to their Scriptures and that it was not illegal under Roman law. He wanted to demonstrate that before the imperial court. He wanted to convince the Jews at Rome of the truth which the Jews at Jerusalem had rejected.

The "hope of Israel" was that God would send Messiah, who would judge the righteous and the wicked on the day of resurrection (24:15). Paul preached that Jesus the crucified is that Messiah, that God raised him from the dead, that he will judge all men on the last day. That preaching was the "crime" for which he had been made a prisoner.

[21]They replied, "We have not received any letters from Judea concerning you, and none of the brothers who has come from

there has reported or said anything bad about you. [22]But we want to hear what your views are, for we know that people everywhere are talking against this sect."

No official letters from the Sanhedrin and no private reports had come from Jerusalem concerning Paul. Still, the Jews at Rome knew that what Paul preached was a matter of dispute. People everywhere were talking against the Christians. The Jewish leaders of Rome were willing, however to give Paul's message a hearing.

[23]They arranged to meet Paul on a certain day, and came in even larger numbers to the place where he was staying. From morning till evening he explained and declared to them the kingdom of God and tried to convince them about Jesus from the law of Moses and from the Prophets. [24]Some were convinced by what he said, but others would not believe. [25]They disagreed among themselves and began to leave after Paul had made this final statement: "The Holy Spirit spoke the truth to your forefathers when he said through Isaiah the prophet:

[26]" 'Go to this people and say,
     You will be ever hearing but never understanding;
       you will be ever seeing but never perceiving."
[27]For this people's heart has become calloused;
       they hardly hear with their ears,
       and they have closed their eyes.
     Otherwise they might see with their eyes,
       hear with their ears,
       understand with their hearts
       and turn and I would heal them.'
[28]"Therefore I want you to know that God's salvation has been sent to the Gentiles, and they will listen!"

Paul, under house arrest, was not free to go to the synagogue. But large numbers of leading Jews made and kept an appointment to meet with him at his quarters. There, all day long, Paul did what he had done in so many synagogues. He spoke of God's gracious rule in working out the salvation of the world. On the basis of their Scriptures and the history of Jesus he tried to convince them that Jesus is the fulfillment of the messianic promises and prophecies.

As so often happened when he preached in the synagogues, there was a division among those who heard him at his place of residence. Some were convinced and others would not believe. The daylong visit and study of God's word ended after Paul reminded them of the word God spoke through the Prophet Isaiah (Isaiah 6:9,10). Notice that Paul regarded the Scriptures as God's speaking, God's word.

God's word, spoken through Isaiah, says that Israel would hear the Scriptures and not understand them. They would see the mighty works of God but not recognize them for what they were. Paul warned his hearers not to let that happen in their case.

How could it happen that people would hear without hearing and see without seeing? It happens when they harden their hearts against God. Israel, in Isaiah's day, did not want to hear God's word or see his ways. They did not want him to control their lives. They wanted him out of their lives, even while they still used his name and professed loyalty to his law.

The result was that God finally did leave them alone, did get out of their lives. Then they couldn't see or hear or understand anymore. They couldn't turn to God for healing any longer. That is, they could not repent.

Those who would not believe Paul's testimony concerning God's kingdom and Jesus Christ were in danger of such hardening. God's word would become something dark and difficult for them. The very gospel which was intended to save them would result in their hardening. It is not the gospel's purpose or God's intention to harden men's hearts. But those who refuse to repent and believe are at last hardened.

In fact that hardening *becomes* God's intention for the gospel after men have hardened themselves. Paul was quoting the Septuagint, the Greek translation of the Old Testament. If we compare Isaiah 6:10 in the NIV with what Paul quoted here, we see that the Hebrew (from which the NIV translates Isaiah), is a stronger statement. It says,

> "*Make* the heart of this people calloused;
> *make* their ears dull
> and *close* their eyes (emphasis added)."

After his people had refused to hear and see, God sent them his messenger to harden them. When they had rejected the word of grace which he offered, God used that same word of grace to confirm them in their unbelief.

At the synagogue in Pisidian Antioch Paul and Barnabas said: "We had to speak the word of God to you first. Since you reject it and do not consider yourselves worthy of eternal life, we now turn to the Gentiles" (13:46). At the synagogue in Corinth, ". . . when the Jews opposed Paul and became abusive, he shook out his clothes in protest and said to them, 'Your blood be on your own heads! I am clear of my responsibility. From now on I will go to the Gentiles' " (18:6).

Paul's words at his house in Rome were the same kind of call to repentance. He had discharged his responsibility to his own countrymen. Some were convinced, and some would not believe. He was now free to preach to the Gentiles in Rome.

"And they will listen!" The same God who spoke the words of judgment in Isaiah 6:9,10 said through the same prophet: "All the ends of the earth will see the salvation of our God" (Isaiah 52:10). That had been happening throughout Paul's ministry and he was confident that the Lord would continue to bless his work among the Gentiles. That was the special call and assurance God gave him when he called him to be an apostle (9:15; 22:15,21; 26:17).

³⁰For two whole years Paul stayed there in his own rented house and welcomed all who came to see him. ³¹Boldly and without hindrance he preached the kingdom of God and taught about the Lord Jesus Christ.

A footnote in the NIV indicates that some manuscripts read, "After he said this, the Jews left, arguing vigorously among themselves." That would really be a restatement of what Luke already reported in verse 25.

Paul's reason for living in a rented house was not that the believers at Rome were lacking in hospitality. It was because he was a prisoner, who always had a guard with him, and because he was constantly receiving visitors who came to hear his message.

After two years his situation changed, but it was not part of Luke's plan to tell his readers why or in what way it changed. We can gather much from Paul's own writings as to what happened after that, and we will do so. First, let us consider the final verse of Luke's history.

Why had God spared Paul and brought him to Rome as a prisoner? To preach God's saving reign and to teach about the Savior. During the two years of house arrest he was able to do that without any interference from the authorities. He did it with that boldness which comes from the Holy Spirit. Thus Luke concludes the story of some of the work of some of the apostles in some parts of the world.

During the two years in Rome Paul wrote several of his epistles: *Philippians, Colossians, Philemon* and possibly *Ephesians*. The result of his trial before the imperial court was that he was acquitted: "I was delivered from the lion's mouth" (2 Timothy 4:17).

Thus Paul was free to continue his work, and it is clear that he revisited many of the places where his earlier journeys had taken him. He worked on Crete and left Titus there to complete the work of organizing the churches on that island (Titus 1:5). He revisited Miletus (2 Timothy 4:20) and probably Ephesus (1 Timothy 1:3). Perhaps he made a visit to Colosse and enjoyed Philemon's hospitality as he had hoped to (Philemon 22). He revisited Troas (2 Timothy 4:13) and went to Macedonia (1 Timothy 1:3).

It had been Paul's intention, before his arrest in Jerusalem and the subsequent voyage to Rome as a prisoner, to go to Spain (Romans 15:24,28). He had expressed the hope that after a visit with the saints in Rome they would help him make that trip (Romans 15:28). Perhaps he was able to do so, but there is no biblical evidence that he did.

Somewhere, for some reason, Paul was arrested a second time. From prison in Rome he wrote his *Second Epistle to Timothy*. He expected to be executed this time. Ancient tradition says that he was beheaded at Rome, probably in A.D. 66. "For I am already being poured out like a drink offering, and the time has come for my departure. I have fought the good fight, I have finished the race, I have kept the faith. Now there is in store for me the crown of righteousness, which the Lord, the righteous Judge, will award to me on that day — and not only to me, but also to all who have longed for his appearing" (2 Timothy 4:6-8).

The Spirit promised by Jesus (1:5) moved and empowered others to continue what the apostles began. To this day there are witnesses to the risen Savior carrying his saving name "to the ends of the earth" (1:8).

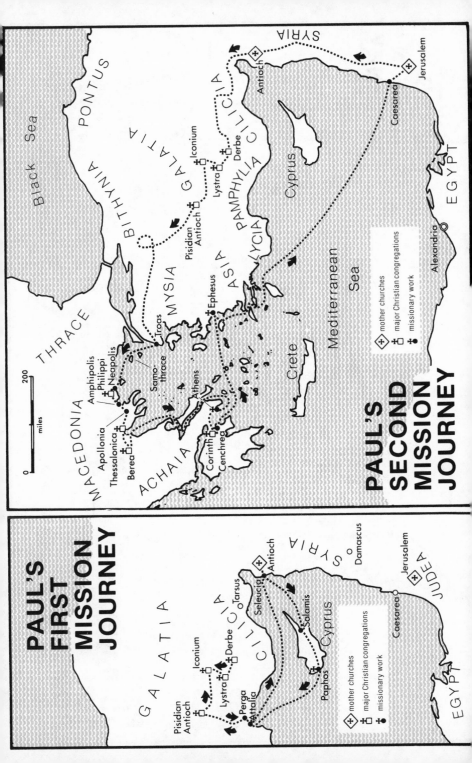

PAUL'S FIRST MISSION JOURNEY

Black Sea

GALATIA

Pisidian Antioch
Iconium
Derbe
Lystra
Tarsus

CILICIA

Perga
Attalia

PAMPHYLIA

Seleucia
Antioch

SYRIA

Damascus

Salamis
Paphos

Cyprus

Jerusalem

JUDEA

Caesarea

EGYPT

mother churches
major Christian congregations
missionary work

PAUL'S SECOND MISSION JOURNEY

Black Sea

PONTUS

BITHYNIA

GALATIA

Iconium
Pisidian Antioch
Lystra
Derbe

PAMPHYLIA

CILICIA

Antioch

SYRIA

LYCIA

ASIA

Ephesus

MYSIA

Troas

Samothrace

THRACE

MACEDONIA

Amphipolis
Philippi
Neapolis
Apollonia
Thessalonica
Berea

ACHAIA

Athens

Corinth
Cenchrea

Crete

Mediterranean Sea

Cyprus

Caesarea

Jerusalem

Alexandria

EGYPT

200
miles
0

mother churches
major Christian congregations
missionary work

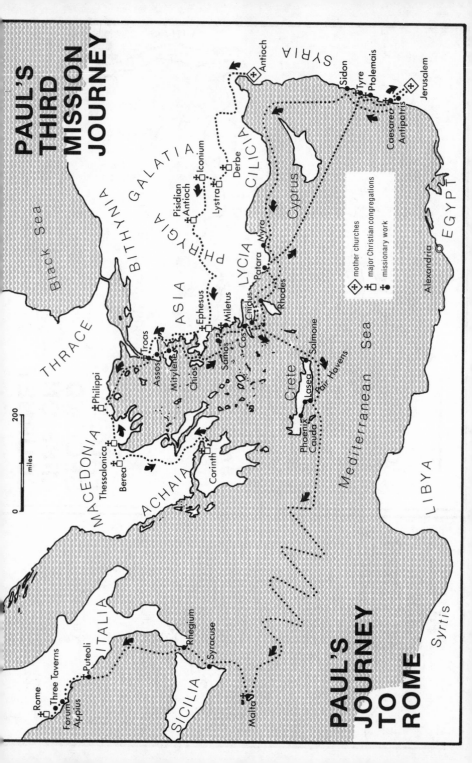

PAUL'S
THIRD
MISSION
JOURNEY

Black Sea

THRACE

BITHYNIA

GALATIA

PHRYGIA

ASIA

Troas
Assos
Mitylene
Chios
Samos
Cos

Pisidian
Antioch
Iconium
Lystra
Derbe

LYCIA

Patara
Myra
Cnidus
Rhodes

Salmone

Crete
Lasea
Cauda
Phoenix
Fair Havens

CILICIA

Cyprus

Antioch

SYRIA

Sidon
Tyre
Ptolemais

Caesarea
Antipatris
Jerusalem

EGYPT

Alexandria

Mediterranean Sea

LIBYA

Ephesus
Miletus

Philippi

MACEDONIA

Thessalonica
Berea

ACHAIA

Corinth

200
miles
0

☩ mother churches
☐ major Christian congregations
● missionary work

ITALIA

Rome
Three Taverns
Forum Appius
Puteoli
Rhegium
Syracuse

SICILIA

Malta

Syrtis

PAUL'S
JOURNEY
TO
ROME